THE DIGITAL CAPABILITY MODEL

77 BUILDING BLOCKS OF DIGITAL TRANSFORMATION

77 BUILDING BLOCKS OF DIGITAL TRANSFORMATION:

THE DIGITAL CAPABILITY MODEL ™

Digital Alignment

Digital Customer Experience Management

Digital Channel Management

Front-office

Digital Commerce

Digital Marketing

Social Interaction

Back-office

Middle-office

Knowledge & Content Management

Customization & Personalization

Digital Intelligence

Digital Data Services

Digital Infrastructure Services

Digital Development & Operations

By Jace An

77 BUILDING BLOCKS OF DIGITAL TRANSFORMATION: THE DIGITAL CAPABILITY MODEL ™

By Jace An

First Edition

DEDICATION

This book is dedicated to my better half, Emily and my precious daughter, Alice for their spiritual support along the journey to completing this book.

ACKNOWLEDGEMENTS

I would like to express my special gratitude to Nick Crowther, Managing Director at Freerange Future, for inspiring me to embark on the journey to creating this book. This book would not have been created if it were not for him.

Throughout the process of creating and publishing this book, many individual professionals have helped me out. I'd like to give a special thanks to Eddie de Jong, Zoran Petrovich, Dayeong Yun, Beenish Qureshi, Todd Emsley, and Edward Oh for actively participating in editorial review, book designing and formatting, and contributions for this book. This work would not have been possible without support from all of them.

TABLE OF CONTENTS

PROLOGUE

The Purpose and Audience of This Book

This is not a theory book that discusses academic concepts of digital capability and digital transformation, but rather a practical field book that describes how to assess and improve digital capabilities of an organization. This book therefore caters best for digital 'practitioners' who are involved in digital business operations, including information technology, digital technology, digital marketing, digital channel management, social media management, online commerce, online customer services and many more operational areas that digital technology may have an impact on.

A digital capability is defined in this book as an organizational capacity and ability to produce intended business outcome in the digital space by combining process, people and technology elements in a way that is unique to each organization.

A Process element includes process flow, input & output information, and business rules, policies & guidelines. A People element includes organizational structure & culture, and people's roles, responsibilities & skills. A Technology element includes applications, data, infrastructure, facilities and equipment around digital technology.

The Social Listening digital capability is for example defined as an organizational capacity to understand what users are talking about on social media and use that for business by combining its well-defined processes, skilled staff and their clear roles & responsibilities, and automation tools. A higher maturity of digital capabilities ensures effective and efficient operations of a digital business.

Digital business operations is a multi-disciplinary area where business and IT converges and works together to produce business outcomes in the digital space. Understanding both business and IT as if these were a single departmental function is therefore critical to the success of digital business. The Digital Capability Model is optimized to meet the needs of those who wish to obtain and increase this cross-boundary, multi-disciplinary knowledge.

The Digital Capability Model is comprehensive in scope, making it best suited for those who desire to have a broad understanding of the entire scope of digital capabilities and want to use a holistic approach to improve the performance of their digital business.

However, the book is focused on 'introducing' digital capabilities by describing their definition and key concepts, as well as the maturity levels and maturity indicators of each digital capability. Although it goes deep enough when necessary, technical details of a digital capability is out of scope.

The definition and key concepts of 'Product Similarity Analytics' capability are for example discussed and the basic analytical method explained, although the detailed formula and algorithms of the analytics are deemed outside the scope of this book. This book may be used as a starter to understand the overarching structure of digital capabilities, while other sources should be used when technical details for implementation of the digital capabilities are required.

Impact of the Digital Trend on Business

I started my career as the marketing manager of an Interactive Marketing Team in a marketing communication company. When my team saw the potential of the Internet as an unprecedented effective marketing channel, we developed an Internet shopping mall in the mid-1990s by using CGI programming[1] and MySQL[2] database. E-business soon became the dominant trend as the first version of digital business in the early 2000s.

Nowadays, new digital technologies are introduced at a rapid pace. As was learned from integrating e-commerce or e-business into the traditional business in the past, other significant potential for further sell-side improvements is possible by applying those contemporary digital technologies to the business.

It is commonly acknowledged that Social, Mobile and Cloud are among the most relevant factors of the contemporary digital era. A closer look at these three elements reveals that they are closely related from a business perspective.

Put simply, those three things are all related to 'digitized user interactions'. Social means users interact with each other for socialization, Mobile means users interact using mobile devices, and Cloud means dynamic provisioning of business services to support unpredictable, massive transaction processing involving the un-structured and semi-structured data those interactions generate.

Before the contemporary digital age, customer behaviour could only be determined through surveys and focus groups interview

---

[1] Common Gateway Interface (CGI) programming is an old way of standard web programming. CGI has been used to provide a webserver with a standard gateway to legacy IT systems to expose the functionalities of the legacy IT systems as web pages to the Internet.

[2] MySQL is an open-source relational database management system.

(FGI), or at best by analysing behaviours of customers who did visit.

Using Social, Mobile and Cloud, previously unseen customers' private reactions to brands through 'digitized interactions' can now be observed and even measured, even if they never visit or shop. Customers reveal themselves to businesses through their digitized interactions. Marketing & sales divisions should be most excited about the digitization of customer behaviours.

The Digital Capability Model

The Digital Capability Model can help you to make the most of these new digital opportunities and make the most out of the digital trends because the Model has Social, Mobile and Cloud at the core of the digital capabilities, and seamlessly integrates them with digital business.

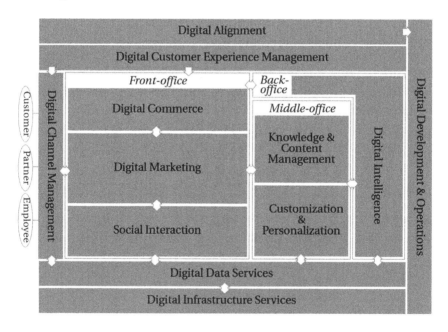

[Figure 1: The Digital Capability Model – Mega Capability View]

The Digital Capability Model is a reference model used to diagnose and design business capabilities required for digital business. It focuses heavily on the operational areas of information technology, marketing, sales and customer service. Several noticeable features in the Model should be of interest.

1. The Model is based on the global best practices for digital business.

The Digital Capability Model consists of 12 mega capabilities and 77 capabilities that are based on global best practices. The digital capabilities of an organization can be benchmarked against the best practices in two ways. Firstly, the digital landscape can be checked to verify if it covers all the mega capabilities and their constituent capabilities contained in the Model. Secondly, an organization's digital practices can be compared with the leading practices described in the maturity indicators of each digital capability.

2. The Model consists of front-office, middle-office and back-office modules to help you respond to customers better.

The front-office interacts with customers directly through digital channels to market and sell products and services. The back-office supports the front-office by providing information needed to interact with customers. In architectural terms, back-office processes are not necessarily integrated with front-office processes seamlessly. Chances are therefore that the front-office is not responsive enough.

This is where the middle-office concept comes in. The middle-office in the Model is responsible for preparing customized content based on analytics insights provided by the back-office and then feeding the customized content to the front-office on demand. The middle-office is seamlessly integrated with front-office operations so that front-office staff are well equipped to interact with, and respond to customers. This enables staff to socialize with customers, and market and sell products and services to them effectively.

3. Most digital capabilities in the Model are aligned with customer journeys toward purchasing

Thanks to digitized customer interactions, customer behaviour and interaction can now be observed objectively. So that the customers can be influenced effectively at multiple touchpoints to move toward a purchasing action during their journey. This is why managing customer experiences and journeys are becoming more critical in the digital age than ever before. All channels, front-office, middle-office, and back-office, should be aligned with strategically developed customer experience journeys. This concept is core to the formation of the Model.

4. The front-office is structured to move interactions with customers from socialization through marketing to sales.

It is not possible to sell to everyone encountered online immediately. Socialization should first be used to build a relationship as per the customer journey map.

The Social Interaction capabilities of the front-office can target a broader audience than customer segments in a marketing plan. This enables the building of brand awareness, interest and preference widely, as well as creating word of mouth through loyal brand supporters.

The relationship evolves beyond socialization to the point where marketing offers can be pitched, and to the next level where potential customers are led to a purchasing transaction. The Model fully supports the concept of managing conversions in the marketing funnel.

5. The Model is relevant to many different marketing approaches.

Marketing practices typically consist of planning, execution and performance evaluation processes. Every business, however, has a different set of marketing processes. The holistic and comprehensive nature of the reference model makes it relevant to any marketing process that conforms to the Plan-Do-See marketing cycle.

INTRODUCTION

The Structure of This Book

The Digital Capability Model consists of 12 mega capabilities and 77 capabilities, where a mega capability is comprised of a set of capabilities. This book is organized to describe the capabilities individually according to the taxonomy of the Digital Capability Model. The diagram of the Digital Capability Model on the next page will facilitate better understanding of the structure of this book.

Digital Customer Experience Management is discussed first. Digital Customer Experience Management is a set of digital capabilities used to improve customer experience across all digital channels and touchpoints. Digital Customer Experience Management capabilities provide overarching directions for the front-office, middle-office and back-office capabilities of the Digital Capability Model.

The **front-office** capabilities are explained next. As mentioned earlier, the front-office is structured to be aligned with the customer relationship moving from socialization to purchasing action. This starts at **Social Interaction** capabilities and moves up to **Digital Marketing** capabilities, and eventually **Digital Commerce** capabilities.

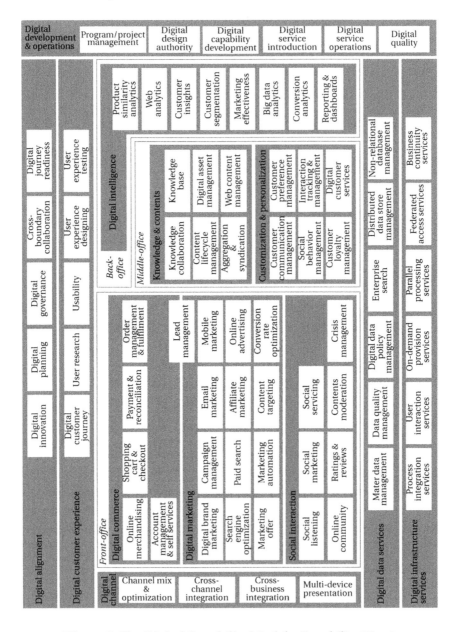

[Figure 2: The Digital Capability Model - Capability View]

Digital Channel capabilities are introduced right after the introduction of the front-office capabilities. This mega capability is closely integrated with the front-office capabilities that use **Digital Channel** capabilities to connect to a broader digital user base, including digital customers.

Following the introduction of Digital Channel capabilities, the **middle-office** and **back-office** capabilities are described.

Digital Data Management capabilities and **Digital Infrastructure Management** capabilities are the technical foundations on which the front-office, middle-office and back-office capabilities are built.

Digital Alignment is a set of capabilities used to develop and execute digital plans that are aligned to corporate and business unit strategies. Digital capabilities are developed based on the digital plans and maintained through the **Digital Development & Operations** capability. These two mega capabilities are discussed at the end of the Digital Capability Model.

In the final part of the Model, the **Digital Transformation Planning Methodology** is introduced. This brief methodology can be employed to make the best use of the Digital Capability Model when digital plans need to be established to improve digital capabilities.

Machine Learning is mentioned a few times in this book, but not established as a standalone capability of The Digital Capability Model for a reason. Machine Learning-based AI is instead discussed briefly in the epilogue.

A Mega Capability and a Capability

Every mega capability in the Digital Capability Model has its constituent capabilities. In this book, a mega capability is introduced first and its constituent capabilities are subsequently explained.

When a capability is introduced, the definition of the capability is described, followed by the maturity levels and examples of indicators of the capability levels. The definition of a capability also includes key concepts that complement the definition and assist with determining the maturity level of the capability.

Maturity Levels of a Capability

While a capability of the Digital Capability Model can be assessed in terms of its level of maturity, a maturity level of a mega capability is calculated by combining the maturity levels of the capabilities that belong to the mega capability.

The results of the assessment of the maturity levels are used to establish a digital strategy and plans to improve overall levels of digital capabilities of an organization. This will be discussed further in a later part of this book.

Below are the overall definitions and indicators of a maturity level of each digital capability, and capability-specific indicators of a maturity level are described in the following chapters. Please note that the maturity indicator examples included in this book should be considered 'signs' of the maturity level rather than absolute criteria, as every organization has unique digital operations that cannot be generalized.

Level 0: Non-existent

- No digital capability exists; neither processes of the capability, people responsible for performing the processes, nor are supporting tools in place.
- The capability may be considered core to the digital business and strategically required, but it has never been built.

Level 1: Ad hoc

- The level exists in ad hoc, once-off, or tactical form.

- It is driven not by digital direction, but by external pressure or urgent internal issues.
- It may be considered strategic core to the digital business and the need for improvement is acknowledged. The overall digital strategy is however absent and the capability may be in the pilot phase or initially implemented, and it has therefore very limited functionalities.

Level 2: Basic

- The ad hoc level is constantly enhanced to leverage bottom-up improvement opportunities, or cope with competition, not to outperform or beat competitors, but to survive.
- More implementations are planned or are in progress.
- Functionality gets rich and upgraded, but is still competitively limited because this is considered as hygiene factors.

Level 3: Defined

- The capability level exists because it is considered strategically required and core to the digital business strategy and operations.
- Digital vision and strategy drives investment in the capability.
- It is regarded as average practice in the market.
- This level is an industry norm.
- This level is not a key differentiator, nor does it provide competitive advantage.

Level 4: Optimized

- The strategic level is constantly optimized to the point where the capability is starting to be differentiated for an organization, enabling it to cope successfully with fierce competition.

- The performance of the capability is traced, measured and improved against pre-defined KPIs (Key Performance Indicators) and metrics.
- The capability level enables the organization to learn internally to outperform, rather than to copy the practices of competitors.

Level 5: Progressive

- The capability level is fully integrated with other digital capabilities so that it gets synergy and exceeds expectation through working together with other digital capabilities.
- It is considered truly market leading and best practices in the industry and market.
- Very few have this capability level.

MEGA CAPABILITY 1.

DIGITAL CUSTOMER EXPERIENCE MANAGEMENT

Digital Customer Experience Management is a set of digital capabilities used to enhance customer experience throughout all digital interactions with all levels of organization, e.g. marketing, sales, delivery, and support. It enables simplified, seamless, and intuitive customer experiences in order to eventually strengthen customer relationships and directly affect the bottom line.

This mega capability should be an integral part of corporate-level customer experience management. The entire customer experience should be managed across digital and non-digital channels for seamless customer experience.

While the Digital Capability Model has extensive implications to almost every operational area of an organization, its primary focus is on improving marketing and sales capabilities and effectiveness by leveraging contemporary digital channels and technologies. This mega capability is therefore at the core of the entire Model, as it provides overarching directions directly to the front-office, middle-office and back-office where daily digital marketing and sales activities are performed.

Digital Customer Experience Management has a significant impact on Digital Brand Marketing capability in particular, because a brand is defined as the collection of all customer experiences with all levels of an organization and the brand is built from the results of the customer experiences.

There are 5 capabilities in this mega capability:

- Digital Customer Journey Management
- User Research
- Usability Analysis
- User Experience Designing
- User Experience Testing

Let's look at the relationships between the capabilities: "How do they collaborate to achieve what Digital Customer Experience Management intends to achieve?" Remember that the end goal of this mega capability is to strengthen customer relationship that affects the bottom line directly.

Here is a quick overview of the relationships:

- Progress from one digital touchpoint to another - from brand awareness to purchasing to servicing - is guided by a digital journey map produced through Digital Customer Journey Management.

- In order to understand how customers behave along the digital customer journey, some research into online users has to be done. User Research will allow user behavioural patterns to be captured.

- The user behavioural patterns will generate ideas on how to design user interactions at each digital touchpoint of the digital customer journey map for User Experience Design to enhance user experience and thus strengthen relationship.

- Ease-of-use is the most important for customer experience enhancement, more important than fun for example, making Usability Analysis another standalone capability. User Experience Designs should take and incorporate usability requirements from Usability Analysis as one of its top priorities.

- Through User Experience Testing, User Experience Designs should be tested to verify whether intended customer responses to the designs would be derived.

CAPABILITY 1-1.
DIGITAL CUSTOMER JOURNEY MANAGEMENT

CAPABILITY DEFINITION

Digital Customer Journey Management is a digital capability that helps customers along their journey from brand awareness to purchase and after-services, and guides them every step along the journey to improve customer experience.

A customer journey begins even before brand awareness, goes through stages where the customer has preference of the brand and keeps thinking about it, until it finally leads to the stages where the customer makes a purchase and receives customer services. After that, the customer embarks on another journey toward another purchase. The Journey should be cumulative and end-to-end, covering the marketing funnel, the sales funnel and the service/aftermarket[3] funnel.

Let's look at the key concepts to understand this capability better.

Digital Customer Journey Map

A digital customer journey map is a visual presentation that describes a Customer Journey on digital channels.

Digital Customer Journey Management should look at the entire spectrum of engagements across many different digital channels, from initial contact with a brand through to post-sales services. This makes a digital customer journey a long process involving many steps. Different people may take different routes to go

---

[3] An aftermarket is a market where customers buy spare parts, accessories, services, and other types of dispensable products needed to maintain the purchased products. When a new ink cartridge is bought to refill a printer, this is done in an aftermarket.

through the steps to complete their journey, resulting in many different customer journeys.

To get started, identify a few key journeys that are critical to the digital business, create a customer journey map to represent the key customer journeys, and then focus on these. A single customer journey will not meet the needs of all customers, nor is it feasible to create and maintain all customer journeys for all customers.

A digital customer journey map is a great tool to visualize the complex end-to-end digital customer journey in a simple way, focusing on key journeys. In general, a digital customer journey map consists of a persona, journey stages, touchpoints, interactions, and route. It describes how a persona interacts with a brand on a digital touchpoint in a journey stage.

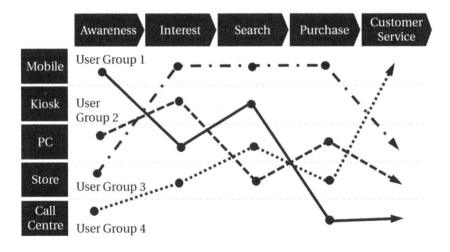

[Figure 3: Digital Customer Journey Map]

Customer Segment

A number of customers share common behaviours, including purchasing patterns in the digital space as well as in the real world. Those who share common behaviours are grouped into a distinctive customer segment.

There may be many customer segments for an organization, but the number of profitable customer segments or heavy user segments are not that many. In general, those groups are target customer segments accounting for 20~40% of total customers, while generating 60~80% of total operating profit or revenue.

A digital customer journey map needs to be created for the target customer segments. A single journey map for every customer is not effective enough and a journey map per customer is not feasible. It is advisable to create a persona representing a customer segment when a journey map for a customer segment is designed. Factors to consider include customer profile, customer preference, and other customer behavioural patterns.

Customer Segments are described in further detail in the section 'Capability 8-3. Customer Segmentation'.

Journey Stage

One of the misconceptions around a digital customer journey is that a customer journey begins when a customer initiates exploring a product or brand, or researches the product or brand. This is the beginning of the marketing or sales phase, not the beginning of an end-to-end customer journey.

A customer journey begins with the very first encounter with a brand, which evolves into full awareness of the brand. An end-to-end customer journey commonly includes the following stages:

- **Awareness stage**: customers make an initial contact with a product or brand, get to know the brand, and recognize the brand name.

- **Interest stage**: customers become interested in the product or brand through interesting interactions the brand provides.

- **Preference stage**: the brand becomes one of the preferred options for consideration when they are to make a purchase.

The preferred options constitute an evoked set[4] for the customers.

- **Search stage**: when customers plan to purchase a product, they gather information on candidate products and the focus of the research is on the evoked set, which is the preferred options for the purchase.

- **Analysis stage**: customers filter and compare products to make a purchasing decision.

- **Purchase stage**: a product is purchased and delivered.

- **Use stage**: the product is installed and used.

- **After-service stage**: customers ask and receive customer services and maintenance, and place complaints or give compliments. The after-service stage is considered another stage for customer purchase if the service or maintenance is out of warranty.

Digital Touchpoint

A touchpoint is where and how a customer interacts with a brand. In the digital space, a digital channel, digital media, or digital device can be a touchpoint through which a customer meets and interacts with a brand. To achieve the objective of the digital journey stage and move on to the next digital journey stage, multiple digital touchpoints can exist.

If the daily routine of a persona of a customer segment were to be followed, the touchpoints the persona purposely accesses, or the touchpoints that are exposed to the persona without the persona knowing it, will be found. This is how digital touchpoints are

---

[4] An evoked set is a set of product choices that a customer believes are viable options for them to purchase based on their wants relating to the product.

identified. Customer interactions with a brand and an organization arise on digital touchpoints.

Customer Interaction

A user may initiate interactions with a brand or an organization at a touchpoint to accomplish his purpose, or the interactions may be initiated by the organization to accomplish the purpose of the organization. The former type of interactions is to 'meet the wants' of the customer, while the latter is to 'create or awaken the needs' of the customer. When designing interactions on a digital touchpoint, both types of interactions should be considered.

Different interactions can be generated at the same touchpoint in different journey stages. These reflect a different state of a customer in progress toward a purchasing action. The context in which a touchpoint is used should also be taken into account.

Digital interactions are initiated and continued by delivering and exchanging messages between a customer and an organization. A description of how to design interactions to invoke a specific reaction is given below.

1. Define the reaction expected from the persona when the messages are sent at the touchpoint. The customer's reaction should drive which messages should be delivered.

2. Define key messages to be delivered at a touchpoint in a journey stage, considering the profile of a persona or a customer segment the persona belongs to, the preferences of the persona or the customer segment, and other behavioural patterns. The messages should be aligned with the expected customer reaction defined in step 1.

3. Repeat the processes; define the next customer reaction expected and define messages to encourage the reaction. When the next messages are designed, consider situations where a customer responds with unexpected reaction after the message has been delivered, and incorporate messages

to respond to the unexpected customer reaction into the next messages.

Route

A persona may prefer to take a few different routes from one journey stage to another in a single customer journey. The designing of customer interactions through message delivery and customer reactions at multiple touchpoints allow for the design of multiple routes optimized for the persona.

Although the shortest route is desirable, the persona may take another route depending on the interactions experienced at the previous touchpoint. As some touchpoints allow a persona to take multiple routes, these should be designed as an 'intersection' of the multiple routes, allowing them to take another route to the same destination on the same journey map, rather than dropping out of the journey.

Requirements of a Customer Journey Management Tool

MS-Office productivity tools such as Visio or PowerPoint may be used to develop a digital customer journey map, as this digital capability does not require robust tool capability. The following requirements may however be considered if there is a budget available for this digital capability.

- Provide standard templates of a digital customer journey map.
- Support users to develop a graphical map of the digital customer journey.
- Provide functionality to manage stages of the digital customer journey map, e.g. definition and profile of each stage, gate control, conversion plans, etc.
- Manage master data for a journey map such as customer segment, persona, journey stages, digital touchpoints, customer interactions, scenario, route, etc.
- Analyse the gap between a current map and a future map.

- Provide collaboration functionality.

MATURITY INDICATOR EXAMPLES

Level 0: Non-existent

- Although customer journey management practices may exist offline, there is nothing defined in the digital space to manage a customer journey. This includes digital customer journey, digital journey stages, digital touchpoint, or anything else that may be required.

Level 1: Ad hoc

- Some touchpoints for the digital space are identified and managed on an ad hoc basis.
- This is a once-off activity for a specific marketing promotion or event, and thus neither comprehensive nor detailed.
- It may have been created upon the request from executives for decision-making. It has however never been a regular part of the digital business operations.

Level 2: Basic

- Only a part of customer journeys in the digital space is managed; commonly a customer journey covering sales processes is defined.
- The digital customer journey map has barely been updated since its creation.
- The entire journey is not identified, nor is the key journey highlighted.
- It is not integrated with the offline journey, nor aligned with the corporate-wide customer journey.

Level 3: Defined

- End-to-end journeys for target customer segments are defined and managed through a few customer journey maps.
- Digital touchpoints, customer interactions on the touchpoints, and multiple routes are identified and defined.
- The online journey is integrated with the offline journey so that the corporate-wide customer journey can be managed seamlessly.
- Specialized staff, standard processes, and standard tools are implemented to perform Digital Customer Journey Management effectively.

Level 4: Optimized

- Digital Customer Journey Management is optimized to the extent that the organization can identify and focus on key customer journeys that can create differentiated interactions and experiences.
- The organization can differentiate itself in the market by demonstrating this level of the capability. It does however not necessarily provide a competitive advantage against major competitors.

Level 5: Progressive

- Many users from the key customer segments interact with the organization at the digital touchpoint as planned, as the organization is well aware of the behavioural patterns of the segments.
- The capability is fully integrated and aligned with other such digital capabilities from the front-office, middle-office, and back-office, enabling them to collectively create seamless experiences under the consistent direction offered by the digital customer journey map.
- The level of the capability provides a competitive advantage by creating higher customer intimacy and customer loyalty.

CAPABILITY 1-2.
USER RESEARCH

CAPABILITY DEFINITION

User Research is a digital capability used to understand customer behaviours, customer wants, customer needs and customer motivations by incorporating experimental and observational research; customer wants are explicitly expressed by customers, while customer needs are hidden or unknown to customers.

The User Research data is also used to design customer interactions and user experiences.

- **Designing of customer interactions at touchpoints**: The research data should provide input to developing concepts for customer interaction design in relation to what messages customers would want and need from the brand and organization at a specific touchpoint.

- **Designing of user experience and usability of touch points**: The research data should provide guiding principles to develop design concepts for improved user experiences and ease-of-use.

Numerous organizations perform user research on a regular basis and the research often targets a broader user base. The results of the user research into the broader user base does however often not lead anywhere. It would be sensible to focus user research on target customer segments of an organization.

When target customer segments are identified through analysis of customer interactions and purchasing behaviours, a profile of each target customer segment can be developed.

There is however a good chance that current databases and information available within an organization would not provide data enough to create an effective profile of a target customer segment. This is why User Research capability needs to be built to produce additional data for the profiling.

A common profile of a customer segment includes, but is not limited to:

- **Demographics**: the statistical characteristics of the customers in the same customer segment, such as age, gender, geographic location, marital status, income, home ownership, disabilities, education, employment status, children, savings, etc.

- **General value, belief & attitude**: common principles, standards, opinions, and even feelings shared by the majority of the customers in the same customer segment.

- **Situational goals**: common goals, purposes, and objectives shared by the same customer segment.

- **Preferred channels**: the access and communication channels most preferred by the customer segment.

- **Information searching patterns**: common patterns of where they go to find information, how they evaluate the information, what type of information they trust the most, etc.

- **Decision making patterns**: common patterns of the type and quantity of information used for decision-making, and a way that purchasing decisions are made, e.g. emotional, analytical, experiential, intuitive, etc.

- **Purchasing patterns**: common patterns of product purchasing, e.g. what product, how much, how many, and how frequent they purchase in which channels.

- **Annual revenue**: the annual purchasing amount by the customer segment.

- **Cost to serve**: the annual cost to support and maintain the customer segment.

User research should fill the gap between the data available in your transactional and analytical databases, and the data required to design interactions and user experiences.

MATURITY INDICATOR EXAMPLES

Level 0: Non-existent

- Some customers may have been analysed through transactional and analytical databases within the organization. Research into users outside the scope of the internal databases has however never been performed.

Level 1: Ad hoc

- User research is performed on an ad hoc basis to answer a tactical question, without clear long-term objectives for the use of the research data.
- User research has for example been performed a few times in the past to develop an executive report as part of marketing and business strategy consulting projects.

Level 2: Basic

- Research on users is conducted on a regular basis to fulfil the bottom-up needs for a quick fix, without longer-term objectives for the use of the research data.
- The user research is not focused on target customer segments.
- It is not aligned with strategic needs for digital customer experience management; it does not help answer strategic questions from the digital marketing strategy.

Level 3: Defined

- Centrally coordinated research into target customer segments is conducted to address strategic needs.

- Research tools, research methodology and aids, and clear roles and responsibilities are implemented.
- The data collected from the user research properly reflects customer wants that are explicitly expressed by the customers.
- Various types of research are employed to address not only quantitative questions, but also qualitative questions, e.g. focus group interviews and surveys.

Level 4: Optimized

- The user research is performed to understand the target customer segments better, rather than a broader customer base.
- The user research is focused on a few key areas where customer interactions and customer experiences need to be improved to facilitate progress from one touchpoint to another.
- The user research practice is optimized to the extent that hidden customer intentions can be captured. This allows for customer interactions at touchpoints to be designed in a way that they align with the hidden intentions of the customers, as well as the wants explicitly expressed by the customers.

Level 5: Progressive

- The result of the user research can facilitate creation of new needs previously unseen by the target customer segments; this is an advanced version of the hidden intention of customers, as it is more the invention of needs, rather than a discovery of needs.
- New ideas are continually generated and tried in the market to innovate customer interactions at touchpoints.
- The organization focuses more on creating new demands, rather than meeting existing demands, believing that

customers in general don't know what they need until it is shown to them.

CAPABILITY 1-3.
USABILITY ANALYSIS

CAPABILITY DEFINITION

Usability Analysis is a digital capability to analyse how users interact with the layout and contents that digital touchpoints provide. This capability is more relevant when it comes to the digital touchpoints with interfaces that are complex to navigate, e.g. desktop-purposed websites and mobile apps.

Usability Analysis is inherently an integral part of a broader concept of user experience design. It therefore aims at providing usability requirements and assessment criteria to the User Experience Design capability, to help create simpler and easier-to-use interfaces.

The usability of a digital touchpoint is commonly measured against learnability, efficiency, memorability, errors, and satisfaction. It also provides specific test scenarios and test cases for user experience testing to determine the usability of the designs.

Usability Analysis often follows industry-leading practices such as the 10 usability heuristics developed by Jakob Nielsen. A summarized version of these is shown below:

- **Visibility of system status**: The system should always keep users informed about what is going on, through feedback within reasonable time.

- **Match between system & the real world**: The system should use words, phrases and concepts familiar to the user, rather than system-oriented terms.

- **User control & freedom**: The system should provide emergency exit for the users to leave the unwanted state, without having to go through an extended dialogue.

- **Consistency & standards**: The system should make sure users do not have to wonder whether different words, situations, or actions mean the same thing.

- **Error prevention**: The system should provide mechanisms to prevent user's unconscious errors such as slips or mistakes, e.g. suggestions, good defaults, forgiving formats, etc.

- **Recognition rather than recall**: The system should minimize the user's memory load by making objects, actions and options visible. The user should not have to remember information from one part of the dialogue to another.

- **Flexibility & efficiency of use**: The system should cater to both inexperienced and experienced users. Accelerators may often speed up the interaction for the expert user. The system should allow users to tailor frequent actions.

- **Aesthetic and minimalist design**: Dialogues should not contain information irrelevant or rarely needed. Every extra unit of information in a dialogue competes with the relevant units of information and diminishes their relative visibility.

- **Help users recognize, diagnose, & recover from errors**: Error messages should be expressed in plain language without programming codes, precisely indicate the problem, and constructively suggest a solution.

- **Help & documentation**: Even though it is better if the system can be used without documentation, it may be necessary to provide help and documentation. Any such information should be easy to search, focused on the user's task, list concrete steps to be carried out, and not be too large.

The current levels of usability of the layouts and contents provided at the touchpoints can be assessed against criteria such as these, and target levels of usability set. Gaps are the difference between the current levels and the target levels. Usability requirements can be developed to address the gaps and provide the requirements for User Experience Design and User Experience Testing.

MATURITY INDICATOR EXAMPLES

Level 0: Non-existent

- Usability requirements are not developed.
- Usability of the interactions on the touchpoints is never assessed.

Level 1: Ad hoc

- Usability of the current touchpoints is assessed on an ad hoc basis.
- The depth and quality of the usability analysis is very limited as the usability analysis concept is merely emerging in the organization.
- The usability analysis does not always create requirements intended to improve the current usability.

Level 2: Basic

- Usability of the current touchpoints is analysed on a regular basis to assess the current level of usability.
- The result of the usability assessment may lead to the creation of usability requirements.

- Some of the digital projects include usability requirements as official part of the project scope, and the result of usability analysis may be spontaneously shared among some of the digital projects.
- The depth and quality of the usability is limited, as it is not a separate discipline or practice in the organization, and the usability analysis is performed without central standards.

Level 3: Defined

- Enterprise-wide usability principles and policies are implemented, e.g. User-centric Design principles.
- Standard methodology for usability analysis, analysis criteria, analysis tools, and official role for Usability Analysis are officially established and enforced by the policies.
- Usability requirements from the usability analysis are incorporated into User Experience Design and User Experience Testing.

Level 4: Optimized

- Usability is constantly measured and enhanced against metrics around learnability, efficiency, memorability, errors and satisfaction.
- Usability is optimized to the point where the organization has been able to create usability design patterns and techniques internally. These are stored in a repository enabling them to be shared and reused as design standards across the organization.
- Usability is a critical part of User Experience Designs and User Experience Testing.

Level 5: Progressive

- Usability is one of the drivers for improved customer experiences for the organization, allowing it to build high customer intimacy with the brand. This forms the basis of the competitive advantage.

- Internally developed usability principles, policies, design patterns and techniques are benchmarked as one of the industry leading practices.

CAPABILITY 1-4.
USER EXPERIENCE DESIGNING

CAPABILITY DEFINITION

User Experience (UX) Designing is a digital capability used to design and maintain user experiences in interactions with a brand, product, and organization. It enhances user satisfaction and loyalty by providing meaningful and personally relevant experiences, as well as improving accessibility, ease-of-use, and pleasure.

User experience design is a multi-disciplinary practice involving designing and marketing. On one hand, this capability is a design practice. It encompasses graphic design, sound & motion design, information & contents design, and interface design. On the other hand, this is a marketing practice. User experience is a type of customer experience in the digital space. A collective experience of a customer with an organization constitutes a brand for the individual customer. Therefore, designing user experiences is to design how to build a brand in the digital space.

Design Interaction First

Although User Experience Designing commonly includes creating products that provide improved customer experiences, the focus of user experiences in the Digital Capability Model is on improving the user experience in interactions on digital touchpoints along the digital customer journey.

From this point of view, the alignment of User Experience Designing to customer interaction plans of a digital customer journey map is its most critical management principle. User experience designs should be aligned with the interactions at touchpoints defined in a digital customer journey map. The designs should make sure the planned customer interactions take place.

Customer interactions on digital touchpoints are the repetitive processes of the message delivery and customer reactions to the messages on digital touchpoints. The exchange of the messages and reactions is the key scope of User Experience Designing. Content and information should be designed in detail as a critical part of User Experience Designing, so that the right messages creating the desired reactions are delivered.

If the majority of customers react unexpectedly to the content and information delivered at a touchpoint, either the messages of the digital customer journey map, or the user experience designs should be changed.

Design Interface Later

After the messages and customer reactions have been designed, the delivery methods for messages and reactions should be designed. This means designing interfaces of the touchpoints where the interactions occur. In-depth requirements for designing detailed interfaces of touchpoints should be available from the information on behavioural patterns of target customer segments. These can be identified from User Research results and customer segment profiles.

MATURITY INDICATOR EXAMPLES

Level 0: Non-existent

- The user interface of a touchpoint has been designed, but the user experience of the touchpoint has not been designed. For example, the user interface of the official company website has been designed from a graphic design perspective, but ways to improve user experiences to build better a brand from a marketing perspective has never been considered. The concept of User Experience Designing has therefore not yet been introduced into the organization.

Level 1: Ad hoc

- The role of user experience designer may have been implemented, but the role actually focuses on graphic design.
- The designer creates graphic elements to improve accessibility and usability at some of the digital touchpoints.
- The concept of User Experience Designing is just introduced into the organization.
- User Experience Designing is not yet accepted as a project management principle or discipline.

Level 2: Basic

- The concept of User Experience Designing is actively discussed and some of design practices are shared across some of the digital projects.
- User experience designs are however not consistent across projects or business units, as there is no enterprise-wide standard of User Experience Designing.
- The design practice and designs have little to do with building a brand, and they are therefore not well aligned with customer journey management.

Level 3: Defined

- The concept of User Experience Designing is officially established as one of the digital practices.

- Central standards design principles, policies, processes, methodology and design tools are in place.
- The user experience designs are aligned with the digital customer journey map.
- The user experience designs are consistent across projects and business units.
- The user experience designs are however still more focused on user interfaces, rather than on user interactions.

Level 4: Optimized

- The user experience designs are more focused on user interactions than on user interfaces.
- The effectiveness of user experience designs is measured against metrics such as accessibility and ease-of-use in user interactions and user interfaces on a regular basis.
- User experience designs are optimized based on the measurement against the metrics. This is done to the extent that customers become satisfied and therefore give positive feedback on their online experiences.

Level 5: Progressive

- Many users express strong preference for the designs of the interfaces and interactions with the brand on the digital touchpoints through customer surveys or online feedback. The collective user experience drives customer intimacy with the digital brand, contributing to building a competitive advantage.
- The design patterns for user experiences are internally developed, as part of internal knowledge built for core competencies supporting the competitive advantage.
- Its patterns for user experience design are often benchmarked as one of the industry leading practices.

CAPABILITY 1-5.
USER EXPERIENCE TESTING

CAPABILITY DEFINITION

User Experience Testing is a digital capability used to evaluate user experience designs across all digital channels and devices at touchpoints. It involves target users during testing to ensure that the user experience designs are implemented as is intended by both the requirements for experience designs, and the directions from a journey map.

User Experience Testing should not be confused with user interface testing, as user interface is just a small part of the user experience. Just as User Experience Designing is a multidisciplinary practice, so is User Experience Testing.

User Experience Testing is not solely meant to test user interfaces. It should test whether the experience designs are achieving what customer interactions at touchpoints of a digital customer journey map intend to achieve. For example, it should test whether the right message is delivered to the right customer through a suitable touchpoint to achieve the expected customer response in a way that is compatible with such a user interface.

Test Scenarios & Test Cases

In order to test user experience designs and implementations, test plans that have test objectives, test scope, tester recruiting, testing tools, testing processes, etc. need to be developed. Test scenarios and test cases also need to be developed to conduct the tests.

A test scenario is a general term used to describe the end-to-end flow of tests used to examine a business process scenario. A test scenario of User Experience Testing in Digital Customer Experience Management is a test flow to test an instance of the business processes scenario and customer navigation scenario on a digital customer journey map from the user experience perspective.

There would be many different instances for the same digital customer journey from brand awareness to product purchasing, depending on who is interacting for what and how. As not all instances that might happen can be tested, a few most likely instances should be chosen and test scenarios developed to test those instances.

A test scenario for user experience testing is commonly derived from a common route a persona of a target customer segment may take on a customer journey map.

A test case is used to perform a specific test for a specific function or step of a test scenario. A test case of user experience testing is to test a single interaction of a customer at a digital touchpoint. A test case for experience testing is commonly derived from an individual interaction at a touchpoint in the scope of a test scenario. A test case should have input, expected output and action to perform a specific test action. A single test scenario has multiple test cases.

MATURITY INDICATOR EXAMPLES

Level 0: Non-existent

- A user interface is tested from a software development perspective during system development, but the user experience is not evaluated before, during, or after the development.

Level 1: Ad hoc

- User experience is evaluated on an ad hoc basis.
- The evaluation is only performed to address critical customer complaints or incidents.

- A high-level test plan may be developed to define the scope or objective, but neither the test scenario, nor the test case is formally documented.

Level 2: Basic

- User experience is evaluated on a regular basis. No overarching principle or standard methodology has however been established to guide the user experience testing.
- Multiple testing scenarios and testing cases are planned and documented. Testing scenarios and testing cases are however not consistent, due to lack of a centralized standard or coordination.
- A testing tool may be used to support the testing processes. The functionality of the tool is however too limited to automate the end-to-end testing processes.

Level 3: Defined

- An overarching user experience testing strategy is defined to provide overall guidance for an individual user experience testing.
- Centralized testing methodology, guidelines and testing roles are implemented and enforced across the organization.
- The quality of testing scenarios and testing cases are consistent across the organization.
- A standard testing tool is implemented. The tool is specialized at user experience testing and the functionality of the tool is comprehensive enough to automate and support end-to-end testing processes.
- User experience designs are tested to verify whether intended customer responses to the designs are derived.

Level 4: Optimized

- User experience testing results are constantly measured against pre-defined metrics so that testing procedures and qualities are optimized based on the measurement.
- A closed feedback loop exists between experience testing and the other capabilities under Digital Customer Experience Management. User experience testing results are provided as input to the other capabilities.
- User experience designs are tested to verify whether the user experience designs facilitate the customer's journey on the customer journey map.

Level 5: Progressive

- A closed feedback loop exists between the target customers and the organization. Some loyal customers from the target customer segment regularly participate as an integral part in the user experience testings. The users and the organization successfully collaborate to perform the testing and thereby discover new ways to enhance customer experience designs and facilitate the customer's journey on the customer journey map.

MEGA CAPABILITY 2.

SOCIAL INTERACTION

Social Interaction is a set of digital capabilities used to facilitate interactions, both between end-users and between end-users and an organization through social media channels. The mega capability is not only to help grow business and improve business operations, but also to benefit the customers by ensuring that they get the right advice and support through Social Interaction, enabling them to make informed decisions.

A relationship through socialization needs to be built before marketing is done. The Social Interaction capabilities of the front-office enables an organization to interact with a wider audience than the target customer segments defined in marketing plans. The mega capability help creates brand awareness, interest and preference for the broader audience, as well as create word of mouth through loyal customers. The relationship often evolves beyond socialization to the extent that marketing offers can be made, and it can eventually lead to the next level where the audience can be convinced to take purchasing actions.

Social Interaction has the following digital capabilities:

- Social Listening
- Social Media Marketing
- Social Media Servicing
- Online Community Management
- Rating & Review Management
- Content Moderation
- Social Crisis Management

CAPABILITY 2-1.
SOCIAL LISTENING

CAPABILITY DEFINITION

Social Listening is a digital capability used to capture, store, and analyse a massive amount of information generated by digital users on social media about a brand and an organization in a (near) real time. This information can be about the company, its customers, its products, its services, its competitors, and its industry. This is done to make the best use of the data for business strategy and operations, and to determine how to respond best to customers and users whenever necessary.

Through the Social Listening capability, organizations can capture and analyse a variety of customer voice and sentiment around the brand, product, promotion, event, customer service, competitors and many more, and apply the findings to their business for many purposes. For example:

- Organizations can sense customers' reactions to their promotion on a (near) real-time basis and adjust the marketing promotion and marketing offers used for the promotion to improve the marketing promotion's effectiveness.

- Organizations can understand customers' decision-making criteria by monitoring how customers make purchasing decisions, and apply the criteria to customer mind positioning, product concept building and product positioning.

- Organizations can capture poor customer experiences in customer services, identify common patterns, and streamline and improve the customer services processes accordingly.

- Organizations can get an early warning of increasing negative customer opinions on its business practices and take preventive actions to reduce these before the negative opinions turn into negative actions.

Requirements of a Social Listening Tool

While Social Listening policies, processes, and workforce are important for Social Listening, Social Listening tools are the key to the successful implementation of the Social Listening capability. The tools are used to crawl social websites and media, and mine text and phrases for a specific keyword or combination of keywords on blogs, discussion forums and other social media, as well as mass media in near real time.

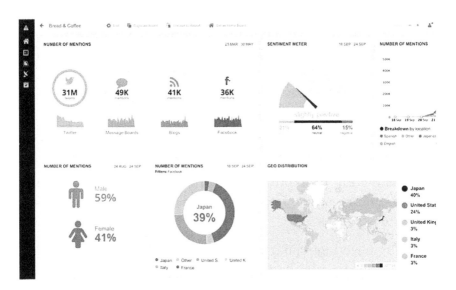

[Figure 4: Hootsuite Social Listening Solution]

The functionality of a Social Listening tool includes, but is not limited to:

- **Data capture**: social website crawling, real-time data stream capture, data transformation, etc.

- **Data store**: data repository, integration with big data platforms, data archiving, etc.

- **Data analysis**: sentiment analysis, influencer categorization & profiling, topic & theme analysis, trend analysis, viral content tracking, word & tag cloud, etc.

- **Data presentation**: alerts & notifications, content publishing, data visualization, dashboard, etc.

A Social Listening tool primarily uses keywords to find, sort, and analyse social website contents for information relevant to the purpose of the Social Listening. Identifying and defining a list of right keywords or phrases that the customers regularly discuss on social websites is critical to gather, capture, analyse, and report relevant information for Social Listening.

This type of information exists in an unstructured format and its volume is so massive that a big data platform is commonly required to perform the analytical processing, as well as storing the data along with Social Listening tools.

Use Cases in Other Business Operations

Information gathered through Social Listening are not only used for marketing and sales purposes, but also for almost all operational areas of an organization. For example:

- **Supply chain management**: customer discussions on social websites may have implication for product demand. This is used by supply chain management departments to plan supply and logistics of the products. Customer opinions are especially effective when the product has just been launched in the market, or is in the early stage of the product life cycle.

- **Product innovation & product quality management**: customers frequently and freely discuss and compare competing products in terms of features and qualities on social websites. These honest opinions from the customers can be utilized by the product development and quality management departments to develop, change, and manage product features and qualities

- **Risk & crisis management**: customers tend to go to social websites after being treated unfairly or finding defects in purchased products. They could for example vent their frustration even before disclosing the problem to the public or mass media. Organizations can capture these incidents and take actions before it turns into a social issue or crisis.

Leading Practice Examples

Some of the commonalities found among the leading practices are:

- They have metrics that are used to measure customer sentiment and decide when to take predefined actions. For example, "If the number of negative opinions on a product is more than 40%, report it to the product manager".

- They analyse trends of the data gathered to identify unseen patterns by integrating Social Listening with Big Data analytics. This takes advantage of correlation analysis functionality of the Big Data analytics. For example, "Users that are more active on social websites will have a stronger preference for screen quality of 3D TV".

- More importantly, they have a governance structure that can integrate Social Listening processes with other operational areas in the organization, so that almost all operation areas in the organization can apply the knowledge captured from the Social Listening to innovate their business operations. For example, negative opinions on a product component that are consistently raised feeds back into product development and quality management processes.

MATURITY INDICATOR EXAMPLES

Level 0: Non-existent

- No organizational ability exists to listen to and analyse the customer voice created on social websites.
- All information that the organization has about its customers comes predominantly from the internal transactional or analytical database, e.g. sales data, customer service data or basket analysis data.
- The organization only becomes aware of a massive crisis after it goes public, or is reported by mass media.

Level 1: Ad hoc

- Due to the lack of a Social listening tool, social websites are manually monitored for the customer's voice. This only happens when it is requested by executives, or when an incident has suspicious symptoms.
- A social manager or marketing practitioner is also responsible for monitoring social websites on an ad hoc basis. The processes and techniques used to monitor and analyse the social websites for customer opinions and voices are however limited.

Level 2: Basic

- A basic tool such as free Social Listening software is used to monitor social websites for customer voices on a regular basis. This is done to understand what is being discussed about the company, product, brand, market, competitor, and industry.
- Monitoring and analytics are not comprehensive due to the limited functionality of the monitoring tool.
- Social Listening principles and policies are missing, and the Social Listening processes and roles and responsibilities to perform the processes are not officially defined.

Level 3: Defined

- Corporate principles, policies, standards, processes, dedicated staff, and tools are implemented to collect and analyse customer voices and opinions generated on social websites.
- Keywords and phrases used to filter and analyse the data are defined, stored, updated and maintained on a regular basis.
- The functionality of the Social Listening tool is comprehensive in terms of data capture and data analysis.
- Overall customer sentiment is captured on a daily basis, and the potential risk of a major crisis is identified.
- The data that is collected from social websites and stored in the data repository remains in a semi-structured or unstructured format.

Level 4: Optimized

- The keywords and phrases have been optimized to such an extent that information that is not relevant to the purpose, the brands, and the industry is filtered out during the data capturing processes. This reduces data storage requirements and improves the effectiveness of data analytics.
- Some of the semi-structured data collected from social websites is transformed and organized into a structured format, enabling a user to use traditional SQL[5]-based analysis on the external data, along with internal structured data such as sales and after-service data. The combined

---

[5] Structured Query Language is a computer language used to create and access structured data held in a relational database management system (RDBMS) in which there are relations between data entities, e.g. the relation between the Customer data entity and the Order data entity is "Customers place Orders"

analysis enables the organization to generate a more comprehensive view into customer behaviours.

Level 5: Progressive

- The results from the analysis of the externally captured data is shared, not only in the marketing department, but also across the entire organization. The enterprise-wide data sharing improves business operations at every level of the organization. The results can for example be used as input into new product development, product quality assurance, customer services, and supply chain planning, as well as a marketing campaign.

CAPABILITY 2-2.
SOCIAL MEDIA MARKETING

CAPABILITY DEFINITION

Social Media Marketing or Social Marketing as defined in the context of the Digital Capability Model is a digital capability used to manage contents and interactions on social websites. It is used to attract the attention of social website users and encourages them to share the contents and information with their social network. This results in the products, services or brands being promoted on the social network.

Organizations can often address a wide range of audiences through Social Media Marketing, including current and potential customers, current and potential employees, journalists, bloggers, and the general public.

The content and information that needs to be delivered to social website users are created and maintained by the Knowledge &

Content Management capabilities of the middle-office of the Digital Capability Model. This will be discussed in detail later in this book.

Social managers and marketers can use content to draw users' attention and initiate interactions with them, encouraging the users to share the content with their social networks. Reproduction of the content can also be encouraged to effectively build customers' relationship with the brand.

Social Media Marketing is an integral part of marketing, and marketing plans for Social Media Marketing should therefore be developed. The plans may include marketing purposes, primary and secondary audience, messages and content, and marketing activity and content posting schedule.

The proper execution of the Social Media Marketing plans should be able to:

- Shape a new brand identity,
- Raise brand awareness,
- Build positive brand reputation,
- Increase website traffic, and
- Improve relationship with prospects.

Integration with Social Listening

Results of Social Listening are commonly used when performing Social Media Marketing activities. The results of Social Listening feed back to Social Media Marketing. When unfavourable behaviours are for example identified through Social Listening, responsive and preventive measures to mitigate the negative impact of the unfavourable behaviours can be implemented through Social Media Marketing.

Social Media Marketing with More Focus on 'Social'

The primary purpose of Social Media Marketing in the Digital Capability Model is to provide users with the right content so that they can easily digest and use to interact with their social network. This approach lets users freely discuss their experience with your brand and share their thoughts on your brand.

This capability is more about socialization than about marketing, and therefore an intruding, aggressive marketing pitch should be avoided.

Requirements of a Social Media Marketing Tool

Below are some of the key functional requirements that comprehensive Social Media Marketing tools should meet in order to effectively automate and support Social Media Marketing processes.

[Figure 5: SproutSocial Social Media Marketing Solution]

A Social Media Marketing tool should be able to:

- Help social managers and marketers to design specific posting patterns and schedules, and post content with a drag-and-drop calendar.

- Allow social managers and marketers to foster and nurture relationships through fast and efficient responses to comments and requests through engagement tracking functionality.

- Provide social managers and marketers with a set of templates to help create customized content to suit the audience of the specific social media of your choice, e.g. simple ads on Facebook, complicated infographics, and beautiful presentations and letters.

- Bulk upload a mass of different updates all at once. social managers and marketers should for example be able to list multiple blog posts in a text file and upload them to be distributed to multiple social media at certain intervals.

- Provide functionalities specialized for a specific social website, e.g. for Twitter, a functionality to recommend people to follow and ultimately help grow audience base.

- Provide functionalities to run contests, quizzes and quick promotions on social media.

- Help measure effectiveness and performance of the posting, create reports measuring key performance metrics, export them via graphs and tables, and adapt to the audience by making suggestions for who should be engaged with, and how to improve content.

MATURITY INDICATOR EXAMPLES

Level 0: Non-existent

- Social media has never been used for marketing communication with customers.
- Social websites have never been considered as a marketing channel.

Level 1: Ad hoc

- Social websites are considered important as a marketing channel, but they have not yet been established in the marketing strategy of the organization.
- Organizational accounts have been created on some of the social websites for tactical purposes, e.g. a sales promotion and event.
- The accounts have not been maintained properly, and the marketing content and messages on the social web sites may therefore not be up to date.
- The tool for Social Media Marketing is focused on a few specific functions, rather than having comprehensive functionalities.

Level 2: Basic

- Social media is constantly used as a marketing channel. They have however not yet been established as an integral part of the marketing channel mix strategy of the organization.
- The marketing content and messages on the social websites are updated on a regular basis. The content and messages are however no more than the information on the official website of the organization; similar content in a similar format is delivered to the audience of the social websites.
- Multiple tools are implemented to manage Social Media Marketing collectively. These are however not integrated.
- Some of the marketing tool functionalities available for traditional customer service management may also be used for Social Media Marketing, but they are limited in terms of performing marketing activities seamlessly on social websites.

Level 3: Defined

- Social media is considered one of the critical channels for marketing, sales and delivery to implement the marketing channel mix strategy.
- Corporate principles, policies, processes, dedicated social managers or marketers, their responsibilities and tool automation are in place to implement the marketing channel mix strategy on social media.
- Detailed plans are also defined to encourage word of mouth among users and their network by the use of the content designed for a specific purpose.

Level 4: Optimized

- The effectiveness and performance of the Social Media Marketing programs and activities are measured against pre-defined metrics, and the results are used to optimize the marketing activities.
- Opinion leaders are actively engaged in conversation with the organization, creating positive reactions from other users.
- The positive reactions help spread out marketing content and messages through social networks.

Level 5: Progressive

- The content and messages on the social websites are non-intrusive, and the interactions with the users are not driven by a marketing pitch.
- Users consider the content and interactions with the social managers and marketer on the social websites more personal and trustworthy than on the official website, and social media users therefore freely discuss their opinions with the social managers and marketers from the organization, and express personal feelings about the organization.

- The less commercial and more personal interactions with the users have contributed to building a positive brand reputation.

CAPABILITY 2-3.
SOCIAL MEDIA SERVICING

CAPABILITY DEFINITION

Social Media Servicing or Social Servicing as defined in the context of the Digital Capability Model is a digital capability used to provide customer service and customer support through social websites.

The majority of customer services and support before, during, and after customer purchase that are delivered by traditional customer service centres can be delivered on social websites.

This capability builds customer services and support operations on social websites and integrates these with the traditional customer service operations in a call centre and offline customer-service centre.

Customer Services Before, During & After Purchase

The responsibilities of customer services and support include fulfilment of customer request throughout the whole customer journey: before, during and after a purchase. After-service, which is provided after a customer purchases, is both the most common type and the most important of all customer service types. Traditional customer services have therefore been well organized to manage after-service.

The same traditional after-service needs to be provided on social websites, so that customers can have seamless experiences across the different service channels. A customer can for example make a request for a repair service on a social website, get a call from the customer contact centre of the organization, and check the status and progress in the repair on the customer service website.

Customer Request Management

In order to provide effective after-service on social websites, the functionality of a Social Servicing tool to manage customer requests on social websites needs to be implemented. The tool also needs to be integrated with warranty management, customer claim management, customer billing management, and service knowledge management so that the end-to-end processes for request fulfilment can be automated.

The seamless integration will prevent swivel chair integration and heavy manual processes, improving customer experiences in customer services across the multiple service channels.

Social websites offer a better environment for organizations to provide services before customer purchase than traditional service channels do, as customers are willing to express what content or services they need in order to make a decision on purchasing a product on social websites.

The request-fulfilment functionalities of a Social Media Servicing tool need to be designed to meet customers' needs for customer services before, or during purchase of a product.

Integration of Social Media Servicing with Product Development & Quality Management

Customer requests, feedback, and even claims are great sources of improvement and innovation in product development and quality management.

Traditional customer service practices have however not been successful in satisfying this expectation. Information gathered through traditional customer service channels is limited, and process and data integration of customer service management with product development and quality management is not effective enough to share the information between the different management processes. One example of this is the lack of integration between claim management processes and product development processes.

Social Servicing can feed far more information into product development and quality management than traditional customer service practices can. This is because of the nature of social websites that encourages and motivates customers to express their opinion and share their ideas freely.

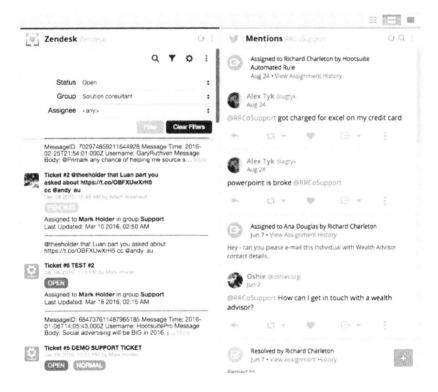

[Figure 6: Zendesk Social Media Servicing Solution]

The data can therefore not be integrated into the systems the other operational areas have access to easily, making it difficult for the other operational areas to access and analyse the data from Social Servicing.

When a big data platform that processes non-structured or semi-structured data is developed, integration of the non-structured or semi-structured data with structured data stored in relational database systems should be considered.

Requirements of a Social Media Servicing Tool

Below are some of the key functional requirements that comprehensive Social Media Servicing tools should meet in order to effectively automate and support Social Media Servicing processes. The tools should be able to:

- Integrate into any social website where the organization has an account.
- Monitor the accounts of the social websites for keywords requesting customer services.
- Alert and notify the customer service team of the posts relevant to customer services.
- Enable a member of the customer service team to respond to messages, comments and mentions promptly through a single dashboard.
- Access customers' conversation history.
- Enable the customer service team to collaborate and assign tasks.
- Analyse customer service performance and generate reports.
- Integrate with the internal customer service systems for management of membership, claim, warranty, repair, billing, etc.

MATURITY INDICATOR EXAMPLES

Level 0: Non-existent

- Social media has never been used for customer services and support.
- Social websites have never been considered as a customer service channel.

Level 1: Ad hoc

- Social websites may be considered important as a customer service channel, but they have not yet been established in the customer service strategy of the organization.
- Accounts for the organization may have been created for customer services in some social websites, but the accounts are no longer used for customer services purposes.
- The accounts have not been properly maintained, and the content and messages for customer services on the social web sites may therefore not be up to date.
- FAQs are provided. Answers may be provided if a customer asks a question for customer services on social websites.
- The tool for Social Media Servicing is focused on a few specific functions, rather than having comprehensive functionalities.

Level 2: Basic

- Social media is used as a customer service channel on a regular basis. They have however not been established as an integral part of the service channel mix strategy of the organization.
- The customer service content and messages on the social websites are updated on a regular basis. The content and messages are however no more than the information on the official website of the organization. Similar content in a similar format is delivered to the audience on the social websites.
- Multiple tools are implemented to manage Social Media Servicing collectively. These are however not seamlessly integrated.

- Some of the customer services and support tool functionalities available for traditional customer service management may also be used for Social Media Servicing, but they are limited in terms of performing customer services and support in a seamless manner on social websites.

Level 3: Defined

- Social media is established as one of the strategic channels for customer services and support to implement the customer-service channel mix strategy.
- Corporate principles, policies, processes, dedicated customer service managers, their responsibilities and tool automation are in place to implement the customer service channel mix strategy on social media.
- Social Media Servicing is still a standalone practice and integration of traditional customer services with Social Media Servicing is therefore limited. Dis-integration of processes and tools causes swivel chair integration and manual intervention to complete the end-to-end processes.
- Customer services are heavily focused on after-service.

Level 4: Optimized

- The effectiveness and performance of the Social Media Servicing activities are measured against pre-defined metrics, and the results are used to optimize the customer service activities.
- Social Media Servicing is well integrated with traditional customer services, including call centre and offline service centres. Processes and tools between the two practices are seamlessly integrated to ensure that there is little swivel chair integration and manual intervention.
- Customer services and support of the organization, both online and offline are provided seamlessly. This improves customer experience significantly.

- The organization has started to expand to customer services to before and during customer purchase.

Level 5: Progressive

- Information such as claims, questions, requests, etc. that is gathered through Social Media Servicing is extracted, stored, analysed and distributed to relevant business units and departments, and reused to innovate brand, products, and business operations.
- Users consider the interactions with the social servicing managers of the organization on the social websites more personal than the customer contact centre, and therefore discuss their opinions with the social servicing managers freely, and express personal feelings about the customer services and the organization.

CAPABILITY 2-4.
ONLINE COMMUNITY MANAGEMENT

CAPABILITY DEFINITION

Online Community Management is a digital capability used to build, grow and guide an online community on social media to support social interactions, marketing activities, and customer services. This digital capability helps enhance brand reputation and power.

Online community is not a new concept. It means a virtual community whose members interact with each other on social networking sites, chat rooms, forums, e-mail lists and discussion boards.

Management of the online community includes building and growing the community and involves managing the community members and interactions among them. Encouraging the online community members to network with one another and share personal stories and experiences is therefore as important as the organization's interactions with the members.

One of the critical missions of online community management is to manage loyal members and help them to lead the community. Community members will willingly follow the opinion leaders.

Requirements of an Online Community Management Tool

The management activities are performed by specialized community managers. To assist with the community management, this capability should provide tools to monitor and report the activities of community members, as well as further tools to manage content and messages that should be communicated to the members in order to proactively respond to their activities, or guide their interactions.

The following are examples of the key functional requirements that an Online Community Management tool commonly offers to automate and support Online Community Management processes effectively.

An Online Community Management tool include the following functionalities:

- Create and manage online communities and user groups.
- Organize community members, discussions, and community content.
- Enable community members to share documents, knowledge, experiences and personal stories.
- Enable community managers to engage internal employees in a discussion automatically.
- Organize online and offline networking.
- Provide functionality to host online conferences and webinars.

- Provide functionality to encourage product knowledge transfer and learning.
- Analyse performance of online communities, e.g. traffic to the community, the number of community members, engagement of the members, etc.

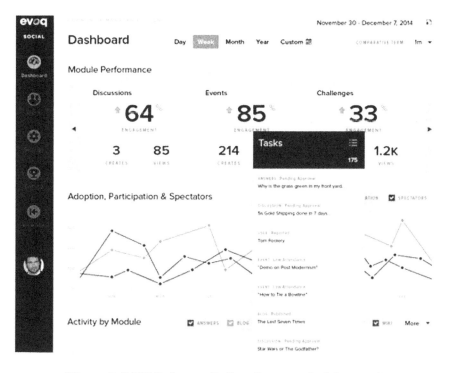

[Figure 7: DNN Software Online Community Manager]

MATURITY INDICATOR EXAMPLES

Level 0: Non-existent

- No online community exists on social media, or on the official website.
- An account on social media may have been created, but there has been no activity to manage the online community since its creation.

Level 1: Ad hoc

- Single or multiple accounts have been created on social websites to build online communities. The communities have however been managed in an ad hoc manner, resulting in outdated content and stagnated activities of the online community members.
- A community manager responsible for managing and maintaining the online communities has not been appointed.

Level 2: Basic

- The organization has set up multiple online communities on social websites, and has maintained the communities and provided content on a regular basis since the creation of the communities.
- The community management efforts are however not managed by a top-down strategy, but from bottom-up needs of the marketing team and staff. The online community management activities are therefore neither aligned with corporate digital strategy, nor consistent across the organization.
- There may be a community manager to maintain and manage the online community. The manager is therefore not dedicated to the community management role.
- The community management tool provides basic functionality for the community manager to create a community and to share content.

Level 3: Defined

- Corporate principles, policies, processes, tools and a dedicated manager are implemented to build, maintain and nurture the online communities.
- Community guideline for community members is officially established and shared on the online communities.

- The functionality of the online community management is comprehensive enough to encourage the community members to actively network and participate in sharing content, knowledge and experiences, and to analyse the performance of the online community management.

Level 4: Optimized

- There are strong supporters for the brand in the online communities, and the communities can therefore be maintained by community members themselves, without heavy involvement or intervention of the community manager, or employees of the organization.
- The performance of the online community management has been analysed against pre-defined metrics to identify improvement opportunities, and the online community management has constantly been optimized based on the performance measurement.

Level 5: Progressive

- The online communities are a critical part of the organizational structure for business innovation. The activities and information generated in the online communities become the integral part of official business processes of the organization for business innovation, and official business information flowing throughout the innovation processes.
- The online communities, as the external part of the organization, provide a core competency for the organization and thus creates competitive advantage in the market.

CAPABILITY 2-5.
RATING & REVIEW MANAGEMENT

CAPABILITY DEFINITION

Rating & Review Management is a digital capability used to monitor, collect, respond, share, and encourage ratings and reviews on company, products and services on rating & review websites, social media, and the official website of an organization.

Monitoring of Ratings & Reviews

Many customers provide ratings and reviews on ecommerce websites when they make a purchase. Customers also tend to go to rating & review websites or social media to compliment or complain about their experience with a company, employee, product and service before, during and after purchase. Organizations should manage how they provide ratings and reviews to the websites outside the company's official websites, and the results of the ratings and reviews.

An organization can start by building an ability to monitor the results of the rating and reviews of customers as soon as they post the content. The monitoring ability can be built as part of the Social Listening capability, or as a standalone monitoring ability specialized for customer rating and review management.

Monitored data should be able to be analysed on a real-time basis to detect negative opinions before it spreads on the Internet, and needs to be gathered and stored into a central repository for later, further analysis and sharing across the organization.

Management of Unfavourable Ratings & Reviews

Rating & Review Management includes all organizational abilities both to encourage customers to provide favourable ratings and reviews on rating & review websites or social media, and to respond quickly and effectively to unfavourable ratings and reviews. Mitigation of the impact of negative feedback and prevention of further negative feedback are in fact far more important than encouraging and sharing positive feedback.

Principles, policies and procedures on how to respond to those negative ratings and reviews needs to be implemented. They should for example provide guidance on:

- How to assess whether it's worth responding.
- How to assess the issues.
- How to follow the different rules of different rating & review websites.
- How to assess whether it is a false accusation.
- How to resolve the issues, including whether to respond privately or publicly.
- How to communicate with the customer in question and the rating & review website.

Requirements of a Rating & Review Management Tool

Organizations can take advantages of Rating & Review Management tools to facilitate the business processes performed to manage customer ratings and reviews effectively.

A Rating & Review Management tool should include the following functionalities:

- Provide functionality for the organization to send customers email invitations or messages to ask for rating and reviews.
- Provide functionality for the customers to respond to the invitation and provide ratings and reviews, and check the progress of their reviews.
- Monitor, gather and display all types of information, e.g. text, photos and videos, on all ratings and reviews relevant to the company, brands, products, services and competitors.
- Consolidate and organize the ratings and reviews according to products, services, or other criteria.

- Alert or notify in real-time when customers post a critical review.
- Automate and facilitate the processes to respond, and manage negative feedback.
- Provide functionality for marketers to reuse the ratings and review content on their websites or elsewhere.
- Analyse the performance of Rating & Review Management.

[Figure 8: Catalyst eMarketing Reputation Manager]

MATURITY INDICATOR EXAMPLES

Level 0: Non-existent

- The company may be aware of the importance of management of online ratings and reviews. No part of the Rating & Review Management capability has however been implemented.
- Any type of information on online ratings and reviews of the company, products, or services have never been monitored, or gathered for management purpose.

- The organization becomes aware of the incident only after the negative review spreads widely on the Internet and mass media report the incident.

Level 1: Ad hoc

- Rating & Review Management is primarily a manual process and performed on an ad hoc basis.
- Customer rating and review information is monitored, gathered, or analysed only when a review involves a critical incident and the organization needs to understand and solve the issue.
- The organization may adopt free software to help monitor and manage customer ratings and reviews. The functionality of the tool is however severely limited.

Level 2: Basic

- Customer ratings and reviews are monitored, gathered, stored and analysed on a regular basis. The management processes have however been built spontaneously from the bottom-up to urgently respond to negative feedback, and all the required processes are therefore not necessarily defined or established.
- Negative ratings and reviews that have significant impact on business may be responded to at a later time due to lack of real-time monitoring functionality.
- Part of the Rating & Review Management processes are automated by a tool that is functionally too limited to facilitate the end-to-end management processes.

Level 3: Defined

- Customer ratings and reviews are monitored, gathered, analysed or responded to according to predefined processes by dedicated personnel.

- Corporate policies and procedures to respond effectively to unfavourable ratings and reviews are implemented.
- The negative reviews that have significant impact on the organization are captured and reported to the organization as soon as they are posted.
- The different business units are coordinated effectively and their responses to a negative feedback are consistent across the organization.
- Corporate standard tools are defined and implemented. The tools collectively have rich functionalities to automate end-to-end processes of Rating & Review Management fully.

Level 4: Optimized

- Users are actively encouraged to rate or review products and services by the organization to promote the word of mouth effect.
- Customers are effectively motivated to populate positive ratings and reviews, and the positive results are actively shared across social websites and the Internet.
- The performance of the Rating & Review Management has been analysed against pre-defined metrics to identify improvement opportunities, and management has been optimized constantly based on the performance measurement.

Level 5: Progressive

- This level of the capability enables the organization to identify root causes of a negative rating and review through end-to-end visibility into business operations. The capability level helps the organization to turn the problems into new opportunities to improve customer experience by getting rid of the root causes.
- The organization is more focused on establishing preventive measures than on efficient corrective measures to reduce the probability of critically negative experiences occurring.

CAPABILITY 2-6.
CONTENT MODERATION

CAPABILITY DEFINITION

Content Moderation is a digital capability used to screen and eliminate content that is irrelevant, obscene, illegal, or insulting to improve the quality of contents and maintain the identity of an online community and a social website. It involves managing users who create that type of unacceptable contents as well.

Clear rules and policies for moderating contents must be implemented to avoid perceptions of bias or unfairness.

Pre-moderation and Post-moderation

Content can be moderated before posting the contents, or after. For pre-moderation, a user submits content and it goes to a queue for review by a content moderator before posting. After moderating the content, the content moderator posts the content. This method is especially effective when the audience is very vulnerable to harmful content.

Pre-moderation however often frustrates users who post content because of the waiting time and becomes the cause of failure in building a robust online community. Post-moderation is therefore more frequently used to ensure better customer experience, in conjunction with automated content moderation tools that can filter out harmful words or sentences when a user posts content.

Centralized & De-centralized Moderation

Centralized moderation is the moderation performed by dedicated content moderator(s). Dedicated content moderators may be professionals hired by the organization, or volunteers selected by the organization from community users.

Decentralized moderation is performed by viewers after content is posted. A popular method for decentralized moderation is to raise a red flag around undesirable content. If the number of red flags reaches or goes beyond a threshold, then the content is moderated.

Centralized modernization can be used in conjunction with decentralized moderation by sharing some of the responsibilities for moderating content. When the number of red flags for content for example reaches the threshold, the content automatically goes under the review by designated content moderators.

Requirements of a Content Moderation Tool

An organization can manage content moderation processes effectively by using a comprehensive Content Moderation tool that is able to:

- Detect unacceptable content and the user creating the content before, or as soon as it is posted. The monitoring and capturing functionality may be implemented as part of a comprehensive Social Listening tool.
- Guide users with example of unacceptable content when composing a post.
- Provide a word filter functionality in which a list of banned words is stored and maintained, and the tool either recommends alternative words, replaces it with a defined alternative, or blocks the entire post.
- Guide content moderators with examples of unacceptable content.
- Guide content moderators and the user who creates the content to moderate the unacceptable content.
- Automate the workflow of the content moderation, review, approval and publish processes.
- Enable community members to raise a red flag on a post.
- Measure the performance of Content Moderation.

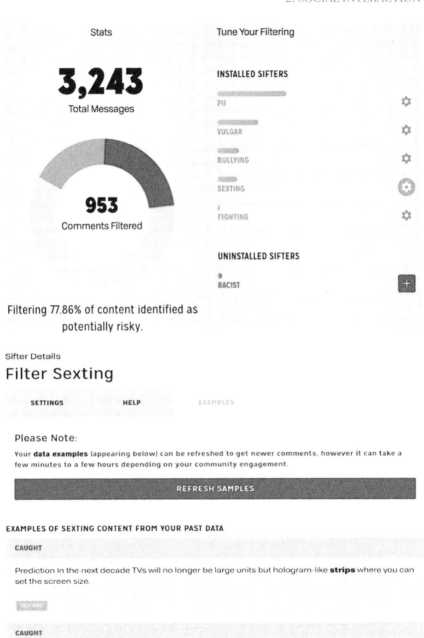

[Figure 9: Sift Ninja Content Moderation Solution]

MATURITY INDICATORS

Level 0: Non-existent

- No action is taken to moderate inappropriate content on the social websites.
- Any customer content can be created, posted and distributed across multiple social websites.
- The organization becomes aware of unacceptable content through an external party such as other customers or mass media, only after the content causes serious issues.

Level 1: Ad hoc

- Inappropriate content is moderated on an ad hoc basis.
- No policies or procedures are defined to manage the content moderation processes. As the role of content moderator is not established, different personnel take joint responsibility to moderate content when it is required.
- Due to the unorganized, intermittent pattern of the content moderation practice of the organization, it often misses the chance to filter out the content that may cause an issue for the organization.
- The tool functionality is limited and the processes are manual.

Level 2: Basic

- The customer content is moderated against the content moderation policies on a regular basis. The management policies and procedures have however been defined spontaneously from bottom-up to get rid of unacceptable content urgently, and the policies and procedures therefore have much room for quick fixes and improvement.
- Customer content is monitored in real time to determine if inappropriate content is posted. An automation tool is employed to detect undesirable content, but is functionally

too limited to automate and support end-to-end content moderation processes.

Level 3: Defined

- Content is monitored, reported and dealt with through corporate policies and processes, a specialized and dedicated content moderator, and comprehensive content moderation tools with rich functionalities.
- The unacceptable content is detected and moderated before, or when the content is posted.
- Both centralized and decentralized content moderations are employed.
- Corporate standard tools are defined and implemented. The tools collectively have rich functionalities to automate the end-to-end processes of Content Moderation fully.

Level 4: Optimized

- Preventive and proactive moderation is implemented and actively enforced. Sophisticated filtering policies and rules used by content moderation tools for automated moderation have for example been developed and deployed.
- The performance of the Content Moderation practice has been analysed against pre-defined metrics to identify improvement opportunities, and management thereof has been optimized constantly based on the performance measurement.

Level 5: Progressive

- Strong self-moderation practice is implemented and actively enforced. As per the decentralized moderation method, more content and users are for example moderated by community members and viewers than by content moderators and content moderation tools.

CAPABILITY 2-7.
SOCIAL CRISIS MANAGEMENT

CAPABILITY DEFINITION

Social Crisis Management is a digital capability used to mitigate the probability and the impact of major incidents that threaten to harm the organization and stakeholders.

The digital capability not only decreases the probability that a major incident occurs, but also reduces the impact of the major incident on business when it actually occurs.

It encompasses abilities to identify a threat before a crisis occurs, and mitigate the threat, and to deal with the crisis when, or after it occurs.

Stories about a food poisoning incident and news of a car accident from a car malfunctioning reported on multiple social websites are for example considered a threat or crisis to the food company and the car company respectively.

Threat Detection & Evaluation

The first step of Social Crisis Management is to build an ability to detect every possible threat to the organization and its stakeholders in social websites and news websites. The ability to detect a threat can be built as part of the Social Listening capability. Not every threat does however become a crisis. Threats that are initially detected should therefore be evaluated against pre-defined evaluation criteria to see which threats should be managed as a priority.

A threat can be evaluated against the two criteria combined as follows:

- **Probability**: the level of likelihood that a threat become a crisis.

- **Business Impact**: the level of negative impact of the threat on business if it becomes a crisis.
- **Threat** = Probability x Business Impact

Threat Mitigation

After evaluating a threat, mitigation plans should be created and communicated to all parties that could be impacted by the threat.

Mitigation plans include the following:

- How to mitigate the probability of the threat becoming a crisis.
- How to mitigate the level of impact of the crisis on business if the threat become a crisis.

Action items to mitigate the probability and the level of business impacts are at the core of threat mitigation plans.

Requirements of a Social Crisis Management Tool

Below are the key functional requirements of a Social Crisis Management Tool. The tool should be able to:

- Capture and store information representing potential threats from social websites, mass media, and other types of content websites.
- Enable users to identify and profile threats from the captured information.
- Enable users to prioritize the threats by calculating the threat level. A threat is calculated in terms of the probability of the threat occurring, and the level of business impact if the threat turns into a crisis.
- Enable users to establish and profile controls to reduce the probability and the level of business impacts.
- Provide functionality to create a mitigation plan including who takes what action, when, and how.
- Automate workflows to handle a crisis when a threat turns into a crisis.

MATURITY INDICATOR EXAMPLES

Level 0: Non-existent

- No activities to assess or mitigate potential threats generated on social websites and online media are implemented.
- The organization becomes aware of the crisis generated in the digital space only after a threat turns into a crisis, and it starts damaging the digital brand significantly and decreases the business value.

Level 1: Ad hoc

- Potential threats generated on the social websites and online media is detected on an ad hoc basis, for example, when asked for by executives, or when required for external compliance purpose.
- Due to the ad hoc pattern of the threat detection practice of the organization, it often misses threats that may turn into a crisis of the organization.
- A threat mitigation plan may have been created, but it has not been updated since the creation of the plan, and is therefore not relevant to the current threats.
- No policies or procedures have been defined to manage a threat and crisis.
- No automation tool is employed to support the Social Crisis Management processes.

Level 2: Basic

- Potential threats generated on social websites and online media are identified on a regular basis before the threats become incidents or crisis.
- The potential threats are not properly prioritized. The Social Crisis Management effort is therefore diffused and is not used to focus on managing critical threats.

- Incidents may also be detected as soon as they occur by using an automated monitoring tool. The tool has however limited functionality that does not enable end-to-end Social Crisis Management processes fully.
- Threats are captured and assessed against the policies on a regular basis. The management policies and procedures have however been defined spontaneously from the bottom-up to respond to a crisis urgently, and the policies and procedures therefore has much room for a quick fix and improvement.

Level 3: Defined

- Potential threats are monitored, reported and dealt with through corporate policies and processes, a specialized crisis manager, and comprehensive Social Crisis Management tools with rich functionalities.
- The threats are assessed to identify priorities.
- Mitigation plans are developed to reduce the probability of the threats and the level of business impact.
- The mitigation plans are executed and the progress of the action items in the mitigation plans are tracked and reported to management.
- Corporate standard tools are defined and implemented. The tools collectively have rich functionalities to automate end-to-end processes of Social Crisis Management fully.

Level 4: Optimized

- The Social Crisis Management efforts are focused on implementing strong corrective measures that address incidents when they happen.
- Effective controls and measures are implemented and actively enforced to mitigate threats turning into crisis actively.
- The performance of the Social Crisis Management practice has been analysed against pre-defined metrics to identify

improvement opportunities, and management of this has been optimized constantly based on the performance measurement.

Level 5: Progressive

- The focus of Social Crisis Management is on implementing preventive measures that can actually contribute to preventing a potential threat from becoming crisis.
- Online community members are also participating in the implementation of preventive measures set up in the threat mitigation plans. The participation of the online community members significantly contributes to implementing preventive measures.

MEGA CAPABILITY 3.

DIGITAL MARKETING

Digital Marketing is a set of digital capabilities used to acquire and retain customers across multiple digital channels by increasing digital traffic and customer engagement. Digital Marketing activities should be based on a single view of customers across multiple digital channels to be seamless across the discrete digital channels, and be guided and directed by the customer routes mapped out on a customer journey map.

Conceptually, a relationship needs to be built through Social Interaction capabilities before making a marketing pitch as per a customer journey map. The relationship between a company and its customers evolves and goes beyond the casual socialization level to the point where marketing offers can be made. The purpose of the Digital Marketing capabilities is to transform socialization relationship into the status where customers can be led to a purchasing transaction.

Digital Marketing includes the following capabilities:

- Digital Brand Marketing
- Search Engine Optimization

- Paid Search
- Content Targeting
- Affiliate Marketing
- Online Advertising
- Digital Campaign Management
- Lead Management
- Marketing Offer Management
- Email Marketing
- Mobile Marketing
- Marketing Automation
- Conversion Rate Optimization

CAPABILITY 3-1.
DIGITAL BRAND MARKETING

CAPABILITY DEFINITION

Digital Brand Marketing is a digital capability used to build and promote a brand to customers in the digital space, so that customer's perception of the brand can move from the initial stage where a customer is aware of the brand, all the way up to the final stage where the customer is loyal to the brand.

This capability should be closely integrated with customer experience management in that a brand is built out of the result of customer experience. By definition, a brand in is a collection of customer experiences with all levels of the organization that owns the brand.

Digital Brand Marketing Funnel and Stages

A brand is all about a customer's perception of the brand, and thus Digital Brand Marketing is all about managing activities to promote customer perception of a brand in the digital space. Customers' perception of a digital brand can be managed effectively through a Digital Brand Marketing funnel consisting of the following stages:

1. **Digital Brand Awareness stage**: Customers see or hear about a brand name and become aware of the existence of the brand, but don't know details about the brand.

2. **Digital Brand Interest stage**: Customers are attracted to some of the features and aspects of the brand, and interested in knowing more about the brand.

3. **Digital Brand Preference stage**: The brand becomes one of the customer's preferred brands. Customers often have preference of multiple brands competing in the same market.

4. **Digital Brand Memory stage**: Customers keep the brand in mind for a proper time when they make a purchase.

5. **Digital Brand Trial stage**: Customers decide to make use of the brand.

6. **Digital Brand Loyalty stage**: Customers are determined to use the brand again because they are satisfied with engaging with the brand.

Digital Brand Marketing plans and activities should focus on moving a customer's mind and perception toward the digital brand loyalty stage. Target customers may probably be scattered across all stages of the funnel. It is however possible that the majority of the target customers are somewhere around the same stage. If that is the case, it will be possible to focus brand marketing programs and activities on moving them from that stage to the next stage. If the majority of the target customers for example seem to be aware of your brand, but do not show interest in your brand, your digital brand marketing activities should focus on providing digital content or messages that can trigger their curiosity, excitement, or interest in the brand, rather than sales promotion messages from a Digital Brand Marketing perspective.

The Digital Brand Marketing funnel is not a sales funnel used to facilitate and manage sales processes. The Digital Brand Marketing funnel focuses on creating a favourable brand image in customers' mind, and does not necessarily increase sales. The Digital Brand Marketing funnel is used to increase the mind share of target customers, whereas a sales funnel is used to increase market share of a target industry.

To make a Digital Brand Marketing funnel work better, the stages of the funnel should be aligned with Digital Customer Journey stages and maps discussed earlier in this book. Digital Customer Journey stages and maps provide overarching directions that the digital brand marketing funnel and the sales funnel should all be aligned to.

Requirements of a Digital Brand Marketing Tool

Very comprehensive automation tools are not necessarily needed to manage Digital Brand Marketing processes. The tool, if any, may however assist with the following tasks.

- Manage digital brand identity data, e.g. digital brand logo, standard colour and font set, headers and footers of website, newsletter template, social account and blog templates, etc.
- Manage stages of Digital Brand Marketing funnel, e.g. definition and profile of each stage, gate control, conversion plans, etc.
- Manage tasks of Digital Brand Marketing programs and routine activities.
- Manage profiles of digital brand influencers and digital media.
- Manage Digital Brand Marketing events.

MATURITY INDICATOR EXAMPLES

Level 0: Non-existent

- The organization may be aware of the importance of digital brand marketing. However, there is neither a plan nor an activity to promote customer perception of the brand in the digital space.
- Sales activities may be performed in the digital space. However, the objectives of the sales activities have nothing to do with increasing brand loyalty or customer mind share.

Level 1: Ad hoc

- The organization performs Digital Marketing Activities on an ad hoc basis. The ad hoc activities are conducted as part of once off marketing events or promotions.
- There is no digital brand marketing plan that drives the Digital Brand Marketing activities.

- No tool is employed to manage the Digital Brand Marketing activities.

Level 2: Basic

- The organization performs activities to promote its brand on a regular basis. An officially defined funnel is not employed, but the marketing activities are mostly focused on increasing brand awareness.
- The Digital Brand Marketing concept has been discussed actively, but has not yet been established as a formal discipline in the organization.
- The equivalent of a Digital Brand Marketing plan is used, but it is focused on short-term quick-wins, rather than on long-term strategic initiatives to improve brand loyalty. The quick-win plans are neither consistent across the organization, nor aligned with the overarching marketing plan.
- Very basic tools are employed to support the development and implementation of digital brand marketing plans partially, e.g. MS-office and free software.

Level 3: Defined

- Digital Brand Marketing is considered an official marketing discipline in the organization, and corporate policies, processes, roles & responsibilities, and automation tools are therefore established to perform Digital Brand Marketing.
- A corporate standard funnel for Digital Brand Marketing is established to ensure consistency in Digital Brand Marketing plans and activities across the multiple business units.
- Long-term strategic initiatives, as well as short-term quick-wins are incorporated into the Digital Brand Marketing plans. The plans for the digital space are aligned with overarching corporate marketing plans.

- An automation tool specialized in brand management is employed to help planning and implementation processes.

Level 4: Optimized

- Progress and conversion from one stage to another in the Digital Brand Marketing funnel are measured and Digital Brand Marketing plans to improve the performance in the funnel are developed based on the result of the measurement.
- The organization can take a clear snapshot of each stage of the funnel to understand where the target customer segments are staying and moving.
- The metric management and performance measurement are supported by a funnel management functionality of the Digital Brand Marketing tool.

Level 5: Progressive

- Digital Brand Marketing activities are fully integrated with other digital capabilities so that Digital Brand Marketing can take advantage of the capabilities and they collectively create marketing synergy, e.g. integration with Campaign Management to promote customer perception, and integration with Customer Loyalty Management to promote brand loyalty.
- The integration with other digital capabilities help achieve the intention of the digital customer journey map. The seamless integration with other digital capabilities also ensures consistency in digital customer experiences, which creates a consistent brand image.
- The practices of Digital Brand Marketing are closely coupled with other digital capabilities so that the Digital Brand Marketing practices cannot be copied easily by competitors.

CAPABILITY 3-2.
SEARCH ENGINE OPTIMIZATION

CAPABILITY DEFINITION

Search Engine Optimization (SEO) is a digital capability used to increase visibility of an organization's web pages in search engine's results of un-paid search, which is also known as organic search. It targets different kinds of search, including image or video search, academic search, local search and so on. The ability to understand search engine's ranking factors and algorithms is critical to successful SEO in order to rank high.

SEO Keywords & Brand Positioning

One of the most important factors for digital professionals to take into consideration for a successful SEO strategy is that an increase in the visibility of a brand on un-paid search engine results is heavily dependent on the increase in customer mind share of a few keywords the brand represents.

A brand cannot always win high visibility for every keyword and must therefore focus on a few keywords, so that the brand can win high visibility for at least those keywords. This is the same reason why the majority of marketers focus on a few segments of a market, rather than on the whole market. The SEO keywords should be consistent with market segmentation, product positioning and mind positioning in the digital space.

Those keywords should represent the languages, behaviours, or preference of a few customer segments an organization is targeting. Without identification of selective and intentional keywords, and heavy focus on them, technical implementation of SEO will end up as expensive mud pits.

It is extremely important to focus strongly on a few keywords by aligning all SEO technical designs to those few keywords. This is how the customer mindshare of a brand for those keywords is increased, leading to increased visibility of the brand on search engine results of those keywords.

It is important to remember that SEO is about marketing and not about technology. SEO technologies and techniques are also being commoditized, and SEO technology alone won't provide any competitive advantage.

SEO Implementation Best Practices

Many of technical details of Search Engine Optimization won't be discussed in this book, as the purpose of this book is to provide an overview only. Many books are available that discuss technical details and techniques to develop a website to be aligned better with SEO principles. That being said, some of the best practices for a successful implementation of SEO are described below.

- Add your own SEO keywords in the HTML[6] <title> tag. These should be consistent with the contents of the web page.
- Use the HTML <meta description> tag to summarize the contents of the web page and include the SEO keywords in the description.
- Use the SEO keywords as part of the URL of the web page.
- Simplify the navigation of the website and provide another site map or XML[7] file for search engines.
- Use text hyperlinks. Do not use image or drop-down menu hyperlinks.

---

[6] HTML (Hyper Text Markup Language) is the standard markup language for creating web pages. HTML tags that are defined by W3C (World Wide Web Consortium) are used for markup and create a HTML document. The latest version is HTML 5.

[7] XML (eXtensible Markup Language) is a markup language that defines markup tags used to encode documents in a format that is both human-readable and machine-readable. XML and HTML are both markup languages. That said, XML tags are used to define the 'content' of a document, whereas HTML tags are used to define the 'structure' of a document.

- Add anchor text in the HTML hyperlink tag and try to use the SEO keywords in the anchor text.
- Use HTML image tags with "alt" attribute to describe the image, and provide an image site map.
- Use the HTML header tags <h1> and <h2> to add the SEO keywords.
- Use a "robot.txt" file to tell search engines whether and where to crawl and index the web pages.
- Add the mobile URL, if any, into the site map.

Requirements of a SEO Management Tool

A SEO management tool commonly provides the functionalities to:

- Track how a website is performing against popular search queries, and alerts when there is an issue.
- Track inbound backlinks of a website and discover broken or low-quality backlinks to the website.
- Track competitor's keywords, SEO activities and SEO performance.
- Test new keywords and make recommendations to confirm whether the new keywords are worth trying.
- Audit a website against ranking factors and make recommendations to improve.
- Help analyse and research keywords to identify different SEO performances, and make recommendations of relevant keyword targets.
- Create performance reports.

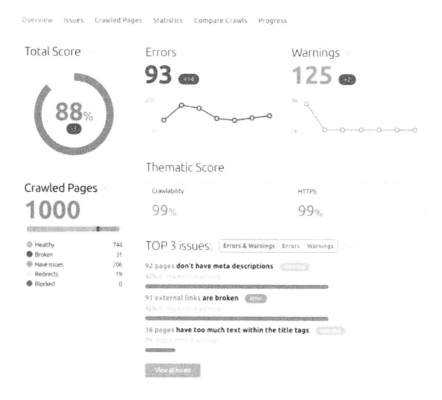

[Figure 10: DigitalGYD SEO Solution]

MATURITY INDICATOR EXAMPLES

Level 0: Non-existent

- The website may be crawled and indexed by a search engine.
- The organization is aware of the importance of SEO. No practice is however implemented in the organization to increase its ranking on the un-paid search results on the search engine, and the website is therefore not seen on the search engine results.

Level 1: Ad hoc

- A few popular SEO techniques of using HTML tags have been implemented on an ad hoc basis.
- Guidance to SEO is not documented and shared across the organization, and the ad hoc SEO practices are therefore inconsistent.
- No official roles and responsibilities are defined for SEO strategy and implementation.

Level 2: Basic

- A few popular SEO techniques of composing contents and using HTML tags have been implemented and are updated on a regular basis.
- The SEO techniques are not standardized in the organization and thus implemented inconsistently by different people across websites.
- No official roles and responsibilities are defined and documented for SEO strategy and implementation. Nobody is however dedicated for the job.
- No formal SEO strategies and plans are established, approved or sponsored.
- SEO keywords are randomly chosen without alignment with digital brand marketing plans.
- There is a SEO tool employed to automate and support SEO implementation. The tool is however limited in functionality and does not cover entire end-to-end SEO processes.

Level 3: Defined

- Corporate SEO strategy, principles, standards, procedures, methodology and guidance are established, documented, approved, sponsored and enforced across the organization.
- There is a SEO practitioner dedicated for the SEO planning and implementation.

- The SEO keywords are planned and selected in such a way that they are aligned with mind positioning of digital brand marketing.
- Multiple SEO tools are employed to automate end-to-end SEO processes. The integration of the tools is however yet to be enhanced.

Level 4: Optimized

- SEO performance is constantly measured against pre-defined metrics, and performance gaps are identified and resolved accordingly.
- A centralized repository for SEO knowledge base containing best practices, proven techniques, recent SEO trends, latest changes to search engine algorithms, and many other types of SEO knowledge is created and maintained.
- Whenever SEO performance is analysed and plans to bridge the performance gaps are developed, new knowledge on SEO techniques are also developed and added to the existing SEO knowledge base.

Level 5: Progressive

- The SEO practices significantly contribute to achieving the objective of Brand Marketing, e.g. conversion from brand awareness to brand interest.
- The SEO is fully integrated with other Digital Marketing and Social Interaction capabilities for maximum marketing synergy. Paid Search, Content Targeting, Affiliate Marketing, Social Media Marketing, Social Media Servicing and a few other digital capabilities are for example used in parallel with SEO to increase the effectiveness of SEO.
- The organization has a great deal of SEO standards, guidelines and techniques in the knowledge base repository. These have been developed internally and they are all up-to-date.

- A few webpages of the organization are ranked on the first page of the unpaid search results for popular keywords.

CAPABILITY 3-3.
PAID SEARCH

CAPABILITY DEFINITION

Paid Search is a digital capability used to increase website traffic by purchasing search results on a search website and search network of the search engine. Paid Search is a type of paid inclusion where ads are shown on a search website or search network of a search engine when a user types in specific keywords.

Paid Search is different from Content Targeting, another type of paid inclusion where ads are shown on 'websites of content network' – a.k.a. display network – of a search engine. Content Targeting will be discussed in the next section.

For Paid Search, there are a number of options, including paying for the number of clicks on ads - CPC (cost-per-click) also known as PPC (pay-per-click) - or the number of impression when ads are displayed - CPM (cost-per-impression).

CPC is more commonly used than CPM, as CPM does not guarantee that the impressions result in website visits. CPM can be a better option when the objective of a Paid Search is to increase awareness of a brand in the digital space, and a visit to a landing page is not necessarily required.

The digital capability encompasses all abilities to plan Paid Search, monitor the progress of its initiatives, evaluate the performance of the initiatives, and revise the Paid Search plan accordingly.

A Paid Search plan includes:

- **Measurable objectives**: the achievement of an objective can be measured with the number of responding users, impressions, clicks, visits, conversion rate, sales etc.

- **Target audience**: the target audience of Paid Search should be aligned with target customer segments of the digital channels.

- **Keywords**: target keywords of Paid Search should be consistent with brand positioning, product positioning, or mind positioning in the digital market.

- **Media**: suitable digital media for the objectives and target audiences should be planned. Search engines, social websites, news websites, or other types of social websites can be used.

- **Messages**: effective messages can be created by considering the objective, target audience, media and expected response from the audience. If the message is consistent with SEO keywords, search engines ranking can be boosted. Keywords and ad copy should be at the core of the messages.

- **Reach & frequency**: planning should be done to determine how far the message should reach into the target audience, and how often the message should be delivered to the same audience.

- **Expected response from audience**: planning should be done to determine how the target audience would feel about the ad copy and how they would respond to the message to help achieve the objectives.

- **Landing page**: a landing page is part of an entire digital marketing campaign just as Paid Search is. A landing page should therefore be consistent with the keywords and ad copy of Paid Search.

It is highly recommended that the keywords you buy for Paid Search are the same as those that have been defined for Search

Engine Optimization. This will improve its ranking on un-paid search results of the search engine where the un-paid search and the Paid Search are performed together.

MATURITY INDICATOR EXAMPLES

Level 0: Non-existent

- Neither CPC nor CPM Paid Search has been planned or tried.

Level 1: Ad hoc

- Paid Search is performed on an ad hoc basis. A Paid Search is for example purchased for once-off promotional event.
- CPC and CPM options from multiple search websites are compared before the purchase of a Paid Search. The ad hoc purchases of the Paid Search services are however not properly planned.

Level 2: Basic

- An individual business unit buys Paid Search on a regular basis to perform their individual digital marketing activities, without an enterprise-wide overarching Paid Search plan or coordination at corporate level.
- Advantages and disadvantages of Paid Search against Content Targeting and Affiliate Marketing are not analysed to determine whether Paid Search is a better option for the specific digital marketing campaign. There is no clear responsibility share between Paid Search and Content Targeting in the digital marketing plan.
- A Paid Search plan is prepared before buying a Paid Search service. The depth and scope of the plan are however limited. It does not define measurable objectives, clear target audiences and expected responses from the audience, and does not measure performance of the paid ads.

Level 3: Defined

- Corporate principles, policies and standards for planning and performing Paid Search are implemented. An individual business unit plans and purchases Paid Search services according to the principles, policies and standards that are used to coordinate different Paid Search campaigns from different business units.
- Role and responsibility around planning and execution of Paid Search are defined.
- A Paid Search plan is prepared whenever there is a Paid Search campaign. The plan defines measurable objective, target audiences, keywords, messages to be delivered to the audiences, expected response from the audiences, message reach and frequency, and performance metrics.
- When Paid Search is performed together with other methods such as Content Targeting, Affiliate Marketing, and/or Online Advertising, the organization cannot ensure that they complement each other and thus increase synergy without too much redundancy.

Level 4: Optimized

- The performance of the Paid Search campaigns is constantly measured against pre-defined metrics, and performance gaps are identified against the measurable Paid Search objectives. Performance improvement plans are developed to fill the performance gaps and implemented according to the plans.
- Paid Search campaigns of the organization intend to achieve very specific objectives and target very specific audiences. The organization has learned from experience that broad targeting and broad match are not highly effective.
- The standards and guidelines are detailed enough to give specific templates and tips to ad design, copy writing, media purchase and many other activities.

Level 5: Progressive

- Paid Search is fully integrated with other Digital Marketing and Social Interaction capabilities. The Paid Search for example contributes significantly to improving ranking on the organic search results by integrating with SEO.
- Paid Search has significantly contributed to achieving the objective of Brand Marketing, e.g. conversion from brand awareness to brand interest.
- The organization has a robust, internally developed knowledge base to make decisions on how to use Paid Search along with other digital marketing capabilities to increase the synergy.

CAPABILITY 3-4.
CONTENT TARGETING

CAPABILITY DEFINITION

Content Targeting is a digital capability used to increase website traffic by showing ads on content publisher websites of the content network where the content of these websites are relevant to the ads.

Content Targeting for an advertisement is done with the assumption that the viewers of the content of the content publisher websites are the potential target audience of the advertisement. Search engines offer a network of content publisher websites - also known as content network or delivery network - for this purpose.

Content Targeting is a type of paid inclusion where an ad is shown on the content network of a search website, whereas Paid Search is another type of paid inclusion where an ad is shown on a search website.

Content Targeting is different from Paid Search in that an advertisement that is relevant to the keywords a user keyed in is delivered to the user in Paid Search, whereas an advertisement that is relevant to the content of a web page a user is viewing is delivered to the user in Content Targeting.

Both Paid Search and Content Targeting are paid advertisement but have different advantages. Content Targeting can be more effective than Paid Search in finding the right customers who are relevant to an advertisement. That being said, a user who is visiting a content publisher website is more likely to be interested in reading the content of the website, and less likely to click on the advertisement to make a purchase.

A survey has suggested that Click Thru Rate[8] (CTR) of Content Targeting is lower than that of Paid Search. It makes sense when you consider the fact that, when a user goes to a search website, the user would click on one of the search results, whereas when a user goes to a content website, the user would want to read the contents rather than click on an ad to move out of the content website.

That is why Content Targeting is used more frequently to increase brand awareness or brand preference, rather than to promote a purchase. If a user clicks on the ad on a content website that leads to the landing page of the ad, then the organization would have a good chance to increase the brand interest or brand preference from the user.

Content Targeting capability is to increase the effectiveness of paid advertising by correctly targeting content on the content

---

[8] Click Thru Rate is a ratio of the number of users that click on a web link to the total users who view the webpage, email, or advertisement containing the web link. (CTR = number of click-throughs ÷ number of impression x 100%)

publisher network, rather than keywords used for search. A Content Targeting plan should therefore clearly define the content it is targeting. The plan should also include measurable objectives, target audience, suitable content publishers and content network provider, ad messages, reach & frequency, and expected response from viewers. Refer to the Paid Search section for further details of the structure of a Content Targeting plan.

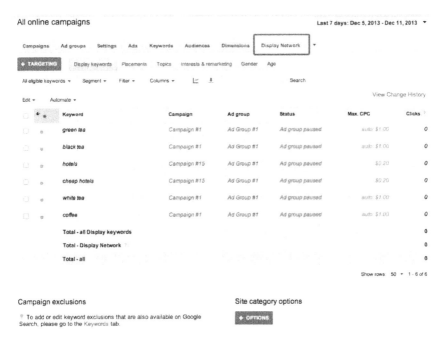

[Figure 11: Google Content Network Management]

MATURITY INDICATOR EXAMPLES

Level 0: Non-existent

- Paid Search may have been conducted. Neither CPC (Cost-Per-Click), nor CPM (Cost-Per-Impression) Content Targeting has been planned or tried.

Level 1: Ad hoc

- Content Targeting is performed on an ad hoc basis. A Content Targeting option is for example purchased for a once-off marketing event.
- CPC and CPM options from multiple content network providers may be compared before the purchase of the Content Targeting option. The ad hoc purchases of the Content Targeting option are however not properly planned.

Level 2: Basic

- An individual business unit buys Content Targeting on a regular basis to perform their individual digital marketing activities, without enterprise-wide an overarching Content Targeting plan, or coordination at corporate level.
- Advantages and disadvantages of Content Targeting against Affiliate Marketing and Paid Search are not analysed to decide whether Content Targeting is a better option for the specific digital marketing campaign. There is no clear responsibility share between Content Targeting, Affiliate Marketing and Paid Search in the digital marketing plan.
- A Content Targeting plan is prepared before buying a Content Targeting service. The depth and scope of the plan are however limited. It does not define measurable objectives, clear target audiences, target contents, and expected responses from the audience, and does not measure performance of the ads.

Level 3: Defined

- Corporate principles, policies and standards for planning and performing Content Targeting are implemented. An individual business unit plans and purchases Content Targeting services according to the principles, policies and standards that are used to coordinate different Content Targeting campaigns from different business units.

- Roles and responsibilities around planning and execution of Content Targeting are defined.
- A Content Targeting plan is prepared whenever there is a Content Targeting campaign. The plan defines measurable objectives, target audiences, target contents, messages to be delivered to the audiences, expected response from the audiences, message reach and frequency and, performance metrics.
- When Content Targeting is performed together with other methods such as Paid Search, Affiliate Marketing, and/or Online Advertising, the organization cannot ensure that they complement each other and thus increase synergy without too much redundancy.

Level 4: Optimized

- The performance of the Content Targeting campaigns is constantly measured against pre-defined metrics, and performance gaps are identified against the measurable Content Targeting objectives. Performance improvement plans are developed to fill the performance gaps and implemented according to the plans.
- Content Targeting campaigns of the organization intend to achieve specific objectives and target specific audiences. The organization has learned from experience that broad targeting and broad match are not highly effective.
- The standards and guidelines are detailed enough to give specific templates and tips to ad design, copy writing, media purchase, and many other activities.
- The organization starts to develop internal knowledge on targeting the right content based on needs of visitors, search engines' content targeting mechanism and keywords that are currently popular.

Level 5: Progressive

- The organization has an internally developed, robust knowledge base to make decisions on how to use Content Targeting along with other digital marketing capabilities to increase synergy.
- Content Targeting is so fine-tuned that the content of the content publishers is well aligned with the content of the advertisement.
- Content Targeting is fully integrated with other Digital Marketing and Social Interaction capabilities. The Content Targeting for example significantly contributes to improving ranking on the organic search results by integrating with SEO.
- Content Targeting has significantly contributed to achieving the objective of Brand Marketing, e.g. conversion from brand awareness to brand interest.

CAPABILITY 3-5.
AFFILIATE MARKETING

CAPABILITY DEFINITION

Affiliate Marketing is a digital capability used to increase website traffic and even promote purchase by showing advertisements on the websites of affiliates of a network that provides an affiliate-marketing program and platform.

The content published on the websites of the affiliates would be relevant to advertisements so that they can attract their visitors to the ad and landing webpage.

Affiliate Marketing is one of the paid advertising methods where an advertiser pays commissions to affiliates - content publishers - for their efforts and performance to bring visitors or traffic to the advertiser. Affiliate Marketing is similar to Content Targeting in that both methods use content publisher websites as digital marketing media.

Whether the advertisement is displayed on a content publisher website is determined by the content publisher in Affiliate Marketing, whereas it is determined by a content matching algorithm developed by a search engine in Content Targeting.

To maintain the integrity of their content websites, affiliates choose which product or service ads to show on their websites. Affiliates can actually decide many aspects of advertisement on their website, including size, shape, layout, location, and even advertisement copy because the affiliate is responsible for editing advertisements to effectively promote the ads as an integral part of the content on their websites.

Affiliates also need to add snippets - a small computer program - into the advertisement to track customer transactions and referrals to the website of the advertiser. Snippets are provided by an affiliate network provider or an advertiser of the product or service.

Affiliate Marketing includes abilities to plan, execute, and measure advertisements on content websites of affiliates to increase visits or purchases through the affiliate's own marketing efforts.

An Affiliate Marketing plan should clearly define the content that is targeted, as does Content Targeting. The plan should also include measurable objectives, target audience, suitable affiliate network provider, suitable content publishers, ad messages, reach & frequency, and expected response from viewers. Refer to the Paid Search section for details of the plan.

If an organization is large enough, it might want to build their own affiliate-marketing program instead of using a public affiliate program, just as Amazon does.

If that is the case, the digital capability includes abilities to develop an affiliate program, build infrastructure to distribute affiliate program, and track customer transactions and referrals from content websites to advertiser websites. It should also be able to calculate rewards for the transactions and make payments without an agent or a network that provides the affiliate marketing platform services. This is however not the case for many organizations.

[Figure 12: iDevAffiliate Affiliate Marketing Management Solution]

MATURITY INDICATOR EXAMPLES

Level 0: Non-existent

- Paid Search or Content Targeting may have been conducted. Neither CPC (Cost-Per-Click), nor CPM (Cost-Per-Impression) Affiliate Marketing has been planned or tried.

Level 1: Ad hoc

- Affiliate Marketing is performed on an ad hoc basis. An Affiliate Marketing option is for example purchased for a once-off marketing event.
- CPC and CPM options from multiple affiliate network providers may be compared before the purchase of the Affiliate Marketing option. The ad hoc purchases of the Affiliate Marketing option are however not properly planned.

Level 2: Basic

- An individual business unit buys Affiliate Marketing services on a regular basis to perform their individual digital marketing activities, without an enterprise-wide overarching Affiliate Marketing plan, or coordination at corporate level.
- Advantages and disadvantages of Affiliate Marketing against Content Targeting and Paid Search are not analysed to decide whether Affiliate Marketing is a better option for the specific digital marketing campaign. There is no clear responsibility share between Content Targeting and Affiliate Marketing in the digital marketing plan.
- An Affiliate Marketing plan is prepared before buying an Affiliate Marketing service. The depth and scope of the plan are however limited. It does not define measurable objectives, clear target audiences, target publishers and their content, expected responses from the audience, and does not measure performance of the ads.

Level 3: Defined

- Corporate principles, policies and standards for planning and performing Affiliate Marketing are implemented. An individual business unit plans and purchases Affiliate Marketing services according to the principles, policies and standards that are used to coordinate different Affiliate Marketing campaigns from different business units.

- Roles and responsibility around planning and execution of Affiliate Marketing are defined.
- An Affiliate Marketing plan is prepared whenever there is an Affiliate Marketing campaign. The plan defines measurable objectives, target audiences, target publishers, target contents, messages to be delivered to the audiences, expected response from the audiences, message reach and frequency, and performance metrics.
- Various offers are provided to the affiliates.
- When Affiliate Marketing is performed together with other methods such as Paid Search, Content Targeting, and Online Advertising, the organization cannot ensure that they complement one another, and thus increase synergy without too much redundancy.

Level 4: Optimized

- The performance of the Affiliate Marketing campaigns is constantly measured against pre-defined metrics, and performance gaps are identified against the measurable Affiliate Marketing objectives. Performance improvement plans are developed to fill the performance gaps and implemented according to the plans.
- Offers are differentiated based on affiliates' needs.
- Affiliate Marketing campaigns of the organization intend to achieve very specific objectives and target very specific audiences. The organization has learned from experience that broad targeting and broad match are not effective.
- The standards and guidelines are detailed enough to give specific templates and tips to ad design, copy writing, media purchase, and many other activities.
- The organization starts to develop internal knowledge on targeting the right publishers and content based on the needs of visitors, and keywords that are currently popular.

Level 5: Progressive

- The organization has a robust, internally developed knowledge base to make decisions on how to use Affiliate Marketing along with other digital marketing capabilities to increase synergy.
- The Affiliate marketing capability is fully integrated with other digital marketing capabilities so that overlaps with other paid advertising methods are minimized, while reach and frequency are maximized. The Affiliate Marketing significantly contributes to improving ranking in the organic search results by integrating with SEO.
- Affiliate Marketing has significantly contributed to achieving the objectives of Brand Marketing.

CAPABILITY 3-6.
ONLINE ADVERTISING

CAPABILITY DEFINITION

Online Advertising, also known as Display Advertising, is a traditional way to buy a section of online media, such as a news channel, to push marketing messages to a customer mass or customer segment through banners or other types of advertisements made of images, flash, videos, audio and text. When a Display Advertisement is shown on a search website, it is not considered part of a search result by users, even though it can be shown based on search keywords.

Online Advertising is a digital capability used to plan, execute, monitor and measure advertisement in digital space. As it is a type of paid advertising, it is planned in a similar way that Paid Search and Content Targeting are planned. Planning for Online Advertising includes the following:

- Measurable goal & objectives

- Target audience
- Messages
- Expected response of the target audience to the messages
- Reach and frequency
- Media mix
- Landing page

It has an advantage when compared to Paid Search, Content Targeting, and Affiliate Marketing, as it can take advantage of graphics, animation, copy designs, and dynamic content, and is not limited to the layout of a search result or HTML text format. Online Advertising requires professional creativity and design skills. Graphic designers and ad copywriters are therefore commonly involved in the creation of the design concept and the design of the advertisement.

It is commonly recommended that Online Advertising is planned and executed along with a non-intrusive way of communications, such as Search Engine Optimization or opt-in emails to increase the marketing communication effectiveness.

MATURITY INDICATOR EXAMPLES

Level 0: Non-existent

- Although other types of paid advertisements may have been conducted, Online Advertising has not been planned or tried.

Level 1: Ad hoc

- Online Advertising is performed on an ad hoc basis. A small section of a news website, social website or other digital media is for example purchased for a once-off marketing event.

- Different options from multiple digital media may be compared before purchasing. The ad hoc purchases of the digital media are however not properly planned.

Level 2: Basic

- An individual business unit conducts Online Advertising on a regular basis to perform their individual digital marketing activities, without an enterprise-wide overarching Online Advertising plan, or coordination at corporate level.
- Advantages and disadvantages of Online Advertising against the other types of paid advertisements are not analysed to determine whether Online Advertising is a better option for the digital marketing campaign.
- An Online Advertising plan is developed. The depth and scope of the plan are however limited. It does not define measurable objectives, target audiences, messages, media mix and expected responses from the audience, and does not measure performance of the ads.

Level 3: Defined

- Corporate principles, policies and standards for planning and performing Online Advertising are implemented. An individual business unit plans and executes Online Advertising according to the principles, policies and standards that are used to coordinate different Online Advertisements from different business units.
- Roles and responsibilities around the planning and execution of Online Advertising are defined.
- An Online Advertising plan is prepared whenever performing Online Advertising. The plan defines measurable objectives, target audiences, messages to be delivered to the audiences, expected response from the audiences, message reach and frequency, media mix and metrics.

- The organization is unable to see whether Online Advertising and other paid ads complement each other and increase synergy without much redundancy.

Level 4: Optimized

- The performance of Online Advertising campaigns is constantly measured against pre-defined metrics, and performance gaps are identified against the measurable objectives. Performance improvement plans are developed to fill the performance gaps and implemented according to the plans.
- Online Advertising campaigns of the organization intend to achieve specific objectives and target specific audiences, understanding that broad targeting and broad match are not effective.
- The standards and guidelines are detailed enough to give specific templates and tips to ad design, copy writing, media purchase and many other activities.
- The organization has developed internal knowledge on designing banners and other multimedia advertisements based on needs of visitors.

Level 5: Progressive

- Online Advertising is planned and performed along with email marketing, paid search, SEO, social marketing and other types of non-intrusive communications so that effectiveness of the ad and synergy of the total communication can be maximized.
- The Online Advertising capability is fully integrated with other digital marketing capabilities so that overlaps with other paid advertising methods are minimized while maximising reach and frequency.
- The organization has robust knowledge base internally developed to make decisions on how to use Online

Advertising along with other digital marketing capabilities to increase synergy.

- The Online Advertising significantly contributes to improving ranking on the organic search results by integrating with SEO.
- Affiliate Marketing has significantly contributed to achieving the objective of Brand Marketing.

CAPABILITY 3-7.
DIGITAL CAMPAIGN MANAGEMENT

CAPABILITY DEFINITION

Digital Campaign Management is a digital capability used to plan, execute, monitor, and measure the marketing campaign in digital space. A digital campaign should address a specific market issue to reach a measurable market achievement such as percentage increase in brand awareness, number of visits, or sales amount. This capability also includes a set of marketing activities and tools to achieve the specific campaign objectives.

Campaign Planning

Campaign planning starts with defining market problems in the digital space and, in general, the marketing problems mean gaps between digital marketing goals and the current state of digital marketing. Information on market problems or gaps can often be collected from the Digital Intelligence capability we will discuss later in this book. If market problems or gaps can be articulated, campaign objectives can also be articulated easily. Campaign planning also includes defining campaign target audiences, campaign scenarios, campaign schedules, messages and channels that can be tailored based on individual preference, and cost.

Marketing Offer Management, another digital capability of Digital Marketing, is critical to the success of a digital campaign, because a digital campaign is done to push messages and marketing offers to target audiences in order to drive marketing results that can solve market problems. Marketing Offers is at the core of what a campaign provides to customers. Marketing Offers should therefore be planned as part of digital campaign plans.

A campaign cascading plan can be created as part of digital campaign plans. Digital campaigns can have a hierarchical structure, where a large digital campaign is divided into smaller digital campaigns. This cascading into multiple digital campaigns is particularly useful when a market problem is too big for a single campaign to address.

Requirements of a Campaign Management Tool

When it comes to campaign management in the digital space, campaign management tools become a critical factor to the successful campaign implementation, as almost all campaign activities should be automated in the digital space, as opposed to the manual processes of campaign management in the offline world. Digital campaign management and offline campaign management do however have many functionalities in common.

A Digital Campaign Management tool commonly includes the following functionalities:

- Campaign opportunity analysis is used to provide functionality to analyse and identify opportunities to improve brand reputation, acquire and retain customers, increase conversion, sales, and profit, increase re-sell, up-sell, and cross-sell opportunities, and decrease costs through a digital campaign.
- Campaign templates are used to provide reusable templates that help configure and set-up a digital campaign.

- Campaign registration is used to facilitate the registering and launching of a campaign and includes the functionalities to:
  - Set measurable objectives of a campaign.
  - Develop a business case for the campaign, e.g. ROI (Return On Investment).
  - Manage automated workflow for campaign approval and execution.
  - Register campaign master data including basic profile, campaign owner and department, campaign products & services, key offerings, campaign scenario, target customers, campaign channels and campaign schedule.
  - Modify existing campaigns.

- Campaign testing & simulation is used to test and simulate a digital campaign before launching.
- Campaign hierarchy & relationship is used to manage hierarchy and relationship of many different campaigns.
- Campaign monitoring is to monitor end-to-end processes and status of a digital campaign.
- Campaign performance evaluation is used to define performance metrics, gather performance source data, analyse performance of a digital campaign against the metrics and generate reports.
- Campaign history management is used to store and view all the campaigns executed in the past for analysis and reuse.
- Comprehensive integration and data exchange with other digital marketing capabilities such as Marketing Offer Management, Lead Management, paid advertisement capabilities, Email Marketing, Mobile Marketing, Marketing automation, and with the middle-office capabilities such as Customer Loyalty Management and Content Lifecycle Management in order to actively reuse the functionalities for automated campaign processes execution and effective campaign management.

[Figure 13: SalesForce Campaign Management Solution]

MATURITY INDICATOR EXAMPLES

Level **0**: Non-existent

- Digital marketing campaigns are neither planned, nor executed.

Level **1**: Ad hoc

- Digital marketing campaigns are performed on an ad hoc basis for once-off promotional events.
- The campaigns are not properly planned. The plan doesn't necessarily include market problems to address, measurable objectives, a business case, target audiences, key marketing offerings, channel mix, etc.

- A very basic campaign management tool may be employed to aid campaign management processes, but most of the campaign processes are performed manually.

Level 2: Basic

- Digital marketing campaigns are planned and executed by individual business units to fulfil their own urgent bottom needs on a regular basis, without strategic coordination by a corporate level campaign strategy, and the individual campaigns are therefore neither aligned, nor consistent across the organization.
- The digital campaigns are planned to include campaign activities in detail. However, the plans don't necessarily include measurable objectives, performance metrics and business cases, and the organization does therefore not fully understand what can be achieved through the digital campaigns.
- The functionalities of the Digital Campaign Management tool are too limited to fully support comprehensive campaign planning and automate the end-to-end processes of campaign execution, monitoring and performance evaluation.
- The Digital Campaign Management tool is not well integrated with the tools of other digital capabilities, resulting in many swivel chair integrations, e.g. sales opportunities from a digital campaign do not automatically feed back into Lead Management, which is used to turn opportunities into sales leads.

Level 3: Defined

- Digital marketing campaigns are performed by individual business units, but their campaign plans are coordinated and harmonized by a corporate level campaign strategy so that their campaigns are aligned and consistent, ensuring synergy across the organization.

- The organization has implemented corporate principles, policies, standards, campaign processes, marketing campaign staff, and campaign management tools to organize, coordinate, and support the individual digital campaigns.
- The digital campaigns are justified through business case analysis, and have measurable campaign objectives and performance metrics.
- The campaign management tools offer functionalities comprehensive enough to automate the end-to-end campaign planning, execution, campaign revision, monitoring and performance measure.

Level 4: Optimized

- The performance of a digital marketing campaign is traced and measured according to the plans during and after the campaign, so that the organization has a clear visibility into whether the campaign is achieving the campaign objectives or not.
- When the performance is not meeting the expectation, the campaign plan is updated to bridge the performance gaps and the organization can adapt to the environment in which the campaign is being performed.
- The campaign standards & guidelines, and campaign knowledge have been optimized enough to make sure the quality levels of digital campaigns are consistent across the organization.
- The integration of digital campaign management tools with other digital capabilities has been optimized so that swivel chair integrations and human intervention for data re-entry are minimized.

Level 5: Progressive

- Digital Campaign Management is at the centre of all digital marketing capabilities and fully integrated with other digital marketing capabilities so that all digital marketing activities are interrelated or aligned with campaign management activities in driving the target customers to move forward in the digital brand marketing funnel and digital customer journey.

- The digital campaign management processes and tools are seamlessly integrated with the processes and tools of other digital capabilities to fully automate and facilitate the collaboration among the multiple digital capabilities.

- The Digital Campaign Management and its integration with Lead Management have been so effective that the campaigns have successfully created opportunities and leads that have created new customers and increased conversions to purchases through Lead Management.

CAPABILITY 3-8.
LEAD MANAGEMENT

CAPABILITY DEFINITION

Lead Management is a digital capability used to generate, capture, qualify, prioritize, and nurture a lead and convert it to sales. A lead refers to the organization's initial contact with a potential customer. Leads are managed by Lead Management capability to convert them into sales. Organizations need to establish a sales funnel - conversion funnel - to manage conversion from leads to sales.

Lead Management Lifecycle

A lead is managed throughout the following lifecycle:

1. **Lead generation**: A lead is generated when consumer interest or enquiry into products or services of the

organization is initiated. Leads generated are not necessarily captured by the organization. A lead can be generated through many different channels and many different digital marketing capabilities. Digital Campaign Management is commonly used to create a substantial amount of leads in a short period.

2. **Lead capture**: When the customer's interest or enquiry is captured by the organization, it becomes a lead. Seamless integration of Lead Management tool with tools of other digital marketing capabilities is critical to automate the capture of a lead as soon as it is generated.

3. **Lead qualification**: When a lead is captured, it is qualified during the process of evaluating if the lead is worthy of investment in marketing effort and money. Lead Qualification is to identify whether there is an urgent need to buy the product or service, and whether the customer has a financial capability to make a purchase if the price range of the product or service is higher.

4. **Lead prioritization**: Once qualified, a lead goes through the process of prioritization of all active leads to see which leads are more important in order to allocate marketing resources in accordance with the priority. The criteria of prioritization may include total deal size, net revenue amount, win probability, relationship with customer, cost, and risk.

5. **Lead nurturing**: A lead is nurtured through the process of developing relationships with the customer at every stage of a brand marketing funnel, a sales funnel and a digital customer journey map. It focuses marketing and communication efforts on listening to the needs of the customer and providing marketing content, marketing offers and customer services to encourage the customer to take a purchasing action.

6. **Lead closing**: When the customer purchases the product or service, the lead is closed.

Requirements of a Lead Management Tool

A comprehensive Lead Management tool should automate and support the end-to-end lifecycle of a lead, and the functionalities of the tool commonly include the following:

- **Funnel management**: the tool should provide functionality to establish a sales funnel that includes a Lead Management lifecycle, the multiple stages of the lifecycle, the control gates between the stages, and be able to manage and monitor the state of the funnel.

- **Lead generation**: a few Lead Management tools may provide the functionality through which customer interest is generated. This is however not Lead Management's strong suit and it is commonly done by other Digital Marketing capabilities and Social Interaction capabilities.

- **Automated lead capture**: the tool should integrate to the tools used by Digital Channel Management capabilities, Digital Marketing capabilities, and Social Interaction capabilities to capture leads that are generated through the interactions and communications on the digital channels automatically.

- **Intelligent lead routing**: new leads should be assigned and routed to the appropriate personnel's inbox automatically, based on pre-determined policies and criteria to accelerate follow-up actions by ensuring that leads are instantly distributed to and received by the right person.

- **Lead qualification & prioritization**: the tool should qualify and prioritize based on pre-defined policies and criteria and present the results back to the personnel so that they can adjust and make a final decision.

- **Automated lead nurturing**: the tool should provide templates for scheduling follow-up actions for lead nurturing, perform marketing activities as scheduled by the personnel, e.g. emailing to a customer as soon as the lead is qualified, track previous follow-up actions and remind them of future follow-up actions.

- **Performance analysis**: the tool should provide functionality to track and measure performance of Lead Management based on pre-defined metrics, and generate performance reports.

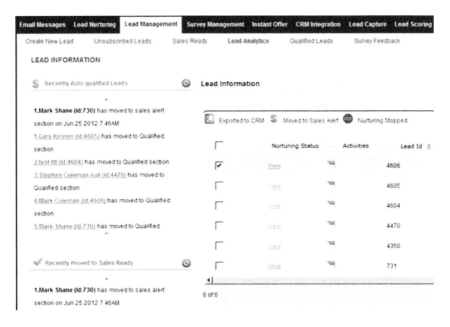

[Figure 14: Leadberry Lead Management Solution]

MATURITY INDICATOR EXAMPLES

Level 0: Non-existent

- No marketing practice has been implemented to capture and nurture marketing leads.
- Even when a customer's interest in the products or services happens to be captured, it is not routed to the right person for follow-ups. It therefore falls through the cracks and is barely noticed.

Level 1: Ad hoc

- The lifecycle of Lead Management is not defined and Lead Management processes are performed on an ad hoc basis.
- When the organization captures a customer's interest in the products or services, people perform follow-up actions. The follow-up actions are however not consistent as there is no structured approach to Lead Management.
- A very basic Lead Management tool may be employed to automate Lead Management processes, but most of the processes are performed manually.

Level 2: Basic

- The stages of Lead Management lifecycle are defined and high-level guidance to follow-up actions are provided. The Lead Management practices are however not shared across the organization and the follow-up actions are therefore not entirely consistent.
- Not all leads are logged into a database, nor are all follow-up actions recorded.
- Leads are qualified and prioritized, but the way that this is done is not consistent across the organization.
- Different business units have introduced different Lead Management tools that are not integrated with one another. Lead information is therefore not shared across the organization.
- The Lead Management tool has fundamental functionality to perform basic processes, but is limited in providing advanced functions such as intelligent routing and lead nurturing.

Level 3: Defined

- Corporate principles, policies, procedures and standards for Lead Management are implemented and strongly enforced to coordinate Lead Management activities across the different business units.

- Sales funnels are officially defined and the gates between the stages of the sales funnel is controlled based on corporate policies. Lead capture, qualification and nurturing are performed as part of the gate control, e.g. a lead that fails to pass a qualification gate cannot be nurtured.
- There are clearly defined criteria used to qualify and prioritize leads, and the criteria are embedded into Lead Management tool so that the policies and procedures can be enforced effectively.
- The Lead Management tools offer functionalities comprehensive enough to automate the end-to-end lead capture, routing, qualification, prioritization, nurturing and closing.

Level 4: Optimized

- The performance of the Lead Management is traced and measured according to pre-defined metrics. The performance measurement is integrated with Conversion Rate Optimization to analyse the performance in conversion rate further. When the performance does not meet the expectation, improvement plans are prepared to bridge the performance gaps, and implemented according to the plans.
- The policies to control the gate of sales funnel has been optimized to accommodate various sales scenarios and cases so that the lead portfolio becomes healthy and sales can eventually be promoted rather than demoted by the gate control.
- Lead nurturing business rules have been fine-tuned and embedded into the policy and rules database to automate the nurturing processes.

Level 5: Progressive

- Lead Management is fully aligned with the brand marketing funnel and the digital customer journey map.
- Lead Management is fully integrated with other front-office digital capabilities so that almost all leads generated through the front-office digital capabilities are seamlessly captured by Lead Management, and the front-office digital capabilities are fully used to nurture the leads.
- The tool is seamlessly integrated with tools for the front-office digital capabilities to enable seamless integration of the end-to-end lead capture and lead nurturing processes.

CAPABILITY 3-9.
MARKETING OFFER MANAGEMENT

CAPABILITY DEFINITION

A marketing offer is a value proposition of a product, a service, or a package of products and services, possibly with dynamic pricing to drive customer engagements with an organization. A discount voucher, a promotional coupon, free subscription, and free trial software are good examples of a marketing offer.

Marketing Offer Management is a digital capability used to create, present, deliver and measure tailored, personalized marketing offers to customers in the digital space.

Use Case of Marketing Offer

A marketing offer is created to meet unique or untapped customer needs without involving re-design or re-development of a product or service. Marketing offers are commonly provided to promote cross-sell, up-sell, or re-sell, but can be any offers to increase the number of members, increase brand loyalty, minimize loss, satisfy customers, or cope with competitor events.

Marketing offers are therefore extensively used for digital campaigns where marketing offers are provided to customers to help address the market problems that the campaigns intend to solve. Marketing offers used for a digital campaign should be designed to contribute to achieving campaign objectives and the overarching marketing goal.

Marketing offers are also actively used by Lead Management to nurture leads. Almost every front-office capability uses marketing offers to initiate and maintain interactions and relationship with customers and users. A marketing offer works best if it is aligned with a customer segment.

Once a marketing offer is created, it is stored in a centralized Marketing Offer repository so that it can be reused for another marketing campaign, Lead Management, or other digital marketing capabilities to move customers forward in the sales funnel.

Designing of Marketing Offer

A marketing offer can be created through the combination of many factors. The following are among the most common factors that could be considered when creating a new marketing offer.

- **Products**: All types of products, including trial products and accessories.
- **Volumes**: How many or much of the products are to be purchased.
- **Services**: All customer services to be provided before, during and after purchase.
- **Pricing**: Pricing structure, including fixed discount and dynamic pricing.
- **Other benefits**: Loyalty points, bonus credit, etc.
- **Digital contents**: Demo video, guidance e-book, blog post, webinar, etc.
- **Customers**: Whom to provide the offer to.
- **Digital channels**: Which channel to use to provide the offer.

- **Offer period**: When to provide the offer.

Requirements of a Marketing Offer Management Tool

A Marketing Offer Management tool should enable and automate the processes to create, maintain, and deliver marketing offers and measure the performance of each marketing offer. The functionalities of the tool should include the following:

- **Offer template management**: To provide standard or frequently used offer templates to create a new marketing offer easily.
- **Offer creation & revision**: To provide functions to combine the offer policies and offer design factors mentioned above to create a new marketing offer, and modify the factors to change the offer.
- **Offer test & simulation**: To provide functions to test and simulate a new marketing offer to validate effectiveness and predict the performance of the offer.
- **Offer cost calculation**: To calculate the cost of a marketing offer automatically.
- **Offer repository management**: To store, search, maintain and distribute all marketing offers and their previous versions.
- **Self-learning engine**: To predict customers' demand by tracking their responses and analysing trends.
- **Intelligent offer recommendation**: To make dynamic recommendations on marketing offers for marketers and customers, considering all relevant customer data.
- **Offer performance management**: To evaluate the performance of a marketing offer and make changes to the marketing offer accordingly.

[Figure15: SAP Marketing Offer Management Solution]

MATURITY INDICATOR EXAMPLES

Level 0: Non-existent

- Other than the standard products or services for digital business, there is no specific marketing offer developed for users with a specific purpose to address a market problem in the digital space.

Level 1: Ad hoc

- A marketing offer is created and provided to a mass of customers on an ad hoc basis.
- The marketing offers are not properly planned. Little planning on the purpose of the offers, target customers, target channels, and the corresponding product & service bundling ends up with a typical discount offer to a customer mass.
- The once-off marketing offers are neither maintained nor reused.

- No tool specialized in Marketing Offer Management is employed, although an office productivity tool may be used.

Level 2: Basic

- Individual business units create and provide different marketing offers on a regular basis without coordination at corporate level, and the marketing offers therefore barely include product bundling that combines multiple products or services from multiple business units.
- Marketing offers are planned to align the offers with the overall digital marketing strategy. The plans are however not comprehensive in scope and depth, and may not necessarily be aligned with corporate-level digital marketing strategy.
- Although marketing offers are stored in a database, they are not maintained to stay up to date. Reusability of the marketing offers is therefore still low.
- A tool specialized in managing marketing offers is employed, although the tool doesn't provide advanced functions such as real-time offer recommendations and self-learning.

Level 3: Defined

- Corporate principles, policies and standards of planning and designing marketing offers are implemented. An individual business unit plans and designs accordingly and can create bundled products or services that combine different products or services from multiple business units.
- Marketing offers are planned, considering digital marketing objectives, digital journey map, brand marketing funnel, digital campaign management, and lead management.
- The marketing offers are stored in a centralized repository, maintained, and reused. Although reusability of the marketing offers is not high, it is increasing.
- A comprehensive Marketing Offer Management tool has been deployed. Advanced functions such as self-learning

and recommendation engines are in place to increase the effectiveness of marketing offers.

Level 4: Optimized

- A marketing offer is traced when provided to customers and the performance of the offer is measured against pre-defined metrics. Performance gaps are identified and the marketing offer is optimized accordingly. The performance optimization may be conducted together with digital campaign performance management.
- Advanced functions such as self-learning and recommendation engines have been optimized as the engines have adapted and learned through previous transactions and massive data feed.
- Marketing offers have been optimized to the extent that marketing offers are actively reused for many digital marketing and ecommerce activities across multiple channels and multiple business units.

Level 5: Progressive

- Marketing Offer Management is fully integrated with other front-office capabilities so that it works effectively to move target customers forward in the brand marketing funnel, the sales funnel, and the digital customer journey.
- The Marketing Offer Management tool and repository is seamlessly integrated with other front-office digital capability tools. The other tools can access Marketing Offer data and provide the offers to users whenever required without swivel chair integration, e.g. the online community manager can provide some of the marketing offers to opinion leaders to incentivize them for their contribution to the online community.

CAPABILITY 3-10.
EMAIL MARKETING

CAPABILITY DEFINITION

Email Marketing is a digital capability used to create, send and monitor emails with marketing messages for promoting brands, products and services.

Before the contemporary digital era, Email Marketing was established and performed standalone without integrating to other marketing capability. This was the online version of direct mail marketing.

In the digital age, Email Marketing has become an integral part of the entire digital marketing capabilities, providing underlying capability to deliver marketing messages through email for other digital capabilities. The Campaign Management capability can for example use the Marketing Automation capability to ask the Email Marketing capability to send an email containing an offer from Marketing Offer Management to a customer as part of the campaign communication.

Requirements of an Email Marketing Tool

As the role of Email Marketing has shifted in the contemporary digital age, an Email Marketing tool does not need to be so comprehensive as to provide additional functionalities such as customer segmentation, content management, workflow management, and complex analytics.

For an effective digital transformation, digital capabilities should be built in an organized way where the roles and boundaries of the digital capabilities are as clear as possible with as little overlap as possible.

An Email marketing tool may therefore include the following core functionalities:

- **Visual editing**: Drag-and-Drop and WYSIWYG[9] (What You See Is What You Get) functionality, built-in-photo editing, pre-built designs and templates, HTML and CSS[10] editing.

- **Mailing list management**: Email recipient list and grouping of the recipients.

- **Opt-in & opt-out option**: Functions for users to opt in or opt out of receiving emails.

- **A/B testing**: Functions to test with different content or locations in the email layout and compare the results, e.g. varying subject lines or banners.

- **Integration to other digital marketing tools**: Pre-built or readily-built integration with Digital Campaign Management, Lead Management, Marketing Offer Management, Marketing Automation, Social Interaction capabilities and Digital Commerce capabilities.

- **Performance measurement**: Analysis of customer reactions and responses to marketing emails.

- **Autoresponders**: Automated or scheduled emailing when triggered internally or by a Marketing Automation tool.

- **Regulatory compliance**: Compliance to spam laws, regulations and proven emailing practices.

---

[9] WYSIWIG is a feature that allows a designer to see what the end-result will look like while the interface of a working product is being created.

[10] CSS (Cascading Style Sheet) is used to describe the format and layout of contents in a HTML document, whereas HTML tags provide the structure of a HTML document.

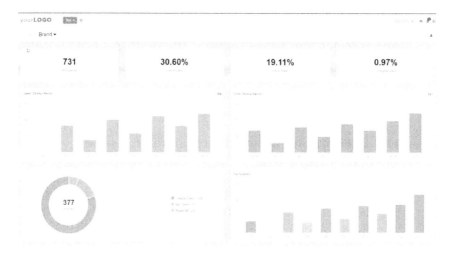

[Figure 16: MailChimp Email Marketing Solution]

MATURITY INDICATOR EXAMPLES

Level 0: Non-existent

- Email is used for the organization to communicate with customers, e.g. for online order management. It is however not used as a marketing method or channel to promote digital marketing communications.

Level 1: Ad hoc

- Email is used for marketing communication purpose on an ad hoc basis. Marketing emails to promote seasonal sales have for example been sent to customers.
- Marketing emails are sent to customers to promote an event or address an urgent issue, regardless of whether or not they have agreed to receive marketing emails.
- The way email messages are designed and developed is neither organized, nor consistent.
- The email messages are not aligned with other digital marketing activities and messages.

- No specialized tool for Email Marketing is employed, but the common SMTP [11] email server for the employee email system is used for marketing emailing.

Level 2: Basic

- Individual business units use email for marketing communication on a regular basis with little coordination at corporate level.
- There are a few common practices shared by business units to design and develop email contents.
- Marketing messages or regular newsletters are sent to customers who agreed to receive them. It is difficult for users to opt-out.
- When customers respond to marketing emails, there are follow-up actions that are inconsistent across the organization.
- Email messages may be aligned to the digital marketing message of the business unit.
- A tool specialized in Email Marketing is implemented, but its functionality is too limited to support marketing emailing and comprehensive integration to other digital marketing tools fully.

Level 3: Defined

- Corporate principles, policies, standards, and guidance to email content development, copy writing, and layout designing are implemented to coordinate marketing emailing performed by individual business units.
- The lifecycle of an email is traced, monitored, and managed.
- Users can easily opt-out.

---

[11] SMTP stands for Simple Mail Transfer Protocol. It is a standard Internet protocol for email transmission.

- The actions to follow up with customers' responses to marketing emails are consistent across the organization.
- Email messages are aligned to enterprise-wide digital marketing communications.
- The Email Marketing tool provides fundamental emailing functionalities and pre-built and custom integration capabilities.

Level 4: Optimized

- The performance of the marketing emails is traced and measured against pre-defined metrics, performance gaps are identified, and the emailing practices are optimized accordingly.
- The standards, tips and guidelines to authoring a marketing email have been internally developed and are considered proven practices of email design and copy writing.
- Integrations of the Email Marketing tools with other digital marketing tools have been further customized and optimized.

Level 5: Progressive

- Email marketing is not only able to work standalone, but also works together with other digital marketing capabilities as an integral component of the other digital capabilities to create synergy from the entire digital marketing perspective.
- Email is positioned not only as one of the communication tools, but is also officially part of the delivery channel mix. Products and services are officially delivered to customers through email, rather than email only being used to notify customers of the delivery of the products or services.

CAPABILITY 3-11.
MOBILE MARKETING

CAPABILITY DEFINITION

Mobile Marketing is a digital capability used to make the best use of features of mobile devices to promote brands, products and services. Due to the nature of real-time, mobile, and personal use of a mobile device, Mobile Marketing best suits time and location sensitive services, augmented reality services, and other personalized and ubiquitously connected services where the other marketing methods and channels are not suitable.

It is common knowledge that real-time messaging functions such as SMS, instant messaging, and push notifications of mobile is the mobile's strong suit when it comes to Mobile Marketing. Among others, location-based services (LBS) and augmented reality services are other reasons why many organizations use Mobile Marketing. Both services are provided based on 'where you are'. Online content is combined with the user's offline location and place.

Location-based services primarily use GPS and map functions to provide relatively simple digital content relevant to the location. Sending a location-based marketing offer is one of the proven practices that make the most of mobile features.

Augmented reality is a real-world image augmented by a virtual image, and requires various technologies that are a lot more complex to render and synchronize digital contents and virtual 3D images on top of moving real-world 3D images. Augmented reality services have great potential for digital marketing, but some organizations struggle to establish a compelling business case due to limited useful use cases and a relatively large investment.

Requirements of a Mobile Marketing Tool

Many mobile marketing tools in the market provide a comprehensive platform for mobile marketing purposes. The scope of these platforms includes mobile campaign management, mobile-format email editor, landing page editor, contact management, mobile personalization, and a lot more.

If only mobile is to be used for digital marketing, the choice of a comprehensive mobile platform makes sense. If not, it would not be a fit-for-purpose solution as many of the additional functionalities are available from other digital capabilities.

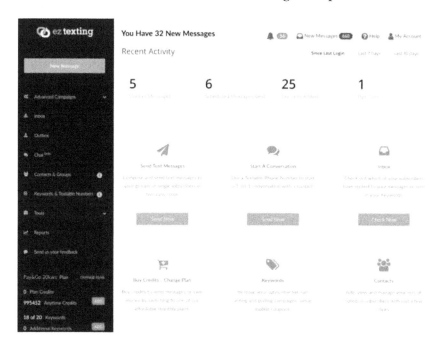

[Figure 17: EZ Texting Mobile Marketing Solution]

A fit-for-purpose Mobile Marketing tool should focus on the following core functionalities, and have a strong ability to integrate with other digital marketing capability tools for the reuse of their functionalities.

- **SMS & MMS[12] messaging**: Easy-to-use messaging functions used to send to individuals or groups as scheduled, or on demand.
- **Instant messaging & chat**: Rich functionalities for interactive messaging.
- **Push notification**: Push messaging with rich content, including images, sounds, etc.
- **In-app messaging**: Messaging with contextual and interactive contents. Active only when the app is used.
- **Autoresponder**: Mobile autoresponders automatically send a response message according to pre-defined policies and rules when a customer sends a message.
- **Barcode & 2D code scanning**: When a code is scanned, it presents a digital content or webpage, e.g. demo video, digital coupon, landing page, product catalogue, product location, etc.
- **Location-based services**: Customized, real-time services are provided based on customers' location, e.g. map services, nearest stores, local events, mobile coupons of local shops, etc.
- **Augmented reality services**: Real-world image are augmented by digital contents and images are provided.
- **User's behaviour tracking**: Users' interactions with a mobile app is captured and stored for real-time response and later analysis.
- **Mobile marketing campaign**: Marketing campaign specialized for mobile is planned and executed through this function. This function can be included in a Digital Campaign Management tool.
- **Mobile channel presentation**: Mobile-friendly user interfaces are designed and developed through this function. This function can be included in a mobile app development platform, or a comprehensive development

---

[12] Multimedia Messages Services.

platform, also known as Integrated Development Environment[13] (IDE).

- **Mobile marketing automation**: This function automates routine marketing activities and processes. The function is commonly included in a Marketing Automation tool.
- **Mobile marketing analytics**: This function supports analysis of marketing activities performed within mobile. In-depth analytics can be covered by many of the Digital Intelligence capabilities.

MATURITY INDICATOR EXAMPLES

Level 0: Non-existent

- Mobile is not used as a marketing channel.

Level 1: Ad hoc

- SMS is primarily used to send marketing messages on an ad hoc basis, e.g. SMS messages to promote seasonal sales have been sent to a customer mass.
- A mobile app has not been developed.
- Mobile messages are sent to customers to promote seasonal sales, or address an urgent issue, regardless of whether or not they agree to receive marketing messages.
- The mobile messages are not aligned with other digital marketing activities and messages.
- Short messaging services are purchased from SMS providers on an ad hoc basis.

Level 2: Basic

---

[13] An Integrated Development Environment (IDE) is a software suite that integrates and consolidates the software development tools needed by developers to write and test software.

- Some individual business units use multiple mobile messaging services for marketing communication on a regular basis with little coordination at corporate level.
- In addition to the mobile messaging services, other common use cases of mobile marketing are shared across business units, e.g. simple location-based services.
- Not all mobile features are used for mobile marketing. The functionalities of the mobile app are too limited to utilize the mobile features fully.
- Mobile messages are sent to customers who have agreed to receive them. It is difficult for users to opt-out.
- A tool specialized in Mobile Marketing is implemented, but its functionality is too limited to support mobile marketing and comprehensive integration to other digital marketing tools fully.

Level 3: Defined

- Corporate principles, policies, standards, and guidance to making the most out of mobile marketing are implemented to coordinate mobile marketing activities performed by individual business units.
- A mobile app is developed to take advantage of many native features of mobile devices.
- Users can easily switch to opt-out of marketing messages.
- The actions to follow up with customers' responses to mobile marketing messages are consistent across the organization.
- The mobile marketing tool provides fundamental mobile marketing functionalities, and pre-built and custom integration capabilities.

Level 4: Optimized

- The performance of the mobile marketing is traced and measured against pre-defined metrics, performance gaps are identified, and the mobile marketing practices are optimized accordingly.

- The use cases and business scenarios of using mobile for marketing have been optimized.
- More advanced features of mobile technologies are used in the mobile app to optimize customer experiences further.
- Integrations of the Mobile Marketing tools with other digital marketing tools have been further customized and optimized.

Level 5: Progressive

- Customers don't feel significant differences in the level of services provided by mobile, desktop, store and other marketing channels. This is due to the seamless integration of the multiple channels while enjoying unique features of mobile service, including location & time-based services, augmented reality-based services and other personalized services.
- Mobile Marketing is not only able to work standalone, but also works together with other digital marketing capabilities. It forms an integral component of the other digital capabilities in order to create synergy from entire digital marketing perspective.

CAPABILITY 3-12.
MARKETING AUTOMATION

CAPABILITY DEFINITION

Marketing Automation is a digital capability used to automate routine marketing tasks, activities and workflows. In theory, the scope of the Marketing Automation capability encompasses the automation of digital marketing planning, execution, monitoring and operational analysis. In reality, the scope of Marketing Automation focuses on automation of the repetitive, routine side of planning, execution, monitoring and analysis, and aims to complement other digital marketing capabilities as an underlying automation platform.

As opposed to offline marketing processes, digital marketing processes can be highly automated by Marketing Automation capabilities. It uses its integration ability to integrate different marketing tools to achieve seamless processes from marketing planning to marketing execution and marketing performance evaluation.

In order to achieve end-to-end automation of the marketing processes, it should integrate and collaborate with other marketing tools such as the Digital Campaign Management tool, Lead Management tool, Marketing Offer Management tool, Email Marketing and Mobile Marketing tool. The purpose of Marketing Automation is not to replace the other digital marketing capabilities, but to complement and help automate them further by providing underlying automation capabilities.

As mentioned as an example in the Email Marketing capability section, Campaign Management can use Marketing Automation to ask the Email Marketing capability to send an email containing a campaign offer managed by Marketing Offer Management to a customer as part of the campaign communication. As demonstrated in the example, Marketing Automation can be used to automate the routine emailing tasks as scheduled by a marketer for a digital campaign. In the same way, SMS messages can automatically be sent by Marketing Automation as part of a digital marketing campaign.

Marketing Automation can also complement and help automate Lead Management further. Marketing Automation can for example help automate lead nurturing processes by automatically sending emails and other messages containing marketing offerings when triggered by an event, or scheduled by a marketer.

Other routine activities of digital marketing, such as blog posting on social media, periodic newsletter publishment and digital advertising can be performed by Marketing Automation automatically when triggered by events, or scheduled by a digital marketer. Marketing Automation also assists digital marketers with their marketing activities by alerting them of their follow-up marketing or sales activities as pre-defined by the digital marketers.

Marketing Automation provides an ability to analyse the performance of routine marketing activities against the pre-defined metrics, e.g. number of emails sent, email open and Click-Through Rate (CTR), and number of customer responses against SMS sent. The performance analytics of Marketing Automation is integrated with the back-office Digital Intelligence capabilities to provide in-depth analysis of website traffic and interactions.

To sum up, Marketing Automation collects all routine, repetitive, and regular marketing tasks required by the other digital marketing capabilities, or as part of ad hoc marketing activities into a central repository, and performs the tasks as pre-defined. Marketing Automation tracks and monitors the progress of the activities it has performed, and, if required, performs follow-up actions as pre-defined.

If there is for example not a response from a customer to whom a Marketing Automation tool has sent an email with a marketing offer, the tool sends a SMS message to remind the customer of the marketing offer as a follow-up action before the offer expires. Marketing Automation also analyses the performance of the routine activities.

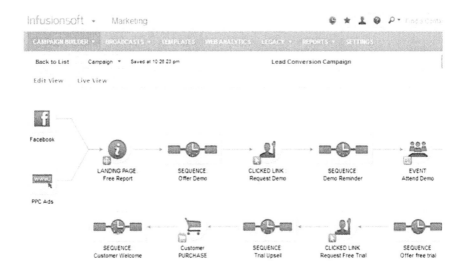

[Figure 18: AdInfusion Marketing Automation Workflow Design]

Functionality of a Marketing Automation Tool

A Marketing Automation tool commonly includes the following functionalities:

- Scheduling of marketing activities.
- Automation of email messaging.
- Automation of mobile messaging.
- Automation of social media posting.
- Automation of delivering marketing offers.
- Automation of follow-up actions.
- Automation of sales rep alerts.
- Automation of landing page personalization.
- Tracking of customer interactions.
- Tracking of website and content usages.
- Automation of campaign execution and monitoring. This functionality may be included in a digital campaign management tool.
- Automation of lead qualification, prioritization and nurturing. This functionality may be included in a lead management tool.

MATURITY INDICATOR EXAMPLES

Level 0: Non-existent

- No Marketing Automation tool has been implemented to perform routine marketing activities automatically. The routine tasks are performed manually.

Level 1: Ad hoc

- Some marketing routines are semi-automated with limited tool capability. A large portion of marketing routine activities is however still performed manually.

Level 2: Basic

- A tool specialized at Marketing Automation is employed, but the tool's functionally is limited and not integrated with other marketing systems.
- Many manual operations and human interventions are still required to manage the marketing workflows.

Level 3: Defined

- A comprehensive marketing automation tool is implemented to automate almost all routine marketing activities across digital campaign management, lead management and other ad hoc marketing activities.
- Integration with other systems has been implemented, but the integrations are not enough to automate end-to-end digital marketing processes fully, and thus manual intervention is required to complete the workflow.

Level 4: Optimized

- The integration of the Marketing Automation tool with other digital marketing tools has been optimized based on refined end-to-end digital marketing processes.
- Campaign execution and lead nurturing processes are fully automated and human intervention is only required for handling exceptions and ad hoc marketing activities.
- Due to the advanced level of marketing automation, every marketing lead and sales opportunity is monitored and followed up if necessary.
- Other parts of the marketing processes, such as marketing planning and collaboration are partly automated.
- Marketing operational efficiency is measured and optimized accordingly.

Level 5: Progressive

- Marketing Automation becomes the underlying enterprise marketing platform on which other digital marketing capabilities can readily be built and integrated with one another. Marketing tools for planning, execution and monitoring are readily built and integrated.
- Marketing Automation releases digital marketers from simple, repetitive marketing tasks with low value so that they can focus on high value marketing analytics, planning and ad hoc activities to facilitate transition and conversion in the marketing funnel.

CAPABILITY 3-13.
CONVERSION RATE OPTIMIZATION

CAPABILITY DEFINITION

Conversion is the transition from one stage to another in a marketing or sales funnel, e.g. transition from visiting stage to purchasing stage, depending on how the funnel has been defined. Conversion rate represents the speed of the transition from one stage to another.

Conversion Rate Optimization is a digital capability used to increase the rate of conversion from a visitor to a customer, or from a lead to a sale. It includes real time abilities to measure the number of leads, qualified leads, and visitors in each stage from a landing page to a destination page, analyse the cause of visitor bounce, and develop and deploy quick-fix solutions to decrease the bounce rate, or increase conversion rate.

This digital capability can increase specific web visitors' actions, such as submitting a form, downloading an asset, requesting for more information, or subscribing to a free trial.

The ways of improving conversion rates may involve revising the website navigation structure, web site layout, digital content, marketing offers and many others that users see and use on the website.

While Conversion Rate Optimization is focused on short-term quick fixes of bottlenecks in conversions, this digital capability collaborates with back-office analytics capabilities, including Conversion Analytics and Web Analytics capabilities, for deeper analysis for root causes of the bottlenecks and longer-term solutions.

Conversion Tracking

The status of conversions should be tracked to analyse and optimize them. Conversion tracking is to monitor what is happening on a website at every possible moment, and to drill down to every user and specific piece of content to examine their effect on conversion rates.

In the example below, conversion and bounce rates with details are analysed.

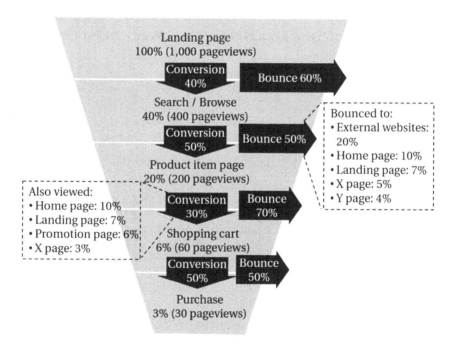

[Figure 19: Conversion Funnel Analysis Example]

Tool functionality for real-time analytics to support traffic segmentation, visitor segregation, and tracking metrics are required for the real-time tracking of conversions.

Traffic Segmentation

For further analysis of a conversion funnel, website traffics need to be broken down into a small number of segments according to such criteria as source of traffic, channel, customer group and so on. Sources of user traffic on a website must for example be identified to understand differences in visitors' collective behaviour from the different source of user traffic. A different source of traffic can result in a different rate of conversion.

It is particularly difficult to analyse visitors' behaviour patterns on a website. In order to identify behaviour patterns of visitors from a different traffic source, many different types of log data and tools are required. This may include standard web server logs, specially purposed webpage scripts to create further web logs, analytics reports from search engines, and specialized conversion rate optimization tools.

Heat Map

A heat map is a visual representation of clicks that resembles thermal imaging. The map shows where people click and what they select on a webpage. It can tell you whether users click on the calls-to-action, or not.

This allows the observation of all visitor activities on a website and allows changes to be made according to the user demand. With the use of heat map analytics, the website's layout, design, navigation, marketing offers and the areas that don't attract visitors can be identified and changed accordingly.

A/B Testing & Multivariate Testing

When the cause of a bottleneck in a conversion funnel is identified, the website needs to be revised and optimized to reduce the bottleneck. This requires evaluation of the multiple options of optimizing the website.

A/B testing is a method of comparing two versions of a website to evaluate which version creates better conversion rates.

Multivariate testing is a method of comparing a few different variable changes on the web site. Multivariate testing compares a higher number of variables than A/B testing and evaluates how the variables interact with one another.

While web development and testing is part of the Digital Capability Development capability, many Conversion Rate Optimization tools provide A/B testing and multivariate testing as part of their functionalities.

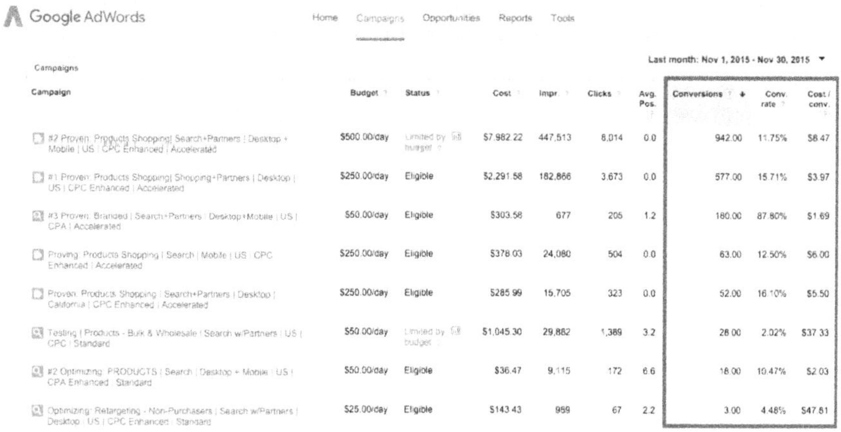

Campaign	Budget	Status	Cost	Impr.	Clicks	Avg. Pos.	Conversions	Conv. rate	Cost / conv.
#2 Proven: Products Shopping| Search+Partners | Desktop + Mobile | US | CPC Enhanced | Accelerated	$500.00/day	Limited by budget	$7,982.22	447,513	6,014	0.0	942.00	11.75%	$8.47
#1 Proven: Products Shopping| Shopping+Partners | Desktop | US | CPC Enhanced | Accelerated	$250.00/day	Eligible	$2,291.58	182,866	3,673	0.0	577.00	15.71%	$3.97
#3 Proven: Branded | Search+Partners | Desktop+Mobile | US | CPA | Accelerated	$50.00/day	Eligible	$303.58	677	205	1.2	180.00	87.80%	$1.69
Proving: Products Shopping | Search | Mobile | US | CPC Enhanced | Accelerated	$250.00/day	Eligible	$378.03	24,080	504	0.0	63.00	12.50%	$6.00
Proven: Products Shopping | Search+Partners | Desktop | California | CPC Enhanced | Accelerated	$250.00/day	Eligible	$285.99	15,705	323	0.0	52.00	16.10%	$5.50
Testing | Products - Bulk & Wholesale | Search w/Partners | US | CPC | Standard	$50.00/day	Limited by budget	$1,045.30	29,882	1,389	3.2	28.00	2.02%	$37.33
#2 Optimizing: PRODUCTS | Search | Desktop + Mobile | US | CPA Enhanced | Standard	$50.00/day	Eligible	$36.47	9,115	172	6.6	18.00	10.47%	$2.03
Optimizing: Retargeting - Non-Purchasers | Search w/Partners | Desktop | US | CPC Enhanced | Standard	$25.00/day	Eligible	$143.43	959	67	2.2	3.00	4.48%	$47.81

[Figure 20: Google Conversion Rate Optimization Dashboard]

Requirements of a Conversion Rate Optimization Tool

A Conversion Rate Optimization tool enables and automates the processes of monitoring, assessing and increasing conversion rates, and it includes the following functionalities:

- **Traffic segmentation**: to divide the total traffic into cohesive groups.
- **Tracking & monitoring**: to track and monitor the status of stages of a conversion funnel.
- **Analytics**: to define metrics such as clicks, scrolls and shopping card abandonment, and evaluate these against the metrics.
- **Heat Map**: to depict which part of a webpage users are interested in.

- **A/B Testing**: to decide which version of a webpage would increase conversion more.

Some of the Conversion Rate Optimization tools may provide functionalities for designing and developing a landing page, and testing usability, performance and browser compatibility of a webpage. This is however not at the core of a Conversion Optimization tool and you may find them in the tools for the Digital Capability Development capability.

MATURITY INDICATOR EXAMPLES

Level 0: Non-existent

- No conversion funnel or funnel stage is established.
- No metrics are defined in relation to conversion rates and nothing is measured in relation to conversion.

Level 1: Ad hoc

- A very simple conversion funnel is established to measure the visit to purchase ratio.
- The visit to purchase ratio is measured on an ad hoc basis.
- The organization has started using basic functions of an analytics tool of a search engine such as Google Analytics, but no tool specialized in conversion analytics is implemented.
- A website optimization solution has not been implemented.

Level 2: Basic

- Different business units have different funnels.
- Conversion rate is measured on a regular basis. There are also further metrics established to analyse reasons behind a conversion rate, e.g. bounce rate during checkout, top exit pages and interactions per visit.

- The organization has implemented a specialized tool, but the functionally of the tool is too limited to analyse customer behaviour patterns, and log data required for the analysis is not readily available.
- Website optimization solutions are partly used.

Level 3: Defined

- The organization has established a standard conversion funnel that is aligned with the brand marketing funnel, lead management funnel and digital customer journey map.
- Corporate principles, policies, procedures, standards and guidance for conversion data collection, problem identification, causal analysis, and problem resolution are established and enforced.
- Proven practices, including traffic segmentation and heat map analysis are employed.
- The functionalities of the Conversion Rate Optimization tool are comprehensive. Not all data required for conversion analysis is available, resulting in incomplete analysis of root causes.
- All solutions required for website optimization are available from other digital capabilities.

Level 4: Optimized

- This level of the digital capability enables the organization to fully understands "what is happening" in the conversion funnel. The maturity level comes from clear visibility into the stages of the funnel.
- Metrics for conversion rate analysis have been optimized.
- Data quantity and quality required for conversion rate analysis have been improved.

Level 5: Progressive

- The level of the digital capability enables the organization to fully understand "why and how it is happening" in the conversion funnel. The maturity level comes from organizational core competency to identify root causes of bottlenecks or other issues which create a competitive advantage.
- The identified root causes are translated into solutions for website optimization.

MEGA CAPABILITY 4.

DIGITAL COMMERCE

Conceptually, an organization starts building a relationship with its potential customers through Social Interaction capabilities and sends marketing communications through Digital Marketing capabilities as the relationship with its customers develops.

Through the social interactions and marketing communications, the customers are ready to purchase the products and services of the organization.

The purpose of the Digital Commerce capabilities is to help with the shopping processes, fulfil customer orders and provide customer services.

Actual conversion to purchase is made during the Digital Commerce processes, and thus the Conversion Rate Optimization of the Digital Marketing capabilities also covers the shopping processes of the Digital Commerce capabilities.

Digital Commerce has the following as its digital capabilities:

- Online Merchandising

- Shopping Cart & Checkout
- Payments & Reconciliation
- Order Management & Fulfilment
- Account Management & Self-service

CAPABILITY 4-1.
ONLINE MERCHANDISING

CAPABILITY DEFINITION

Online Merchandising is a digital capability used to arrange a variety of products and services available for sales, and display them in such a way that they can stimulate interest and entice customers to make a purchase, and customers can find whichever product they wish to purchase.

Dynamic Merchandising & Product Recommendation

Online Merchandising should ensure high customer engagement, low rate of website bounce, and quality customer conversions. It requires dynamic merchandising and customized content publishing to deliver a personalized experience that contributes to increasing customer engagement, sales and customer satisfaction.

Dynamic and personalized display of products, services, and digital contents can be performed based on 'Mega Capability 7. Customization & Personalization' and 'Mega Capability 8. Digital Intelligence' of the Digital Capability Model.

Product Similarity Analytics capability of Digital Intelligence can create rules for real-time recommendation of products, services and digital content. The mechanism will be discussed in detail in 'Capability 8-1 Product Similarity Analytics'. When a customer clicks on a product, the Online Merchandising capability can use the rules to display and recommend products that have close relationship with the product the customer has selected, without knowing who the customer is.

Customer Segmentation capability of Digital Intelligence can also provide Online Merchandising with information on products that can be displayed and recommended to a customer, without knowing what product the customer is interested in at the time when the customer logs in. This type of recommendation is performed by using the customer segment profile that has information on products commonly preferred by the customer segment.

Online Merchandising can also use information on personal preference for digital contents that is provided by the Customer Preference Management capability. There is a lot more information in the middle-office and back-office capability for Online Merchandising capability to use for dynamic merchandising and product recommendation.

Online Merchandising Functionality

Online Merchandising websites commonly provide the following functionalities:

- Functionality to create and maintain an online catalogue of products and services, and display them.
- Functionality for product browsing and keyword search.
- Functionality to collect data on customer preference for products and services from the middle-office or back-office capabilities, and dynamically display relevant products and services.
- Functionality to recommend other products or services complementary to the product a customer is perusing.

MATURITY INDICATOR EXAMPLES

Level 0: Non-existent

- No online product catalogue exists.
- No product is available for view and sales online.

Level 1: Ad hoc

- An online catalogue of products is available online, but the catalogue is static HTML webpages that are not dynamically created.
- Limited products with limited information are available on the catalogue.
- The online catalogue is updated on an ad hoc basis.
- There may be an offline merchandising strategy, but there is no strategy for Online Merchandising.

Level 2: Basic

- A merchandising tool helps merchandisers to create and update the online catalogue.
- Merchandising itself is done by the merchandisers, but there are no central principles or policies to guide what to display where and when.
- Not all products suitable for online sales are registered in the online catalogue database.
- The online catalogue is updated on a regular basis.
- Real-time product recommendation are not available.

Level 3: Defined

- Corporate principles, policies, strategy and guidance to Online Merchandising are implemented.
- The merchandising policies are embedded in the online merchandising websites as business rules for standard merchandising.
- All products suitable for online sales are registered in the online catalogue database.
- Real-time product recommendations are available. The effectiveness of the recommendations is however low due to the limited functionality of the recommendation tool and the limited feed of personalized data.

Level 4: Optimized

- The effectiveness of the recommendation tool has been optimized with the optimized algorithm of the recommendation tool and a substantial amount of personalized data feed.
- Online Merchandising has been optimized by integrating the standard merchandising with personalized merchandising, to the extent that it goes beyond the simple display of products and services pre-defined by standard merchandising policies.
- Various recommendation logic for up-sell, cross-sell, and re-sell of products and services are developed based on the product similarity, and the preference of an individual customer and a customer segment.

Level 5: Progressive

- Effective recommendation of products and services is made possible even with the limited feed of information that a customer may give such as a click on a link, without knowledge of the customer. This level of capability comes from in-depth knowledge of collective patterns of online customer behaviour towards products and services.
- When a customer reveals himself by logging in, the personal information is combined with the collective patterns toward products and services, producing recommendations and merchandising of products, services, and digital contents that are more effective.

CAPABILITY 4-2.
SHOPPING CART & CHECKOUT

CAPABILITY DEFINITION

Shopping Cart & Checkout is a digital capability used to collect product or service items for purchase in a shopping cart, and calculate a total for the order.

Shopping Cart & Checkout include the following functionalities:

- Calculation of total amount of discount from multiple sources, including coupons and discount promotions.
- Calculation of packing and shipping charges and associated taxes.
- Integration with a loyalty program.
- Integration with Payment & Reconciliation capability.
- Invoice management.
- Express checkout.

MATURITY INDICATOR EXAMPLES

Level 0: Non-existent

- Neither shopping cart, nor checkout functions are provided.

Level 1: Ad hoc

- Shopping cart and checkout functions are very limited. There is a single shopping cart available that does not support marketing offers, sales promotions, multiple payment options, etc.

Level 2: Basic

- Various shopping carts are provided for different purposes, e.g. a shopping cart for buying with a coupon or voucher, a shopping cart for special products on sales promotion, and a shopping cart for credit card promotion.
- These various shopping carts exist and should be processed independently from one another, and are not consolidated into a single shopping cart. If for example two products are put into two different shopping carts, checkout is done twice.

Level 3: Defined

- A single shopping cart can handle all different types of marketing offers, sales promotions, payment methods, etc.
- All functionalities required for managing Point of Sales (PoS) are provided, e.g. real-time inventory, express checkout, saved cart, favourites, wish list, gift registry, rain-checks, bulk order, email shopping cart and many more.

Level 4: Optimized

- Long and complicated checkout processes have been streamlined to prevent cart abandonment.
- Customers have a clear visibility of the total price of an order before proceeding with checkout, and there is therefore no surprise during the checkout process.

Level 5: Progressive

- Dynamic propositions of promotions or rewards are made during shopping cart and checkout processes to prevent cart abandonment and increase conversion rate.
- When customers don't proceed with checkout or abandon the shopping cart, the organization can identify the reasons and come up with marketing offers or incentives for the customers to come back to the shopping cart and complete the checkout.

CAPABILITY 4-3.
PAYMENTS & RECONCILIATION

CAPABILITY DEFINITION

Payments & Reconciliation is a digital capability used to enable a retailer to calculate deductions for partners as soon as a customer makes payment. Payment functions should enable customers to make payments with various electronic payment methods over the Internet to complete the purchase process. Reconciliation functions should be able to calculate the amount of money to be allocated to partners according to their contribution to the sale and deduction items. These may include commissions for introducing customers, payment fees, shipping charges, and statutory taxes.

Payment functions include:

- Payment by debit and credit card.
- Payment by gift card, coupons, and loyalty points.
- Payment by a combination of multiple payment options.
- Receipt management.
- Recurring payments.
- Signature capture.

Reconciliation functions include:

- Master data management for reconciliation.
- Real time calculation for reconciliation.
- Weekly or monthly batch calculation for reconciliation.
- Reconciliation data transfer to internal financial system.

MATURITY INDICATOR EXAMPLES

Level **0**: Non-existent

- Online payment is not available, but manual bank transfers are used to make a payment.

Level 1: Ad hoc

- Beside a manual bank transfer, a single online payment option is available.
- Reconciliation is performed manually and is not real-time based.

Level 2: Basic

- A couple of online payment options are available.
- Payment with multiple payment options is not allowed.
- Some of the data used for reconciliation is gathered automatically, but manual intervention is needed throughout the reconciliation process.

Level 3: Defined

- Many payment options are available and the payment function supports saved payment option, ad hoc payment option, gift certificate, coupons, check/money order, etc.
- Payment with multiple payment options is not always possible.
- Reconciliation is done on a real-time basis, but it still needs intermittent human intervention, for example, to calculate deductions from discount promotions on a monthly basis.

Level 4: Optimized

- Payments with multiple payment options are always possible.
- Multi-currency payment is supported.
- Reconciliation processes are fully automated for every transaction, except for refund and exchange transactions

that requires re-calculation of deductions on a case-by-case basis.

Level 5: Progressive

- Dynamic provisioning of a new payment option is made through secure and non-intrusive integration with external payment options whenever needed.
- Reconciliation processes are fully automated and human intervention is required only when there is an exception.

CAPABILITY 4-4.
ORDER MANAGEMENT & FULFILMENT

CAPABILITY DEFINITION

Order Management & Fulfilment is a digital capability used to take an order of product or service items that are available at the time of the order, and pick, pack, and ship the items as instructed in the order statement. It also includes keeping track of progress of the order fulfilment, and managing returns, refunds, exchanges, re-orders, and backorders.

Order Management & Fulfilment functionalities include:

- **Order management**: Functionalities to create customer order, fulfilment order, delivery order, shipping order, back order, recurring order, return order, exchange order and other types of order for order fulfilment purpose, and keep track of the different types of orders.

- **Warehouse management**: Functionalities to pick and pack stocks for customer orders and manage inventory levels. Some of the functionalities may be provided through integration with warehouse management modules of existing supply chain management systems.

- **Logistics management**: Functionalities to manage delivery of products. Some of the functionalities may be provided through integration with logistics management modules of existing supply chain management systems.

- **Order fulfilment tracking**: Functionalities to track the status of the end-to-end order fulfilment processes.

MATURITY INDICATOR EXAMPLES

Level 0: Non-existent

- Online order taking functionality is unavailable.

Level 1: Ad hoc

- Customers can create a simple customer order online.
- The customer order is delivered through email or file transfer to a warehouse for order fulfilment, without creating a fulfilment order. Order fulfilment processes are therefore performed manually.
- There is no integration between the digital commerce system and the existing warehouse management system.

Level 2: Basic

- Fulfilment orders are automatically created based on customer orders. The fulfilment orders are used to facilitate the processes to pick, pack and ship the products in the warehouse.
- There is moderate level integration between the digital commerce system and the existing warehouse management system.

- Standard processes for online order fulfilment are not available and different business units have different order fulfilment practices.

Level 3: Defined

- Corporate policies, procedures and standards are implemented for online order fulfilment.
- Different types of orders are created to facilitate fulfilment responsibilities and tasks, e.g. customer order for customer team, fulfilment order for order fulfilment team, picking & packing order for warehouse team, and delivery order for logistics team.
- Delivery status is tracked when in distribution hubs and centres.
- Simple order changes can be made online, but customers must call the customer contact centre to make further changes to orders, e.g. return of one out of three books.

Level 4: Optimized

- Order fulfilment processes have been streamlined and optimized through seamless integration between ecommerce systems and existing supply-chain management systems, without swivel chair integrations.
- Complicated changes to a customer order can be made online, but it requires human intervention to make corresponding changes to fulfilment orders, e.g. manual changes to warehouse and delivery orders.

Level 5: Progressive

- Customers can make any changes to their order, and the changes to corresponding fulfilment orders are done automatically without human intervention.
- When a customer wishes to return or exchange part or all the products that have already been delivered, the customer can

place a return or exchange order online without calling the customer contact centre.

CAPABILITY 4-5.
ACCOUNT MANAGEMENT & SELF-SERVICE

CAPABILITY DEFINITION

Account Management & Self Service is a digital capability used to maintain customer information, including membership profile, and purchasing and transaction history, and enables customers using their credentials to serve themselves before, during, and after purchase.

Account Management & Self-Service includes the following functionalities:

- Membership registration.
- Member profile, membership category and loyalty points.
- Preference management including communication tool, website layout, newsletters, etc.
- Purchasing, search and view history.
- Watch list and wish list management.
- Order change management.
- Warranty & claim management.
- Feedback & complaints management.
- Online service desk services, including online help topics, FAQs and live chat.

MATURITY INDICATOR EXAMPLES

Level 0: Non-existent

- There is no functionality available for member registration online, but customers may view their orders via an order reference number.

Level 1: Ad hoc

- A customer can register for an online account, but the profile information is limited.
- Customers can view their order history online, but other than that, there is no further online self-service available.

Level 2: Basic

- Customers can change some of their information such as a phone number online, but must call the customer contact centre to make changes to the other customer information.
- Customer preferences are partly managed online.
- Online FAQs for self-service purpose are provided.
- Customers cannot make a change to their order online and must make a call to the customer contact centre.

Level 3: Defined

- Customer can apply for a loyalty membership online without going to the offline customer centre.
- Most of the customer information, including loyalty membership information can be managed online by customers, except for changes to critical information that requires confirmation by the customer contact centre.
- Customers can make simple changes to their order online, e.g. change to the delivery address.
- An online chat tool and comprehensive online help topics are provided.

Level 4: Optimized

- All customer information can be managed by customers online.
- Changes to critical information can be made online through a multi-factor authentication processes.
- Most of the customer services that are provided offline are available online, except a few services, e.g. warranty management.

Level 5: Progressive

- All customer services that are provided offline are available online.
- Customers' experience in online self-services are seamless and consistent to offline customer services, as there is little difference in the scope of customer services between offline and online.

MEGA CAPABILITY 5.

DIGITAL CHANNEL MANAGEMENT

Digital Channel Management is a set of digital capabilities used to harmonize, consolidate, or integrate multiple digital channels that are used for the interactions between target customers and all levels of an organization, to streamline customer experience across the multiple digital channels.

Most customers accessed more than a single online channel to interact with an organization long before the contemporary digital era. The customer behaviour of using multiple digital channels has since been far more complicated due to the proliferation of multiple digital devices.

The only solution to respond to the proliferation of the digital devices and channels best, is not to become channel-intelligent, but to become channel-agnostic. Organizations should stop building channel-specific marketing services and IT services, and start building unified marketing services and supporting IT services that can be provided on any channel, so that customers barely recognize the difference in services between multiple channels. This approach will improve customer experiences in the digital space significantly, and reduce the complexity of digital channel management. This is the key to successful Omni-channel management.

Digital Channel Management has the following digital capabilities:

- Channel Mix & Optimization
- Cross-Business Integration
- Cross-Channel Integration
- Multi-Device Presentation

CAPABILITY 5-1.
CHANNEL MIX & OPTIMIZATION

CAPABILITY DEFINITION

Channel Mix & Optimization is a digital capability used to build and fine-tune a digital channel portfolio to achieve the customer interactions intended at touchpoints on customer journey maps.

Channel Mix

In order to develop an effective digital channel mix, organizations need to understand the unique features that different digital channels and devices have, and the unique functions they can perform. This understanding can lead to further understanding of how different digital channels and devices best fit specific search, interaction and purchase behaviours defined in the profile of a target customer segment.

It is a good idea to start looking at the preferred channels of a target customer segment that are defined in the profile of the customer segment, if one already exists.

Secondary backup channels should also be part of a digital channel mix.

Channel Mix Optimization

The traditional way to optimize a channel mix is to analyse the return on investment, profitability, and/or sales volume for each channel, and reshuffle the channel portfolio according to their financial performance. The primary purpose of the traditional optimization approach is to manage the final results, rather than the customer journey itself, often making the different channels compete against one another.

Channel collaboration is much more important for online than for offline, because online channels should collaborate for a

171

customer to complete his end-to-end journey with an improved customer experience. Making multiple digital channels compete against one another would prevent achieving an omni-channel strategy and eventually hinder the digital channels from working together for corporate-level synergy.

In the digital space, a digital channel portfolio should be optimized against performance indicators and metrics around conversion from one touchpoint and channel of a lower stage, to another touchpoint and channel of an upper stage as planned on a customer journey map, thus promoting collaboration and integration between the different digital channels.

MATURITY INDICATOR EXAMPLES

Level 0: Non-existent

- The organization may think the digital channel mix is critical to the success of its digital business, but the digital channel mix has neither been planned, nor implemented.

Level 1: Ad hoc

- Features of several digital channels and devices have been analysed and a digital channel mix has been implemented on an ad hoc basis.
- The digital channel mix has been neither continuous, nor consistent.

Level 2: Basic

- The digital channel mix is planned annually and aligned with annual business or marketing strategy.
- The digital channel mix plan of a business unit may be aligned with the target customer segments of the business unit, but the digital channel mix plans of individual business units are not coordinated at corporate level.

- The digital channel mix is optimized based on the financial performance of each digital channel.

Level 3: Defined

- Corporate strategy, principles, policies and standards are implemented to coordinate the digital channel mix of business units.
- Besides a business unit-level digital channel mix, a corporate-level digital channel mix plan is established and implemented to target corporate-level customer segments.
- Digital channels are optimized based on contribution to conversions along the entire customer journey, but the organization has limited ability to measure a reasonable portion of the contribution of each channel when sales occur.

Level 4: Optimized

- Effectiveness of each channel and the entire channel portfolio is measured against pre-defined metrics such as conversion from one journey stage to another. The organization has clear policies to measure the contribution of each channel and abilities to track the contribution automatically.
- Monthly or quarterly reviews of the metrics enables continuous optimization in the digital touchpoint portfolio, digital channel mix planning and implementation.
- The digital channel mix is an integral part of entire channel mix across online and offline.

Level 5: Progressive

- The digital channel mix is not optimized for channel-specific financial performance, but for cross-channel financial performance including ROI, revenue and profitability, without each channel being siloed.

- Channel Mix & Optimization capability is seamlessly integrated with the Social Interaction for Social channel mix, Digital Marketing for the marketing channel mix, and Digital Commerce for the sales channel mix. This allows the digital channels to work better as planned in the digital customer journey map.

CAPABILITY 5-2.
CROSS-BUSINESS INTEGRATION

CAPABILITY DEFINITION

Each business unit tends to develop its own silo set of digital channels, resulting in different business units investing in redundant channels that are not coordinated at corporate level. It often confuses customers with inconsistent marketing offers and reduces opportunities for cross-sell and up-sell of different products and different services from different business units.

Cross-Business Integration is a digital capability used to consolidate, integrate, or harmonize the different digital plans and policies across the different business units, to achieve a single face to the same customers and provide consistent messages, content and offers throughout Social Interaction, Digital Marketing and Digital Commerce.

Cross-Business Integration prevents each business unit from sprouting its silo channel without corporate-level synergy across the entire organization, and ensures that an organization can build a consistent brand image for its customers.

There is no single right operating model to implement Cross-Business Integration, but rather a range of options as follows:

- **Centralized model**: A central digital organization is established and tasked with planning and performing all responsibilities for digital channel management with assistance from business units.

- **De-centralized model**: Each business unit is responsible for planning and performing all responsibilities for digital channel management, and all business units participate in a committee where digital channel strategy is shared, discussed and agreed on.

- **Federal model**: Each business unit is responsible for implementing digital channel strategy, but the strategy is drafted and coordinated by a central digital organization, and agreed to by both the central digital organization and all business units.

MATURITY INDICATOR EXAMPLES

Level 0: Non-existent

- There is no collaboration or coordination for digital channel management between individual business units.

Level 1: Ad hoc

- Collaboration between business units for digital channel management occurs on an ad hoc basis, e.g. they may plan a channel mix together for a seasonal sales promotion.

Level 2: Basic

- A few business units are engaged in collaboration for digital channel management on a regular basis to pursue strategic use of multiple channels for synergy among the business units involved. There is however no coordination at corporate-level.

Level 3: Defined

- Corporate strategy, principles, policies and procedures of collaboration for digital channel management between business units are implemented.
- The principles, policies and procedures articulate how digital channels should be managed, how business units make decisions on digital channel management and the responsibilities of the central digital organization.

Level 4: Optimized

- Collaboration between business units on the channel has been optimized to the extent that the enterprise can offer joint marketing offerings and bundled product and services through integrated channels.

Level 5: Progressive

- This level of the capability allows the organization to make a competitive value proposition through the collaboration on digital channel management. This provides a competitive advantage through the joint offerings, products and services.

CAPABILITY 5-3.
CROSS-CHANNEL INTEGRATION

CAPABILITY DEFINITION

Cross-Channel Integration is a digital capability to have all digital channels integrated and connected seamlessly to deliver consistent and seamless customer experiences across different digital channels.

This digital capability aims to achieve the vision of channel agnostic integration or omni-channel convergence, in which customers barely recognize difference of services provisioned and provided in different channels.

The traditional multi-channel approach allows, or even encourages competition between multiple channels by comparing and rewarding their financial performances, making each channel a silo that does not collaborate with others. The multi-channel approach had merit as it delivered immediate financial results.

In the modern digital era, it is believed that collaboration between different digital channels provides more advantages than competition between them. Put simply, the total financial benefits gained from fast conversion resulting from seamless transition between channels are better than those obtained from promoting competition between different channels are.

Cross-Channel Integration of Policies and Processes

Cross-Channel Integration capability involves harmonising marketing and sales policies and processes across different channels, to make sure that different digital channels offer consistent customer experiences. Traditionally, different channels have provided different marketing offers, different products, or different service levels, partly because of different governance structures of the channels.

The inconsistent customer experiences resulting from different offerings of different channels have caused many problems building a consistent brand image. For example:

- A customer buys a product online, but may not be able to return it in a store. The customer may be not willing to use multiple channels with the brand.

- A customer buys a product with 5% off the list price online and later finds out the same product was 10% off in stores on the same day. The next time the customer shops with the brand, he may not believe that the price he sees online or in a store is the best price he can get with the brand.

Such inconsistent customer experiences will ruin a brand's reputation. Make sure different marketing offers or service levels for different channels are used only as a tactical measure that does not have a negative impact on brand building.

Cross-Channel Integration of IT Architecture

Cross-Channel Integration also involves consolidating and integrating different IT solutions supporting different channels. The Multi-Channel Integration (MCI) architecture is an IT solution used to integrate different digital channels, so that separate business applications for different channels don't have to be developed.

The multi-channel integration architecture is extremely important for ensuring seamless transitions from one journey stage to another and from one touchpoint to another, in that it can make customer interactions with an organization seamless for improved digital customer experiences.

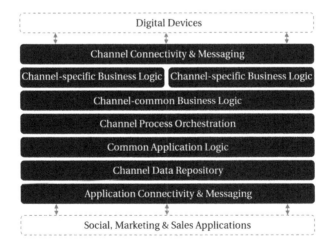

[Figure 21: Multi-channel Integration (MCI) Architecture]

MCI architecture is employed to integrate different channels seamlessly to enable harmonized channel policies and processes. A multi-channel integration architecture includes the following components.

- **Channel Connectivity & Messaging**: This component of MCI is used to connect many different channel devices with MCI architecture. For example, communication protocol conversion, message transformation and formatting, code mapping, transcoding, conversation control, and portal services are provided.

- **Channel-specific Business Logic**: This component is used to deliver business Logic that is unique to a channel. A cash withdrawal service is available on an ATM channel, but not on a mobile channel. Channel Connectivity functions recognize which device is connecting to the MCI architecture, and Channel-specific Business Logic component uses the information to deliver services available to the device.

- **Channel-common Business Logic**: This component of MCI is used to deliver business Logic that is common to all digital channels, e.g. basic product and service management, customer profile management, and marketing offer management. These are synchronized to the front-office digital capabilities.

- **Channel Process Orchestration**: Channel Process Orchestration services are used when the navigation of a specific channel should be changed. It can also be used when a route from one touchpoint to another in a digital customer journey map changes.

- **Common Application Logic**: This component is used to deliver non-business Logic services required for business Logic services to function, e.g. database and file access service, single-sign on, logging, error handling, etc.

- **Channel Data Repository**: All channel information, including customer information, customer contact history, marketing offer, and sales funnel status from different digital channels are consolidated in this centralized database, so that a single truth of the data can be shared across all digital channels.

- **Application Connectivity & Messaging**: This component is used to connect the MCI architecture to core digital applications. Functions such as application connectors or adaptors, message routing, messaging, and data formatting are provided by this component.

MATURITY INDICATOR EXAMPLES

Level 0: Non-existent

- The organization may use one or more digital channels, but each of the digital channels is in its own silo and they are neither coordinated, nor integrated.

Level 1: Ad hoc

- Integration between the digital channels is planned and implemented on an ad hoc basis, e.g. some of the multiple channels are jointly used for a seasonal sales promotion in which marketing offers are coordinated for the channels involved.
- Multi-channel integration architecture supporting the ad hoc channel integration is not implemented, and different programs for the different channels should be developed.

Level 2: Basic

- Multi-channel integration is planned and implemented on a regular basis within a business unit without corporate-level coordination.

- The multi-channel integration is initiated to fulfil bottom-up, short-term, quick-fix needs, rather than the digital customer journey map.
- IT architecture services supporting multi-channel integration is partially implemented with limited multi-channel architecture capabilities, resulting in low reusability of the architecture services.

Level 3: Defined

- Corporate-level cross-channel integration strategy, principles, policies and procedures are implemented and aligned to the digital customer journey map.
- Comprehensive multi-channel IT architecture services are deployed. The architecture has multiple components that can be readily reused for different digital channels with little re-programming.

Level 4: Optimized

- Multi-channel integration policies and procedures have been optimized to the extent that customers are comfortable with accessing a digital channel different to the channel previously accessed.
- Multi-channel IT architecture reusability is high. Multi-channel integration architecture has been optimized to the extent that a new channel can be added with much less effort, e.g. a new channel can be added to the channel portfolio by only developing the user interface of the new device.

Level 5: Progressive

- Customers barely notice the difference between different channels. Due to the highly optimized multi-channel integration architecture, the multiple digital channels are perceived by customers as a mega single channel, also known as omni-channel.

- The multiple digital channels are seamlessly integrated with the brick and mortar channels, so that customers can enjoy maximized customer experience with whichever channels they access.

CAPABILITY 5-4.
MULTI-DEVICE PRESENTATION

CAPABILITY DEFINITION

Multi-Device Presentation is a digital capability used to reuse a single computer program for multiple devices. It is commonly known as 'one-source multi-use' for the presentation layer. The digital capability should handle different computing languages, different platforms and communication protocols that different devices use, different sizes, layouts and content suitable for different devices, and so on.

As digital devices proliferate, the ability to reuse existing applications while successfully meeting different demands from digital users becomes a critical factor to sustainable digital operations. It is the case when it comes to application presentation Logic for digital devices.

To increase the reusability, the presentation Logic of a mobile app and a desktop application should be designed and developed by the architecture principle of Separation of Concerns [14] (SoC).

---

[14] Separation of Concerns is a design principle for dividing an application into separate components that address separate concerns of the application.

According to the principle, presentation Logic should be divided into three 'concerns':

- A concern that handles what the user's request is and how to fulfil it.
- A concern that handles what to present to a user to fulfil the request.
- A concern that handles how to present it to the user.

This design principle for presentation Logic is referred to as the MVC (Model, View and Controller) pattern in the architecture practice.

- '**Controller**' components concern what the user's request is and how to fulfil it. Controller is the interaction components that interact between a user, View components and Model components when a user provides input through the View, or when the Model delivers data to a user.

- '**Model**' components concern what to present to a user to fulfil the request. Model is data components that are responsible for containing data that are delivered between back-end core applications and a user.

- '**View**' components concern how to present it to the user. View is user-interface components that are shown to users on screens of a device such as buttons, text boxes, dropdowns, tables, graphs, diagrams, etc.

Let's consider a very simple scenario to understand how the three components of the MVC model work together. When a user makes a change to his home address:

- The user inputs a new home address on the home address text box of the View component and clicks on the change button of the View component.

- The change button of the View component calls a Controller component – the Controller component may re-format or transform the data if necessary.

- The Controller component delivers the new home address to a Model component that handles home address data.

- The Model component stores the new home address in the database.

- The Model component informs the Controller component that the new home address is successfully stored.

- The Controller component calls an appropriate View component that shows a success message to the user.

Below is another example to understand how the MVC components share responsibilities to perform as presentation Logic in an enterprise environment. In this use case, a portal application and a CRM application are working together for a customer to make a change to the Delivery Address of a customer order.

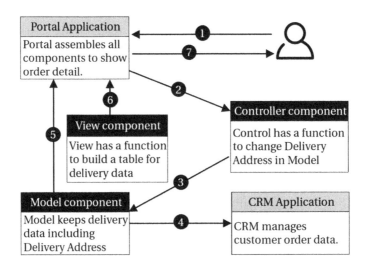

[Figure 22: Collaboration of MVC Components]

1. Customer changes delivery Address

2. Portal delivers customer request to Controller

3. Controller asks Model to change Address in Model

4. Model changes delivery Address in itself and asks CRM to change Delivery Address in customer order database

5. Portal fetches all delivery data including changed Delivery Address from Model

6. Portal asks View to put the data in a table

7. Portal shows order detail with delivery data including changed Delivery Address

The portal application in Figure 22 is used to assemble delivery data, product data, payment data and all the rest of the customer order into a single page. The Controller component is responsible for making sure that the customer's request for the change to the Delivery Address is fulfilled. The Model component is responsible for maintaining delivery data, including the Delivery Address, communicating with the CRM application that manages all customer orders stored in the customer order database. The View component is responsible for formatting the delivery data into a neat table.

If there is a need for the table to be changed to a new table with a different layout, colour, or font, only the View component needs to be changed with no changes to the other components. For a different digital device with a different size, Controller components and Model components can be extensively reused, while View components need to be re-designed to fit into the different screen size. The portal application in the example needs to switch View components based only on request elements, such as a type of Web browser, while still re-using Controllers and Models for the multiple View components.

When organizations take Web app or Hybrid app approaches, rather than the Native app approach to mobile app development, the reusability can increase significantly. A single set of web applications may for example be able to run on desktops and mobile devices. We will have a closer look at the app development approach in the 'Capability 10-2. User Interaction Services'.

Every device has its own display format and size. If a single version of Model and possibly Controller components can be used while developing different View components that best fit to the different display formats and sizes, the reusability of the presentation logic for multiple devices will be maximized.

MATURITY INDICATOR EXAMPLES

Level 0: Non-existent

- Reusability from an enterprise architecture perspective may have been discussed, but a MVC or similar architecture pattern has never been implemented.

Level 1: Ad hoc

- A MVC or similar architecture pattern has been tested and developed as a pilot system. There is however no official standard architecture pattern within the organization, nor are binary components[15] of presentation Logic ready for reuse by other applications.
- Some developers may share the source code[16] of device presentation Logic that implement the MVC pattern, but the device presentation Logic is not reused at binary code[17] level.

Level 2: Basic

---

[15] A binary component is a piece of software that is executable by a computer. A binary component consists of a bunch of binary code. When source code is compiled, it becomes binary code.

[16] Source codes is human-readable programming code that is written by a developer.

[17] Binary code is computer-executable code.

- A MVC or similar architecture pattern has been employed across several projects. The architecture pattern is agreed on and accepted by several architects and developers as the de-facto standard.
- Based on the architecture pattern, a few binary components of Models or Controllers have been built for reuse by other applications. The binary components are however not actively used due to limited functionalities of the components and limited governance of software reuse.

Level 3: Defined

- Corporate standard architecture services for the device presentation layer are officially defined and documented for architectural guidance to implement a MVC pattern.
- Reusable programming codes, APIs [18] (Application Programming Interfaces), libraries and designs are established along with the corporate architecture governance structure in which architecture policies and procedures are available for architects and developers to reuse. Reuse of device presentation Logic is enforced by architecture governance and design authority policies.
- Multiple digital devices with different sizes on the same platform can take advantage of the standard architecture services by reusing the established binary components.

Level 4: Optimized

- A generic MVC model has been customized and optimized for the organization to accommodate unique business requirements.
- Controller and Model components are highly reusable at both the source code and binary code level across multiple

---

[18] APIs are computer programs that expose interfaces that a programmer can reuse to create new computer programs that access the features or data of the programs that provide the interfaces.

desktop and mobile devices running on different platforms, and only View components need to be redeveloped to build new presentation Logic for a new device

Level 5: Progressive

- There is little redundancy in programming Logic between multi-channel architecture Logic and presentation Logic, as multi-channel architecture focuses on channel business Logic, whereas presentation Logic only deals with device presentation Logic.
- Reusability of the presentation Logic is maximized due to the high reusability of existing binary components. Source code is reused on an ad hoc basis.

MEGA CAPABILITY **6**.

KNOWLEDGE & CONTENT MANAGEMENT

Knowledge & Content Management is a set of digital capabilities used to gather, store, distribute and publish knowledge and content that exists in an un-structured data format such as binary documents [19], image, audio and video, as well as those in structured data in a relational database.

The purpose of Knowledge & Content Management is to provide knowledge or content upon demand by a customer to the front-office capabilities, which are Social Interaction, Digital Marketing and Digital Commerce. Knowledge and content can for example be used as input to creation of a blog post, a marketing campaign message and a product review.

Combined with 'Mega Capability 7. Customization & Personalization', which will be discussed in the next section,

---

[19] A binary document is a computer-generated document that is not in a text file format, e.g. MS-Office documents and PDF documents.

Knowledge & Content Management can deliver customized and personalized knowledge and content to a customer segment, or an individual customer.

Knowledge & Content Management and Customization & Personalization have middle-office functionality in IT architectural terms. The middle-office capabilities are integrated seamlessly with the front-office capabilities so that front-office staff and digital applications are equipped with customized or personalized contents to interact with, and respond to, an individual customer or a customer segment. This enables effective socialization with the customers, and marketing and selling of products and services.

Knowledge & Content Management has the following digital capabilities:

- Knowledge Collaboration
- Knowledge Base Management
- Content Lifecycle Management
- Digital Asset Management
- Aggregation & Syndication
- Web Content Management

CAPABILITY 6-1.
KNOWLEDGE COLLABORATION

CAPABILITY DEFINITION

Knowledge Collaboration is a digital capability to facilitate collaboration between people and between organizations to generate and share knowledge. Knowledge Collaboration is one of the critical factors for success in knowledge management.

Knowledge Collaboration commonly includes the following:

- A knowledge map that is used to define and organize knowledge.
- Automated workflow for knowledge creation, addition, review and distribution.
- Social features such as tagging, liking, commenting and rating of a knowledge item.
- Knowledge community management such as a subject expert network, Q&A and discussion forums.

Knowledge Map

A knowledge map is a way to define and organize knowledge that an organization has, and locate a specific knowledge item in the organized knowledge pool.

The scope of knowledge in the context of the Digital Capability Model does not cover all levels of an organization, but rather includes information required to better socialize, market, sell and serve digital customers. The knowledge for the Digital Commerce capability may include proven merchandising practices, or new merchandising ideas. The knowledge for the Digital Marketing capability may include successful marketing campaigns, the latest changes in the ranking algorithm of search engine optimization of Google, proven marketing offers and their use cases in the conversion funnel, or recent marketing events of major competitors.

Much more knowledge can also be created by taking advantage of the back-office capabilities of Digital Intelligence. The most successful marketing offers that lead customers back to Shopping Cart pages to complete purchasing processes for the last 6 months, or a new customer segmentation idea targeting a niche market based on analysis of recent purchasing trends are good examples of the knowledge captured from Digital Intelligence. Digital Intelligence capabilities will be discussed later in this book.

MATURITY INDICATOR EXAMPLES

Level 0: Non-existent

- Knowledge required for digital business or digital capability has never been defined or created.

Level 1: Ad hoc

- A small piece of knowledge required for digital business or digital capability has once been created and there have been ad hoc updates to the knowledge. Knowledge collaboration to increase or update the knowledge since creation has however barely been performed.

Level 2: Basic

- Basic processes of knowledge creation have been shaped to meet the immediate needs for short-term quick-wins.
- Some employees perform the knowledge process on a regular basis, but knowledge collaboration through the processes are barely encouraged by the organization.
- A tool for knowledge creation, collaboration and distribution exists, but its functionalities are limited.

Level 3: Defined

- Corporate knowledge principles, policies and processes, knowledge maps, knowledge communities, and knowledge managers and owners are implemented.
- Multiple tools for knowledge creation, collaboration and distribution are also employed to facilitate knowledge collaboration, but functionality and integration of the tools are not fully implemented.
- New knowledge is created for a few subject areas on a regular basis. Employees don't however actively collaborate and share their knowledge, because knowledge sharing is not yet accepted by employees as a critical part of daily operations, and many employees are not willing to share their own knowledge.

Level 4: Optimized

- Knowledge collaboration and sharing is focused on a few critical subject areas. The knowledge of the focused subject areas is actively created and shared.
- Employees actively involved in the knowledge collaboration consider knowledge sharing a critical part of their daily operations and they believe they are rewarded for knowledge collaboration.
- Knowledge is actively shared through the knowledge collaboration tools that feature the functionalities common to Social websites.

Level 5: Progressive

- Knowledge Collaboration has been a part of the strategic business initiatives to create and maintain core competency and competitive advantage of the organization.
- The core knowledge that is active in creation and sharing is aligned to the key success factors defined in the corporate business strategy.

CAPABILITY 6-2.
KNOWLEDGE BASE MANAGEMENT

CAPABILITY DEFINITION

Knowledge Base Management is a digital capability used to store and maintain knowledge data in knowledge repositories. The knowledge that is created, revised, added, reviewed and shared through the Knowledge Collaboration capability is stored in a knowledge base as organized by a knowledge map. Content management systems are commonly used for Knowledge Base Management, as knowledge is managed as part of enterprise content.

Knowledge Base Management capability includes an ability to increase the knowledge base, as well as the current volume and quality of knowledge.

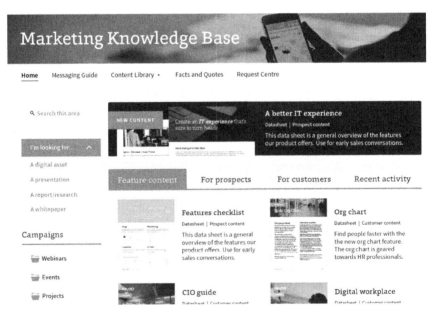

[Figure 23: Igloo Knowledge Base Management Solution]

MATURITY INDICATOR EXAMPLES

Level 0: Non-existent

- A Knowledge base required for digital business or digital capability doesn't exist.

Level 1: Ad hoc

- A dedicated Knowledge base for digital capability does not exist, but the enterprise-wide knowledge base includes some of the knowledge for digital business or digital capability.
- The Knowledge base for digital business or digital capability is available in a simple bulletin board format and is updated on an ad hoc basis.

Level 2: Basic

- There may be a good deal of knowledge required for digital business or digital capability, but the knowledge base is not properly organized, e.g. lack of knowledge map.
- There is no proper governance structure to manage the knowledge base, making the quality of the knowledge relatively poor in terms of accuracy and correctness.

Level 3: Defined

- Corporate knowledge principles, policies, processes, roles of knowledge administrator and knowledge base tools to manage knowledge base arc implemented.
- The quantity of knowledge is growing, but the knowledge has a substantial amount of poor quality data that needs to be fixed through active knowledge filtering and cleansing.
- Several knowledge repositories exist, but these are not integrated.

Level 4: Optimized

- The quality and quantity of the knowledge are measured against pre-defined metrics on a regular basis, and optimized accordingly.
- The amount of good quality knowledge increases, but is only valuable to a small portion of the digital practitioners.

Level 5: Progressive

- The Knowledge Base is one of the sources of core competency and competitive advantage of the organization.
- Core knowledge is defined and aligned to key success factors defined in the corporate business strategy. Increasing the core Knowledge base has been one of the strategic business initiatives.

CAPABILITY 6-3.
CONTENT LIFECYCLE MANAGEMENT

CAPABILITY DEFINITION

Content Lifecycle Management is a digital capability used to create contents, add additional information to use and publish content better, approve content to be released, and maintain content until its end of life.

Content Type

Content types define how content is managed throughout its lifecycle. Different content types require different sets of metadata[20] with which content is created, stored, searched and maintained. White paper content type in an organization may for example require a specific set of metadata, such as product name, version, workflow and target users. Content types enables organizations to manage their digital content consistently throughout the content's lifecycle.

Content Creation

A content management system as a technology tool of Content Lifecycle Management automates content creation processes, or supports employees to create content. Content such as binary documents, multimedia, or software files are frequently created elsewhere, and uploaded to a content management system.

A Knowledge Base is commonly stored and maintained in a content management system. Some Digital Assets are created through Digital Asset Management, but a content management system usually provides storage capability for Digital Asset Management. This will be discussed further later in the next section.

If a content author wishes to create a document from scratch through Content Lifecycle Management, the capability offers very basic document creation tools. The tools may provide such functionalities as content creation templates, WYSIWYG (What You See Is What You Get) editors, spell checker, preview, multi-language support, check in & out, version control, or document creation & collaboration workflow.

Content can be created through the processes of converting a paper-based image or document into an electronic format. This

---

[20] Metadata is a set of data that describes information about other data, e.g. definition of the data, purpose of the data, creator of the data, and creation date and time of the data, e.g. metadata of an MS-Office report document may include title, subtitle, purpose of document, report summary, status (draft or release), tags, creation date, approval date, author, author's organization, reviewer, approver, pages, etc.

capability automates the conversion processes through capture functionalities such as image scanning or content recognition. The final product of image scanning is an image file, whereas content recognition produces readable or editable data or documents.

Content Maintenance

Once content is developed, it is processed further for additional information to make sharing and maintaining the content easier. The additional information is saved as metadata of the content. The content metadata is added to facilitate content search, publishing, access, and retention, and the metadata includes the following:

- **Search**: Author, date published, summary, keywords and topics.
- **Publishing**: Release date, audience, channel and touchpoint.
- **Access**: Rights to view, save and edit.
- **Retention**: Archiving and retention period.

Content metadata can also be combined with Customization & Personalization capabilities to deliver customized content to a customer segment, or personalized contents to an individual customer.

Content indexing, content format conversion, document assembly, content tagging and rule-based content publishing are also supported to manage content better.

Besides content archiving and retention performed by IT administrators, content nearing the end of its life, such as content nobody has viewed for the last couple of years, should be identified and disposed of as defined by content disposal policies. This capability should be able to automate or support this process to maintain the quality of content.

Content Taxonomy

A content taxonomy is a way to organize digital content into hierarchical classification. A content taxonomy is used for content browsing or search, a navigation tree and site map of a website, knowledge base and knowledge map, Cloud-drive folder structure, data exchange such as XML (eXtensible Markup Language) , and many other purposes.

All digital content, including digital assets and web content, are organized into a content taxonomy. Content taxonomy is also used to implement a knowledge map to organize knowledge into a knowledge base in a structured way.

The value of a content taxonomy lies in improved access to the right content and increased employee productivity through reduced time needed to find the right content. It is believed that a content taxonomy is critical to the success of digital content management. Enough time and efforts should therefore be invested to identify a right content taxonomy.

Requirements of a Content Management Tool

Many of the critical requirements were mentioned in the discussion above. A summarized list of the requirements is given below.

- Functionalities to create content, e.g. content templates and editors.
- Functionalities to collaborate, review, and approve content, e.g. check in & check out, and automated workflow.
- Functionalities to share and publish content, e.g. publish scheduling, conversion to different formats for different devices, publishing to social websites and access control.
- Functionalities to search content. This may be provided by the Enterprise Search capability of Digital Data management.
- Functionalities to support SEO, e.g. URLs and metadata for SEO.

- Functionalities to maintain content, e.g. content versioning and archiving.
- Functionalities to analyse the performance of Content Lifecycle Management, e.g. content usages, quantities and quality.

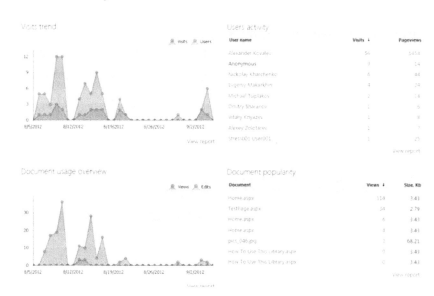

[Figure 24: HarePoint Content Usage Analytics Tool]

MATURITY INDICATOR EXAMPLES

Level 0: Non-existent

- Digital contents may exist somewhere within the organization, e.g. product brochures and technical whitepapers in MS-Word format on a personal desktop. They are however neither identified, nor maintained as digital content.

Level 1: Ad hoc

- Digital content is created and stored in a content management system on an ad hoc basis.
- Some digital content types are identified.
- There is no official implementation of content taxonomy, or content metadata structure.
- The content management tool is a simple file server. Its functionality is too limited to manage the content metadata.

Level 2: Basic

- Digital content is created as needed by individual business units on a regular basis and the content creation and maintenance are not coordinated at corporate level.
- Digital content is focused only on electronic documents.
- The Content management tool is functionally limited and can't fully automate or support the end-to-end lifecycle of content.
- Content taxonomy and metadata structure are established partially.

Level 3: Defined

- Centralized content policies, content creation and management processes, content manager, and content management tools are implemented.
- Workflow automation is supported for content creation, collaboration, distribution and approval.
- The functionalities of the content management tools are comprehensive enough to automate and support the end-to-end lifecycle of content.
- A content taxonomy is established, but there are many complaints from employees about the inconvenience of the taxonomy when they create and search content.
- Content metadata is not rich enough.

Level 4: Optimized

- Content has rich metadata so that it can be searched, accessed, and shared easily.
- Existing content taxonomy has been optimized and multiple new taxonomies are developed to meet further needs from employees.
- All different taxonomy structures and metadata structures across all content, including knowledge, documents, and digital assets are consolidated respectively.
- Content is frequently updated and cleansed, and the reusability of contents is therefore high.
- Content is starting to be created through crowd sourcing.

Level 5: Progressive

- The Content Lifecycle Management capability is seamlessly integrated with the Customization & Personalization capability, as well as with other digital capabilities from the front-office and back-office operations. This allows the intelligence created by back-office capabilities to be captured into personalized digital content that is seamlessly published to users through the front-office capabilities.
- The lifecycle of digital content is well managed, e.g. content at end of life is identified and disposed of on a regular basis.

CAPABILITY 6-4.
DIGITAL ASSET MANAGEMENT

CAPABILITY DEFINITION

On one hand, a digital asset is a subset of digital content mentioned earlier and a digital asset is therefore managed as digital content is managed. On the other hand, a digital asset is a subset of organizational assets that has significant monetary value and should therefore be created, maintained and protected as an enterprise asset of an organization.

The characteristics of a digital asset comes from both the digital content and enterprise asset aspects, and the Digital Asset Management capability manages the combined characteristics of a digital asset.

Digital Asset Management is a digital capability used to organize, manipulate, store, retrieve, distribute, secure and back up digital assets, such as textual content and media content that have significant value to an organization. The majority of the functionalities provided by a content management system can be reused for Digital Asset Management, including metadata and taxonomy, because the asset lifecycle is managed the same way as the content lifecycle is across creation, publishing maintenance and archiving.

Digital Asset Development & Maintenance

Digital assets are developed through specialized editing tools, for example videos, music, or photos. Some of the content creation functionalities of the Content Lifecycle Management capability may be reused for digital asset development.

Further editing functionalities for asset merging, media transcoding, digital file re-sizing, asset cataloguing, or asset curation should however be provided for a digital asset to be delivered or managed as an enterprise asset.

A Digital Asset Management system should also provide functionalities for asset disposal and recovery.

Digital Rights Management

Copyright of a digital asset should be protected and managed properly. The purpose of Digital Rights Management is to manage access to digital assets and prevent unauthorized access to them.

Digital Rights Management is commonly implemented by embedding programming codes into the digital asset to prevent illegal copying, allowing access to and use of the digital asset during a specific period, or limiting the number of devices the digital asset is saved or installed on.

Digital Rights Management is at the core of Digital Asset Management and commonly provides the following functionalities.

- Copyright and intellectual property protection.
- Encryption and decryption management.
- Access control management.
- Usage tracking and metering.

[Figure 25: Libris Digital Asset Management Solution]

MATURITY INDICATOR EXAMPLES

Level 0: Non-existent

- There may be assets that can be converted, or have already been converted, to digital content that can be managed as digital assets, but they are not defined as digital assets, and are therefore not managed as digital assets.

Level 1: Ad hoc

- There is no formal practice of Digital Asset Management, and digital assets are created and maintained on an ad hoc basis.
- No digital asset management tool is available, but a content management tool is used for cataloguing digital assets.

Level 2: Basic

- Digital assets are managed by individual business units on a regular basis, but digital asset has a different meaning and scope to different business units.
- A digital asset management tool is available, but its functionalities are limited to support sophisticated asset cataloguing, asset manipulation and asset usage.
- Little to no effort is made to protect digital copyright or intellectual property.

Level 3: Defined

- Corporate principles, policies, processes, managers and work manuals for digital asset management are implemented.
- A comprehensive and sophisticated digital asset management tool is implemented.
- Integration with a content management and web-publishing tool is limited. Metadata and taxonomy are not well integrated across the different systems, and redundant copies of digital assets exist outside Digital Asset Management scope without proper control, e.g. it is unknown how many copies of a digital asset exist across the organization.

- Cyber security measures are implemented to protect the digital rights of digital assets.

Level 4: Optimized

- The taxonomy has been optimized to be more user friendly and the metadata has become richer, and the searchability and usability of digital assets has therefore improved.
- Integration with content management tools and web publishing tools is optimized enough to share the same metadata and taxonomy across the systems.
- The multiple copies of digital assets that exist in different systems are properly controlled and synchronized to maintain a single truth of the digital assets.

Level 5: Progressive

- The Digital Asset Management capability is seamlessly integrated with the Customization & Personalization capability, as well as with the front-office digital capabilities. This integration allows personalized digital asset data to be published seamlessly to users through the front-office capabilities.
- The Digital asset lifecycle is well managed, e.g. whether to sustain a digital asset or when to end its life is properly planned and executed, balancing costs and benefits of each digital asset.
- Business communities consider digital assets a critical part of enterprise assets, and therefore make business decisions on investment in and maintenance of the digital asset accordingly.

CAPABILITY 6-5.
CONTENT AGGREGATION & SYNDICATION

CAPABILITY DEFINITION

Aggregation as part of the Content Aggregation & Syndication capability is the process of pulling or receiving digital content from different content sources inside and outside an organization, according to pre-configured aggregation rules. It also includes the processes of sanitizing, organizing and storing the pulled data for reuse.

In contrast, the syndication part of the Content Aggregation & Syndication capability is the process of pushing or sending digital contents to different content consumers other than the organization's own websites, according to pre-configured syndication rules. From the perspective of the content consumers who are receiving the content, they are aggregating content when the organization is syndicating the content.

Content Aggregation & Syndication is a digital capability used to manage the content receiving and sending activities with pre-configured business rules and highly automated processes.

Content aggregation includes the functionalities to:

- Recommend and help users discover content relevant to internal digital content needs.
- Enable users to fine-tune, customize and categorize content sources.
- Store aggregated content in a centralized repository for reuse in content development.

Content syndication includes the functionalities to:

- Manage distribution partners.
- Manage digital content to be distributed.
- Control digital asset license usage.

- Help with Search Engine Optimization (SEO).

Content syndication may have a negative impact on your Search Engine Optimization if the syndication is not properly planned. For example, Aa famous website that you syndicated your blog posts to may for example have a better ranking on Google than your website has for the same blog posts. There are several ways to avoid the negative result and even help with your search engine optimization (SEO) efforts, by adding right HTML tags for example. These tips are available on the Internet.

Aggregating and syndicating contents requires underlying technical integration of internal systems with content providers and content consumers. The underlying technical integration is provided by 'Capability 10-3. Process Integration Services'.

MATURITY INDICATOR EXAMPLES

Level 0: Non-existent

- Content is neither aggregated nor syndicated.

Level 1: Ad hoc

- Either content aggregation or content syndication is performed partially on an ad hoc basis.
- There is a tool employed to support Content Aggregation & Syndication, but the tool has limited functionality and therefore the end-to-end aggregation and syndication processes are manual.

Level 2: Basic

- Content aggregation or syndication processes are performed on a regular basis by individual business units, but the content aggregated or syndicated is neither consolidated, nor shared across the organization.

- Multiple tools are deployed for content aggregation and syndication, but the functionalities of the tools are too limited to automate end-to-end content aggregation and syndication processes fully.

Level 3: Defined

- Centralized principles, policies, processes for content aggregation and syndication are implemented at corporate level.
- Multiple tools demonstrate functionalities comprehensive enough to automate the end-to end aggregation and syndication processes fully.
- Integration of the internal systems with content providers and consumers is limited due to the heterogeneous platforms and high complexity of the other parties.

Level 4: Optimized

- The business rules in the tools that are used to automate the processes of content aggregation and syndication can be dynamically changed by business users without assistance from IT staff.
- Integration of the internal systems with content providers and consumers has been optimized and streamlined to enable end-to-end automation of aggregation and syndication processes.

Level 5: Progressive

- The purpose and scope of aggregated content go beyond collecting reference information for content creation. It becomes one of the primary sources for content creation.
- Content aggregation and syndication significantly contributes to improving performance of search engine optimization (SEO).

CAPABILITY 6-6.
WEB CONTENT MANAGEMENT

CAPABILITY DEFINITION

Web Content Management is a digital capability used to author, publish and manage web pages, and enable collaboration to create and revise the web pages, even with little understanding of programming languages or mark-up languages.

Web Content Management uses such content as images, audio, videos, or documents that are already stored in the content management system to organize the content into web page templates and to create web pages. The assembled content, web page templates, and complete web pages to be published may be stored in the Web Content Management system.

All types of content are published onto a web site through Web Content Management. Digital assets may for example be produced through Digital Asset Management processes, stored and maintained in a content repository of the Content Lifecycle Management capability, and published on a web site through a Web Content Management tool.

A comprehensive content management system such as enterprise content management (ECM) systems, often provides Web Content Management functionalities as a component of the total solution.

The Web Content Management capability includes the following functionalities:

- Web page template management, e.g. product catalogue, merchandising, promotion, blog and community.
- Web page editor with WYSIWYG function.
- Web page metadata editor, e.g. Title tag, Meta tag and Headings.

- SEO management, e.g. HTML code optimization, URL management and sitemap creation.
- Web page version control.
- Collaboration for web site development.
- Web site search.
- Web page access control.
- Rule-based publishing and workflow, e.g. who publishes what, when and where.
- Deployment to multiple Internet domains.

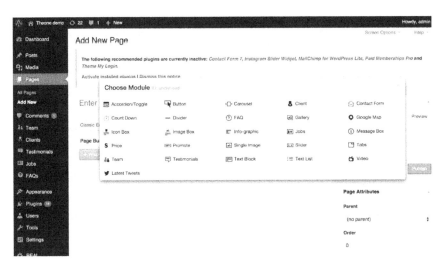

[Figure 26: WordPress Web Content Management Platform]

MATURITY INDICATOR EXAMPLES

Level 0: Non-existent

- Web pages have never been published.

Level 1: Ad hoc

- Web pages have been published and updated on an ad hoc basis through a text-editing tool that is not specialized in web content editing and publishing.

- Web page development and publishing processes are predominantly manual based. No web page template or other toolset for web content management is used.

Level 2: Basic

- An official web site is created and published to meet the individual needs of a few business units.
- The website is updated and maintained on a regular basis.
- Digital content is not actively reused to create web content and develop webpages.
- A basic Web Content Management tool is introduced, but is functionally limited.
- Webpage metadata and SEO-friendly features are not managed.

Level 3: Defined

- Centralized principles, policies and processes required to create, publish and maintain web contents and webpages are implemented.
- A comprehensive web content management tool is employed.
- Workflow and collaboration functionalities are provided to automate collaboration between content creators, web designers, web application developers and a web-publishing manager.
- Web page metadata and SEO-friendly features are developed during the web page creation processes, but the practice is not aligned with content metadata management and corporate level SEO management.

Level 4: Optimized

- Rule-based web publishing has been optimized to automate the publishing processes further.

- Initial creation of web page metadata and SEO-friendly features during web development are compliant and aligned with enterprise content metadata management, and corporate level SEO management.
- Redundancy of content between web content management and digital content management is minimized. Fewer copies of content are created for web publishing by reusing more of the digital content.
- Web programming is significantly reduced due to automation and non-technical staff can edit web content with little help from front-end web developers.

Level 5: Progressive

- Web content management capability is integrated seamlessly with Social Integration, Digital Marketing, Digital Commerce and Customization & Personalization, and little swivel chair integration between them is therefore required to publish individualized social content, marketing messages and ecommerce contents.
- The web content lifecycle is well managed, e.g. web pages at end of life are identified and disposed of on a regular basis.

MEGA CAPABILITY 7.

CUSTOMIZATION & PERSONALIZATION

Customization & Personalization is a set of digital capabilities used to manage the relationship between an organization and its customers by knowing more about their customized wants and personalized needs.

By definition, customization is performed to meet 'Wants' that customers express explicitly because they know what they want, whereas Personalization is conducted to meet 'Needs' that an organization identifies through analysis of customer behaviours because customers are often unaware of what they need.

Digital content including web content, knowledge, and digital assets from Knowledge & Content Management is delivered through Social Interaction, Digital Marketing and Digital Commerce capabilities to a customer segment, or an individual customer, as per the information on customer relationship maintained in Customization & Personalization capabilities.

Customization & Personalization capabilities have a middle-office processing style in terms of the IT architectural pattern: small transactions occur frequently on a real-time basis in the front-office, while large transactions occur intermittently in the back-office and middle-office processing style is in between the front-office and back-office processing styles.

The middle-office operations are integrated seamlessly with the customer-facing front-office operations so that front-office staff or IT systems are well equipped with customized or personalized content to interact with and respond to an individual customer, or customer segment, to socialize with them, and market and sell to them effectively.

Customization & Personalization has the following digital capabilities.

- Customer Preference Management
- Customer Communication Management
- Social Behaviour Management
- Interaction Tracking & Management
- Customer Loyalty Management
- Digital Customer Services

CAPABILITY 7-1.
CUSTOMER PREFERENCE MANAGEMENT

CAPABILITY DEFINITION

Customer Preference Management is a digital capability used to collect and maintain information on customers' preference. The preference data is either 'Wants' collected directly from a customer, or 'Needs' perceived and captured through internal analysis of customer behaviours.

Customer Preference Data

Customer preference data includes, but is not limited to:

- Preferred products or services.
- Preferred marketing offers, e.g. prefers high rate of loyalty point to low rate of discount.
- Preferred digital content.
- Preferred channels and touchpoints through which a customer explores an organization.
- Preferred channels and touchpoints through which a customer is contacted by an organization.
- Preferred channels and touchpoints through which a product or service is delivered.
- Preferred communication patterns, e.g. when and how often.
- Preferred checkout, e.g. payment methods and delivery methods.
- Personal favourites, such as favourite music, sports, and many more.

Capturing Preference Data

Customer 'Wants' are gathered from front-office operations. 'Wants' data is given by customers submitting the preference data directly to the preference management system through multiple tough points.

The collection and the use of the preference data may need permission from a customer for opt-in marketing purposes, as well as regulatory reasons, e.g. asking whether a customer prefers email contact to other communication channels. For the same reason, an opt-out option should always be readily available to customers on any channels accessible to them.

'Wants' are different from 'Needs'. 'Needs' are captured in the back-office operations and given to Customer Preference Management. 'Needs' data is analysed and discovered by data analysts or analytics tools that identify customer preference patterns and extract preference data from the patterns.

A customer's preferred products identified in 'Mega Capability 8 Digital Intelligence' are not always consistent with the products a customer indicates as their preference on a preference setting on a webpage. More often than not, the preferences identified from digital analytics is more effective in building relationships with customers than the preferences customers indicate, because many customers don't know what they really want.

Not many organizations are successful in feeding the back-office analytics data back into Customer Preference Management for use in the front-office interactions with customers.

Consolidating Preference Data

Preference data is gathered across different functional departments including marketing, sales, service and call centres, and across different IT systems including campaign management system, lead management system, call centre system and official websites. Chances are these different sources of preference data are not integrated or consolidated into a single repository, because the departments operate autonomously and independently of one another. These discrete systems have their own preference management functionalities and data that is not integrated with one another.

This is one of the most common challenges organizations face when it comes to customer preference management. Many companies embark on a strategic business initiative to establish a single truth of customer data across all levels of their organizations. If this is the case, customer preference data should be part of the scope of the customer data-integration initiative.

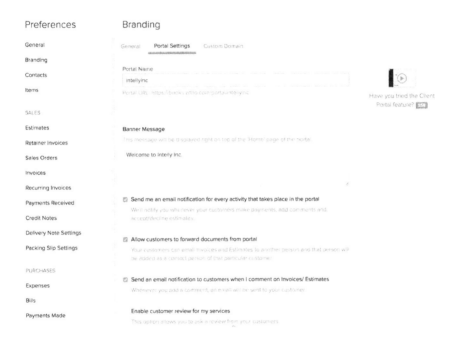

[Figure 27: Zoho Customer Preference Management Solution]

Keeping Preference Data Up-to-date

Another challenge of maintaining customer preference data is that once the data is collected from customers, it becomes outdated quickly and the cost of keeping it up-to-date can be expensive.

One of the ways to encourage customers to self-update their preference data is to remind them of their preference data by presenting the opt-in information on their preferred touchpoints, saying, "I am giving you a coupon for this product because you told us you are interested in the product and promotion campaign".

For the preference data from the back-office capabilities, periodic feedback processes should be established so that the analytical data can return to the preference database automatically, or manually.

MATURITY INDICATOR EXAMPLES

Level 0: Non-existent

- A small piece of customer preference information may be captured during interactions with customers, e.g. during the checkout process, without the organization realizing it. The captured preference data is neither kept, nor maintained as customer preference data for customization or personalization later, e.g. email, is identified as a preferred communication channel, but is only used for notification of product delivery.

Level 1: Ad hoc

- A piece of customer preference information is captured during customer interactions and stored as customer preference data.
- The customer preference information is used to communicate once-off promotional events or marketing campaigns only, and is barely used to build a close relationship with the customers through on-going customization or personalization.
- The information has barely been updated since the initial creation.

Level 2: Basic

- The basic amount of customer preference information is gathered by each department or each business unit on regular basis.
- The customer preference data is neither consolidated, nor coordinated by a single preference management plan across the organization, and each set of preference data therefore has a different scope, value and format, while there are many redundancies in the data.

Level 3: Defined

- A central framework of customer preference data-management is implemented at corporate level. This framework provides centralized principles, compliance requirements, data capturing & maintenance processes, and management tools.
- The scope of customer preference information to be captured is comprehensive, but a significant piece of preference information is still missing.
- Much of the customer preference data has been consolidated, but some in-scope preference data stays unconsolidated and is not integrated across multiple departments and multiple IT systems.
- The organization is struggling to keep the data up-to-date due to lack of strong enforcement of policies and procedures.
- The Customer Preference Management is focused on managing 'Wants' collected directly from customers.

Level 4: Optimized

- The 'Needs' part of customer preference data is provided by Digital Intelligence capabilities, allowing the organization to be aware of untapped needs of an individual customer and a customer segment.

THE DIGITAL CAPABILITY MODEL

- Customer preference data is consolidated into a single repository that is shared by all departments, all business units and all IT systems that manage the preference data
- Customers are willing to provide and update their preference data to get the right content and more benefits, without fear of privacy breaches.

Level 5: Progressive

- More information and insights into customer preference come from what the analytics find in the back-office, than what customers express in the front-office.
- Accuracy and relevance of customer preference data is so high that customer responses to the customized or personalized messages and services is positive.
- Customer Preference Management is integrated seamlessly with Knowledge & Content Management, Digital Intelligence, Social Integration, Digital Marketing, and Digital Commerce capabilities, and little swivel chair integration between them is therefore required to collect and exchange customer preference data.

CAPABILITY 7-2.
CUSTOMER COMMUNICATION MANAGEMENT

CAPABILITY DEFINITION

Customer Communication Management is a digital capability used to plan, implement, monitor and adjust how an organization communicates with customers to improve customized and personalized communications. At the core are the functionalities to extract, compose, author, format, print, deliver, store, or retrieve communication messages such as letters, bills & invoices, statements, policies, quotations, proposals, contracts, manuals, or customer correspondence as per the customer's preferred and available communication options to better communicate with a customer or a segment of customers.

High-level Communication Management Processes

Digital contents are re-produced through Customer Communication Management to format and individualize customer-specific contents as instructed by customer preference information, and deliver the individualized contents through the individualized media to the specific customer. Below is a high-level view of the customer communication processes:

- **Create template**: Select a communication message template from the template library. The template should provide documentation guidelines.
- **Populate content**: Extract source content from content management systems. Customize or personalize the source content and compose new content.
- **Customize format**: Create a completely new message with customized format and graphics.
- **Deliver messages**: Send the new message through the customer's preferred channels at the preferred time.

Requirements of a Communication Management Tool

A Customer Communication Management tool should support the following:

- Multiple document file formats, e.g. PDF, EPUB, RTF, HTML, XML etc.
- Multiple channels or touchpoints delivery, e.g. print, fax, email, SMS, web, kiosk etc.
- Multiple ways of creating a document.
- Document creation on demand, e.g. Insurance policy document delivered upon request by a customer on a website.

- Batch style document creation, e.g. monthly batch processing creating monthly bills.
- Interactive creation of document, e.g. quotation document creation & delivery through interactive negotiation or conversation on a website.
- Rule engine to select contents dynamically based on customer preference information to create customized and personalized communications.
- Mini-BPM (Business Process Management) [21] style workflow design functionality to change the processes of composition and approval of content, documents, and messages easily.
- Customer journey mapping functionality to align customer communications with the customer journey map.
- Compliance functionalities to comply with regulatory requirements.

Relationship with Other Capabilities

Content Lifecycle Management provides source content that is used by Customer Communication Management to compose a new message. Both digital capabilities should be seamlessly integrated for this reason. A few Enterprise Content Management (ECM) solution vendors provide both capabilities in a single suite to offer the integration readily.

Multi-Channel Integration (MCI) applications of Cross-Channel Integration capability should be integrated for multi-channel delivery of customer communications to reduce redundancy in channel functionalities between Customer Communication Management and Cross-Channel Integration.

---

[21] BPM (Business Process Management) is a discipline that uses various methods to design, automate and monitor business processes. Its focus is on enabling business users to change the business processes implemented in IT systems, without involvement of IT professionals.

Customer Communication Management belongs to middle-office operations, and channel application Logic is therefore not part of the responsibilities of Customer Communication Management. The channel application Logic should be implemented in MCI applications.

Social Interaction, Digital Marketing and Digital Commerce should also be seamlessly integrated with this capability to deliver customized messages, documents, and content to customers through socialization, marketing, and sales processes, e.g. claim application creation for Social Servicing, white paper creation for Marketing Offer Management and contract document creation for Order Management & Fulfilment.

MATURITY INDICATOR EXAMPLES

Level 0: Non-existent

- The organization focuses only on traditional customer communication methods, such as printing and mailing a paper-based statement. There are no equivalent digital practices to the traditional communications.

Level 1: Ad hoc

- The same formats of digital documents as stored in a content management system or a file server are delivered to customers without reformatting or reproduction for customization or personalization, because there is no capability to extract multiple content and compose them for a new document in the Customer Communication Management.
- The format of the documents may be able to be changed in the content management system. The reformatting function is however not integrated with Customer Communication Management.

Level 2: Basic

- Digital content is extracted from only a few content sources and transformed to new formats customized and personalized for customers due to limited integration ability.
- Multiple document file formats are supported with format changes, while multiple channels are partially supported for communications of the new content with the changed format.
- Both batch-type and on-demand creation of documents are supported, but interactive creation of documents is not supported.
- Many of the processes from document creation to delivery are manual.

Level 3: Defined

- Digital content is extracted from almost all content repositories.
- Centralized principles, policies, processes, dedicated staff and specialized tools for customer communications are implemented.
- Multiple document file formats, multiple delivery channels and multiple ways of document creation are supported.
- Simple business rules are deployed into the customer-communication management tools to capture customer preference and apply them to content creation and delivery.

Level 4: Optimized

- The processes from message designing and authoring to delivery can change dynamically as soon as business staff change the process flow implemented in the mini-BPM functions, without assistance of IT staff.

- Changes in compliance requirements can be applied dynamically to document creation without help from IT staff.
- The rule engine has been optimized and has become sophisticated and comprehensive by learning from historical data.

Level 5: Progressive

- Content management systems and back-end legacy systems such as ERP (Enterprise Resource Planning) and CRM (Customer Relationship Management) are integrated with each other to provide source data seamlessly to create further sophisticated new content, documents, or messages.
- Communication designs are highly optimized for the unique features of each touchpoint on the digital customer journey map.
- Customer Communication Management tools are seamlessly integrated with the multi-channel architecture and the front-office systems.

CAPABILITY 7-3.
SOCIAL BEHAVIOUR MANAGEMENT

CAPABILITY DEFINITION

Social behaviour is defined as a type of customer behaviour on social media and online communities.

Customer behaviour is analysed as part of the analysis for Customer Insights and Customer Segmentation to develop an insight into customers and a profile of a customer segment in the Digital Intelligence capability. Critical behavioural patterns can be identified to separate and organize customers into a few segments of customers.

Analysis of Social Behaviour

Social behaviour is analysed to find patterns in a similar way that customer behaviour is analysed, and such activities as tweeting, sharing, posting, liking, commenting, or befriending are analysed to identify the patterns of those activities.

Source data processed to detect unseen patterns of social behaviour would result in massive data volume. It would therefore not be a good idea to let Social Behaviour Management take care of the analytics of the data.

The unseen patterns should be analysed and captured primarily through Big Data Analytics of Digital Intelligence, considering its data analytics ability. Source data required for the Big Data analysis is commonly provided through the Social Listening capability.

Social behaviour patterns vary depending on the circumstances of an organization. Loyal, Leading, Onlooking, Chatting, and Complaining are among common examples of social behaviour patterns. Each pattern may have different needs for content and interactions between users and an organization.

Once data analysts or decision makers decide to use the social behaviour patterns and needs that the patterns implicate, the behavioural patterns and needs are stored for later use by Social Behaviour Management.

Social Behaviour Management

Social Behaviour Management is a digital capability used to store the information on behavioural patterns and needs in a structure that can be accessed readily. The patterns and needs information is later used to provide customized and personalized content. Social Interaction capabilities can also use the information to respond to users on social websites best.

The customer segment displaying a 'Chatting' behaviour pattern is for example more likely to respond to a new product launch by posting reviews of their experience with the product launch, whereas the customer segment displaying a 'Leading' pattern is more likely to write a blog post analysing the new product itself. The 'Onlooking' users may be more interested in content on flash sales for the new product launch.

This information and guideline need to be maintained in Social Behaviour Management and be readily available for use by community managers or social media managers through automation tools.

The Social Servicing capability may use the information when dealing with users displaying a 'Complaining' behaviour pattern. The Rating & Review Management capability can be used to ask 'Loyal' users to share their experience with a few review websites where negative reviews and ratings are emerging.

MATURITY INDICATOR EXAMPLES

Level 0: Non-existent

- The organization may have big data analytics capability and some statistics about its customers may be available through the analytics. Customer behaviour patterns are however neither defined, nor stored in a database. The organization therefore has little to no idea who the social members on the social websites are, what they are sharing and why.

Level 1: Ad hoc

- User behaviours on social media are defined and used on an ad hoc basis, e.g. age, gender, active hours and most viewed contents, to see who they are and how they use social media, but it does not lead to the level where the organization can respond to different needs of different segments properly.

- This is an ad hoc activity performed upon request by executives, or management.
- Captured behaviours and needs are not properly stored and managed.

Level 2: Basic

- Behavioural patterns of users are defined and updated on a regular basis. This helps understand very basic patterns in the behaviour, leading to identifying a few groups of users that demonstrate similar behaviour.
- Different needs of the different groups may be identified, but the identified needs are not consistently used for social interactions or digital marketing across the organization.

Level 3: Defined

- Social behaviour-based segmentation is officially implemented at corporate level.
- Corporate principles, policies, processes, managers and tools are implemented to capture the analytics results from Digital Intelligence for social behaviour-based segmentations and their needs.
- The social behaviour segmentation is either seamlessly integrated with, or consolidated into the customer segmentation practice for marketing purpose, so that the profiles of customer segments have social profile data in addition to traditional customer profile data.

Level 4: Optimized

- The social behaviour-based segments, their profiles and their needs have been optimized to the extent that provisioning and recommendation of different content to the different segments across the Social Interaction capability can be automated to a certain degree.

- The Social Behaviour Management tool is integrated with Social Interaction capabilities seamlessly, so that the social behaviour data can be readily reused for the Social Interaction capabilities to provide customized and personalized interactions with users.

Level 5: Progressive

- The Social Behaviour Management capability is integrated seamlessly with Customer Insights, Customer Segmentation, Digital Customer Journey and Digital Marketing so that the organization's ability to predict customer behaviour has increased significantly.

CAPABILITY 7-4.
INTERACTION TRACKING & MANAGEMENT

CAPABILITY DEFINITION

Interaction Tracking & Management is a digital capability used to track and manage customer interactions at all levels of an organization by providing interaction data and automating the interaction processes.

By tracing every single interaction between customers and the organization, a specific interaction can be managed better. The digital capability keeps track not only of purchasing customers, but also of prospects.

Every single interaction of a customer with an organization is managed as a ticket in the Interaction Tracking & Management capability as follows:

- When a customer makes a call to a sales representative to ask for a proposal with a question about technical specification, a ticket is issued.
- If the request is transferred to a technician for an answer, the ticket is assigned to the technician.
- When the request is fulfilled and the answer provided, the ticket is closed.

This digital capability is shaped around functionalities to manage an interaction ticket. The ticket resolving processes is automated and supported by the digital capability across the organization.

Requirements of an Interaction Tracking & Management Tool

Interaction Tracking & Management provides the ticket functionalities including the following:

- Automated processes to create, transfer and close a ticket.
- Rule-based ticket routing.
- Automated processes to capture and store information of customer interactions.
- Automated processes to provide context of an interaction with a customer based on the last interaction, or interaction history of the customer.
- Support function to respond to customers, e.g. canned responses.
- Automated processes to track the time spent on interactions.
- Support function to create reports with real-time operational statistics of the customer interactions across multiple channels.
- Support function to manage service levels.
- Mini-BPM style workflow design and execution.
- Integration with multi-channels, e.g. email, phone, online chat and SMS.

MATURITY INDICATOR EXAMPLES

Level 0: Non-existent

- Customers can interact with the organization, but the status of an interaction is neither recorded, nor traced.

Level 1: Ad hoc

- Some of the customer interactions with the organization are recorded when the interaction is initiated, e.g. request for quotation over the official website, but the interactions are not fully tracked.
- The interactions are not shared across the organization.
- A very limited tool is used to record the interaction, e.g. MS-Excel.

Level 2: Basic

- Many interactions are recorded, e.g. request through online help desk, and customer responses to marketing offers.
- The interactions are tracked in each silo of individual departments or business unit, but they are not shared across the organization.
- Interaction history is maintained so that interactions can be tracked further back. It is however difficult to track interaction history of a customer and understand the context of past interactions because interaction tracking is poorly managed.

Level 3: Defined

- A comprehensive automation tool is implemented to record, track and manage customer interactions. The tool provides comprehensive functionalities to manage comprehensive data scope of a customer interaction within all levels of the organization.

- Corporate-level ticketing principles, policies and procedures are well implemented.
- Real time statistical reports are provided periodically.
- Not all interactions are captured and managed by this capability, and tracking of all interactions of a single customer is still challenging.

Level 4: Optimized

- All customer interactions within all levels of the organization are tracked automatically.
- The customer interactions are tracked from creation of a ticket to close of the ticket.
- Human interactions with customers are further automated through automated workflow with a rule engine that routes the interaction tickets dynamically.
- Ticket routing is fully automated as per an automated rule-based engine.
- Service level objectives can be dynamically configured into the rule engine to automate interactions further.
- All interactions are centrally managed by this capability and all interactions of a single customer can therefore be tracked in most cases.

Level 5: Progressive

- This level of the capability enables humans to take full advantage of a knowledge base so that common responses to customer requests and common answers to customer questions can be found easily.
- This capability is seamlessly integrated with the other capabilities of Customization & Personalization, e.g. integration with Customer Preference Management to use preference data dynamically, and integration with Customer Communication Management to use dynamic documents or messages.

CAPABILITY 7-5.
CUSTOMER LOYALTY MANAGEMENT

CAPABILITY DEFINITION

Customer Loyalty Management is a digital capability used to plan and implement a loyalty program to increase brand loyalty of customers. It includes abilities to gather and analyse data representing customer loyalty, to plan and measure their loyalty to a brand. A loyalty program is used to reward and thus encourage loyal buying behaviours by using a membership structure and membership benefits.

The Customer Loyalty Management concept has been around for many decades. Common functionalities of the capability include the following:

- Member classification.
- Membership card management, i.e. physical loyalty cards, gift cards, or digital cards.
- Member credential management: whether social media credential can be shared.
- Member referral tracking.
- Membership portal, web and mobile.
- Points management: how points are earned and spent.
- Other benefits management: discounts, premium contents, events, etc.
- Partnership: how points are earned and shared across partner networks.

The key to the success of Customer Loyalty Management does not lie in the loyalty program itself, because recent loyalty programs are all quite similar and customers don't find any significant differentiation among them that drives loyalty to a specific brand.

The key to the success of Customer Loyalty Management rather lies in its integration with other digital capabilities.

Here is an example. Let's presume a company interacts with a Gold member for product repairs through Interaction Tracking & Management. They then discover that the customer has been at the final stage of the conversion funnel longer than the pre-defined waiting days in Conversion Rate Optimization. As email has previously been identified as the customer's preferred communication channel in the Customer Preference Management, the company sends a marketing offer via email in Marketing Offer Management. This marketing offer is only available to Gold members.

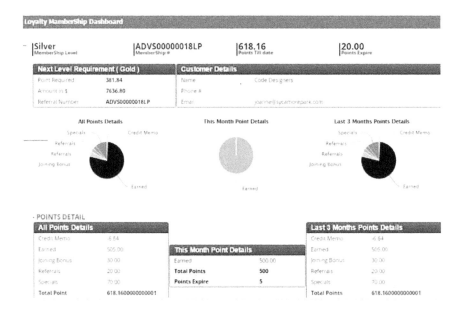

[Figure 28: Advectus Customer Loyalty Management Solution]

For this business scenario to work, the following six digital capabilities should be integrated seamlessly without swivel chair integration: Interaction Tracking & Management, Customer Loyalty Management, Conversion Rate Optimization, Marketing Offer Management, Email Marketing, and Customer Preference Management. Although this might be a very sophisticated scenario, this level of integration is the best way to give an organization a competitive advantage as this integration practice can't be copied easily by competitors.

MATURITY INDICATOR EXAMPLES

Level 0: Non-existent

- No loyalty program has been implemented.

Level 1: Ad hoc

- There is a rewards program, but it is not active because it has been launched recently, or it has barely been managed since its launch.
- Temporary bonus promotions for members are launched on an ad hoc basis to promote or revitalize the loyalty program, but it only encourages cherry picking behaviour, rather than encouraging loyal buying behaviour.

Level 2: Basic

- A membership program exists, but it is only focused on loyalty points and customers can earn points against the purchasing amount.
- Other than points management, many other loyal functionalities such as member classification and corresponding benefit management are missing.

Level 3: Defined

- All common functionalities for Customer Loyalty Management are implemented, e.g. membership classification, qualification & benefits, membership portals and a member support organization.
- The online loyalty program is integrated with the offline loyalty program as a single program.
- Membership levels are only determined by purchasing amount.

Level 4: Optimized

- Member levels are determined by more sophisticate logic, such as lifetime value that takes purchasing frequency, purchasing recency, purchased product variety, as well as purchasing amount into account.
- Member benefits are offered as per the customer's preference.
- Online purchasing history and offline purchasing history are integrated for a combined basket analysis across the organization.

Level 5: Progressive

- Customer loyalty is measured against all interactions, including social interactions. Loyal members active on social media are also managed in the loyalty program.
- Customer Loyalty Management is integrated seamlessly with other capabilities to effectively plan and implement the loyalty program.

CAPABILITY 7-6.
DIGITAL CUSTOMER SERVICES

CAPABILITY DEFINITION

Digital Customer Services is a digital capability used to assist customers with products or services before, during and after purchase throughout the digital customer journey, to ensure customer satisfaction with an organization.

Customer services before purchase helps customers to choose products or services, e.g. co-browsing on an ecommerce website. Customer service during purchase helps customers to place orders, including product or service selection, payment and checkout. It includes assistance with product returns or exchanges. Customer service after purchase helps customers to use products and services cost effectively and correctly. It includes assistance in planning, installing, training, troubleshooting, maintaining, upgrading and disposing of a product or a service that a customer has purchased.

Requirements of a Digital Customer Service Tool

A Digital Customer Service tool has much in common with traditional customer support applications. Digital Customer Service tools should however have more functionalities to automate end-to-end customer support online and enable extensive self-help services.

A Digital Customer Service tool commonly supports the following functionalities:

- **Service desk management**: to design and manage a service desk and staff.
- **Issue management**: to capture issues and provide the first line of support.
- **Request management**: to take and fulfil customer requests.
- **Problem management**: to identify the root cause of unknown errors and provide resolutions.
- **Work order management**: to create, allocate, track and evaluate work orders to address the issues, problems and requests.
- **Appointment management**: to schedule customer appointments.
- **Communication tool management**: to manage various types of communication tools.
- **Claim & warranty management**: to check warranty conditions and process claims.
- **Rule-based work routing management**: to create and dynamically change the service and work processes, without the assistance of IT staff.
- **Self-service portal**: to provide self-services and self-help functions in a consolidated website.

- **Customer satisfaction management**: to perform online customer surveys and analysis.
- **Analysis & reporting**: to analyse service performance and create performance reports.
- **SLA management**: to monitor whether SLAs (Service Level Agreements) are met, and follow-up where service levels are breached.

[Figure 29: Zendesk Customer Service Solution]

The Digital Customer Services capability uses Interaction Tracking & Management as an underlying capability to interact with customers in order to provide customer services.

MATURITY INDICATOR EXAMPLES

Level **0**: Non-existent

- Customer services are only provided by means of phone calls to a call centre.

- Information on how to contact the call centre is available on a website, but customer service is not available online.

Level 1: Ad hoc

- Very few customer services are provided on the website, e.g. FAQs and enquiry form submission.
- Customer service operations are only available through offline customer service centres and call centres.

Level 2: Basic

- Service requests are made online and these requests are then redirected to offline customer service centres and call centres. These processes use multiple communications tools such as live chat, SMS, email and phone calls.
- The basic online help facilities including an online manual and a help repository are available, while a bulletin board is provided for customer self-service. A comprehensive self-service portal is however not available.
- Workflow and routing for handling issue, request, problem and service work is not automated.

Level 3: Defined

- Many customer services that are available at offline customer service-centres, or call centres are also available on the customer self-service portal.
- For a few critical services, customers must visit an offline customer service-centre, or make a phone call to the call centre, e.g. password change and product repair.
- Workflow and routing for handling issue, request, problem and work are automated, but the routing logic cannot be changed easily because rule-based routing ability is limited.

Level 4: Optimized

- Most customer services that are available at an offline customer service-centre, or a call centre, are also available on the customer self service portal so that in most cases customers don't need to make a phone call or pay a visit to the offline customer centre.
- A Known error database[22] (KEDB) has been developed in the knowledge base to provide resolutions to the issues with known errors as soon as the issues are identified.

Level 5: Progressive

- Self-help functions have significantly improved due to the robust service knowledge base in the self-service portal.
- Customer service-desk staff can readily access any information that is needed to respond to a customer service request. This is possible because the Digital Customer Service capability is integrated seamlessly with other digital capabilities, e.g. service desk staff can see customer preference data, recent interactions, contract documents, warranty information, agreed service levels, and for example, technical manuals for quick reference. These manuals can be used without having to open other applications or log in to them.
- To effectively identify a root cause of unknown errors and provide faster resolutions to these issues, service knowledge specifically designed for solving unknown issues has been built into the knowledge base.

---

[22] KEDB is a database in which all known errors in products are recorded as they are and when they happened. KEDB is commonly part of a knowledge base.

MEGA CAPABILITY 8.

DIGITAL INTELLIGENCE

Digital Intelligence is a set of digital capabilities used to extract and transform transactional data from the front-office and middle-office capabilities, populate data suitable for deep-dive analysis in the back office, analyse for trends and patterns in the business transactions, and help executives and managers derive insights into the transactions for them to make informed decisions.

As Digital Intelligence is a subset of business intelligence for use by the entire organization, a significant portion of the functionalities provided by existing business intelligence capabilities can be reused to build Digital Intelligence capabilities, e.g. reuse of the data population, data store, data mining and reporting functionalities of the existing business intelligence systems.

Digital Intelligence has the following digital capabilities:

- Product Similarity Analytics
- Customer Insights
- Customer Segmentation

- Conversion Analytics
- Marketing Effectiveness
- Big Data Analytics
- Web Analytics
- Reporting & Dashboards

CAPABILITY 8-1.
PRODUCT SIMILARITY ANALYTICS

CAPABILITY DEFINITION

Product Similarity Analytics is a digital capability used to analyse similarity among products in terms of which products and services are viewed, moved into carts, or purchased either 'together' or 'in a row'.

The product similarity analysis can be performed in two ways:

- Association analysis
- Item-based collaborative filtering

Association Analysis

The association analysis shows products that are close enough to each other to be used as a basis of product recommendation. When product X is for example closely related to product Y, product Y is recommended to a customer who bought, or showed interest in, product X.

It enables business to recommend not only products, but also services and content effectively. The recommendations are based on a rule table of the association, without knowing the visitor when they show an interest through actions, such as a click on a link on a website.

The terms Support, Confidence, and Lift are introduced briefly below, as they are frequently used for the association analysis of a shopping basket.

In the example below, the association between the purchase of milk and diapers, and the purchase of beer are analysed by the rules of Support, Confidence and Lift.

Support represents how often the items are purchased together in total orders. In the example, milk and diapers are purchased together in 3 out of 5 orders, beer is purchased in 3 out of 5 orders, and milk, diapers and beer are purchased together in 2 out of 5 orders. Thus, Support is measured as follows:

Order ID	Purchased items
1	Bread, **Milk**
2	Bread, **Diapers**, **Beer**, Butter
3	**Milk**, **Diapers**, **Beer**, Butter
4	Bread, **Milk**, **Diapers**, **Beer**
5	Bread, **Milk**, **Diapers**, Butter

- **Support** (Milk, Diapers) = 3 / 5 = 0.6
- **Support** (Beer) = 3 / 5 = 0.6
- **Support** (Milk, Diapers, Beer) = 2 / 5 = 0.4

Confidence indicates how often the items are purchased together under the condition of how often other items are purchased together. Confidence of how often milk, diapers and beer are purchased together under the condition of how often milk and diapers are purchased together, is measured as follows:

- **Confidence** = Support (Milk, Diapers, Beer) / Support (Milk, Diapers) = 0.4 / 0.6 = 0.67

Lift shows how often the items are purchased together when compared to how often the items are purchased independently. If they are purchased more often together than independently, the Lift value is greater than 1, which means that the items have a positive effect on one another, and are therefore more likely to be purchased together. If the Lift value is smaller than 1, they are negatively associated. If the value is 1, they have almost no effect on each other. In this example, Lift value is as follows:

- **Lift** = Support (Milk, Diapers, Beer) / {(Support (Milk, Diapers) X (Support (Beer)} = 0.4 / (0.6 X 0.6) = 1.11

Each of the association rules has its strengths and drawbacks. It is recommended that all options be considered to see which option works best for different business scenarios and use cases.

Item-based Collaborative Filtering

Item-based Collaborative Filtering, a.k.a. Item-to-item Collaborative Filtering, is used to identify which products are highly correlated by comparing the historical preferences of 'customers' who have purchased the same products.

Item-based Collaborative Filtering is different from the association analysis in that customers enter into the equation as well.

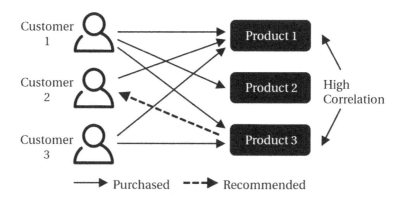

[Figure 30: Item-based Collaborative Filtering]

In Figure 30, it is revealed that product 1 and product 3 are highly correlated by comparing users' purchasing history.

Because customers' preference is factored into the product similarity analysis, Item-based Collaborative Filtering is considered more personal than the association analysis. It does however not necessarily mean the association analysis is less effective than Item-based Collaborative Filtering. The association analysis is more suitable for the product items that are purchased together in the same shopping basket, while Item-based

Collaborative Filtering is suitable for those purchased across different shopping baskets.

Apache Mahout is a famous Machine Learning framework for implementation of collaborative filtering ready for immediate use. Apache Mahout is deployed on top of Hadoop using MapReduce. Refer to 'Capability 10-4. Parallel Processing Services' for overview of MapReduce.

MATURITY INDICATOR EXAMPLES

Level 0: Non-existent

- Association of purchased products have never been analysed.

Level 1: Ad hoc

- Purchased products are analysed on an ad hoc basis for simple dependencies in the products.
- The analysis is done as part of performance analysis, and product recommendations do not necessarily follow.
- The level of analysis is not deep enough to identify unseen patterns, due to lack of a specialized data-mining tool.

Level 2: Basic

- Products and services purchased are analysed for patterns on a regular basis.
- The limited functionalities of the analytics tool do not support sophisticated association analysis fully.
- The architecture and capacity of the analysis platform is not enough for the analytical processing of massive basket data.

Level 3: Defined

- All standard processes, analysis model, experts and data mining tools are available for the association analysis of the basket data.
- Sophisticate data mining algorithms and tools specialized for association analysis are used.
- Product-similarity analytics tools are built on top of the enterprise-data warehouse platform to take advantage of its analytical processing capacity.
- Merchandisers consider the results of Product Similarity Analytics for dynamic merchandising online, but the results are not necessarily transferred into the product recommendation engine in the front-office.

Level 4: Optimized

- The organization has optimized its association model used to analyse product similarity.
- Product similarity results are integrated to the product recommendation engine in the front-office for real-time product recommendations.
- Association analysis are performed for the majority of marketing offerings and digital contents to identify similarity among them.

Level 5: Progressive

- Product similarity analytics is integrated with other analytics such as customer insights and customer segmentation to identify products in common, e.g. Product-based recommendations from Product Similarity Analytics is combined with customer-based recommendations from Customer Insight and Customer Segmentation.
- Parallel processing of Big Data Analytics provides underlying data handling functionalities to Product Similarity Analytics for advanced correlational analysis.

CAPABILITY 8-2.
CUSTOMER INSIGHTS

CAPABILITY DEFINITION

Customer Insights is a digital capability used to analyse and understand customer behaviours and intentions behind the behaviours to help acquire, develop and retain customers. Whereas the Product Similarity Analytics capability focuses on products, the Customer Insight capability focuses more on customers than on products.

This digital capability requires an ability to capture and maintain enterprise-wide customer data regularly to drive insights into the Voice of the Customer (VoC). It may model customer tendencies, predict frequency and time lapse of purchasing items and other behaviours, and measure the lifetime value of a customer.

Customer Data

The ability to capture customer data is fundamental to building a Customer Insights capability. The customer data includes information on customer master data, demographics, interactions, preferences, privacy, product, events and campaigns, behaviours, 3rd party data for data enrichment and security profile.

The customer data comes from On-Line Transaction Processing[23] (OLTP) applications such as CRM (Customer Relationship Management), ERP (Enterprise Resource Planning), and SCM

---

[23] OLTP applications represent computer programs that process simple, but frequent business transactions, typically in the front office and middle office on a real-time basis, whereas OLAP (On-Line Analytical Processing) applications are computer programs that process complex, intermittent analytics in batches, typically in the back office.

(Supply Chain Management). Source data collected from the OLTP applications goes through data ETL [24] (Extraction, Transformation, and Load) processes to populate the target state customer data that can be used to analyse and develop Customer Insights.

Customer Analytics

Insights into customers involve understanding of customer needs, modelling of customer behaviours including purchasing actions, and an estimation of the customer lifetime value.

Although many different models for understanding and modelling customer needs, behaviour and profitability are available, a discussion of these are beyond the scope of this book. For detail of the modelling, refer to traditional marketing books specialized in modelling customer needs, behaviours and values.

Customer Insights can be developed for a mass of customers, customer segments, or an individual customer. Customer Insights developed for a mass of customers is not very effective, while Customer Insights developed for individual customers is costly. Development of Customer Insights for customer segments is therefore common practice.

Insights into individual customers are however now gaining momentum, since contemporary digital technologies enable real time analysis of the massive data from individual customers. Insights into customer segments and individual customers can therefore complement each other when combined for joint analysis.

---

[24] ETL stands for the processes of extraction, transformation, and loading of data when the data is pulled out of one database and placed into another for different data usage. ETL processes are commonly performed when moving data from OLTP systems in the front and middle offices to OLAP systems in the back office for deep-dive data analysis.

Customer Insights are performed in parallel with Customer Segmentation. Customer Segmentation is commonly performed as part of business strategy planning and execution processes, while Customer Insights are developed on an on-going basis.

Customer Insights can be developed before target customer segments are identified. Insights into the customer segments are refined and developed further to understand target customer segments better, once the target segments are established.

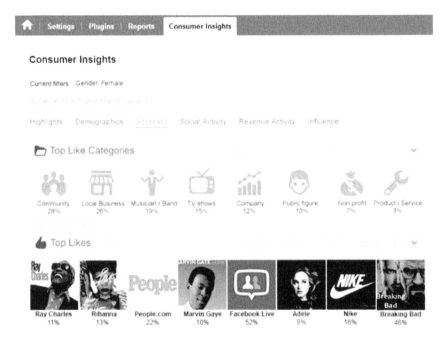

[Figure 31: Gigya Customer Insights Management Solution]

MATURITY INDICATOR EXAMPLES

Level 0: Non-existent

- Some customer data residing in OLTP applications may be analysed to understand customers, but this is never transformed to analytical data suitable for analysis of customer insights.

- The capability to analyse customer behaviour is not available.

Level 1: Ad hoc

- Customer data capture and analysis are performed on an ad hoc basis.
- Some customer behaviour data is collected for analysis in a productivity tool, such as MS-Excel, on an ad hoc basis.
- The organization does not know the location of the data required for customer insight analysis, nor how to use it.
- The organization can describe customers by simple metrics, such as sales volume.

Level 2: Basic

- Customer data is captured from a variety of systems inconsistently, without integration of the customer data that represents customer profile attributes.
- Customer transaction data is obtained and turned into basic insights.
- Basic customer surveys are conducted, or customer satisfaction data is captured on ad hoc basis.
- The tool supports basic analytics functionality, e.g. canned reports.
- Limited data management and data cleansing techniques are employed.
- The data warehouse and/or data mart[25] that store customer data are not consolidated.

---

[25] The data mart is a subset of the data warehouse. Operational data is extracted from the front-office systems, transformed and loaded into the data warehouse, and then the data in the data warehouse is broken down into multiple subject areas that are stored into multiple data marts for further analysis by each business division and department.

Level 3: Defined

- Corporate principles, policies, processes, techniques and sophisticated tools are available to collect and analyse the data, and standard customer insight generation processes are established across the organization.
- Basic customer surveys or customer satisfaction data is captured on a regular basis.
- The organization has an integrated view of multiple sources of data representing customer profile attributes.
- Customer profile and experience data are comprehensive.
- The tool supports comprehensive analytics functionalities.
- Customer data cleansing practice is in place and cleansing occurs regularly.
- Comprehensive customer profile and customer experience data allows reprioritization of customer segments.

Level 4: Optimized

- Customer Insight capability has optimized to the extent that some of the hidden patterns of customer behaviours and intentions are visible. The organization optimizes customer experience based on the patterns.
- Some advanced audit data representing customer experience is analysed, e.g. call monitoring data.
- Customer insight data is used by all customer-facing systems.
- Corporate data governance policies and procedures are well enforced.
- A single, consolidated customer information data-repository is in place.
- Changing needs and preferences of customer segments are monitored over time.
- The organization tracks customer operational metrics representing critical success factors.

Level 5: Progressive

- All hidden patterns of customer behaviours and intentions can be articulated. The organization has complete understanding of customer needs and priorities across customer lifecycles.
- All advanced customer experience audit techniques, including data derived from persona evaluations are used to capture the real voice of customers.
- Customer Insights data is readily available to management and executives for strategic planning and decision making.

CAPABILITY 8-3.
CUSTOMER SEGMENTATION

CAPABILITY DEFINITION

Customer Segmentation is a digital capability used to divide a customer base into a few segments of customers that share similar characteristics, including demographics, behaviours and mindsets, and spending habits.

While the basics of traditional customer segmentation methodologies have not changed in the contemporary digital era, a few more considerations relevant to digital technology and digital business can be added on top of the traditional basics of segmenting customers.

Segmentation Methods

There are various ways of performing customer segmentations by combining the following dimensions.

- **Demographics-based segmentation**: segmentation by customer demographic characteristics such as age, gender, education and occupation.
- **Behaviour-based segmentation**: segmentation by shopping behaviours such as purchased products and services, and RFM (Recency, Frequency, and Monetary: recency of latest purchases, frequency of purchases and volume of purchases)
- **Value-based segmentation**: segmentation by total benefit and cost of a customer.
- **Need-based segmentation**: segmentation by needs that are often unfulfilled and unmet.
- **Attitude-based segmentation**: segmentation by attitude toward a brand such as brand loyalty, promotion sensitivity and sensitivity to brand switch.

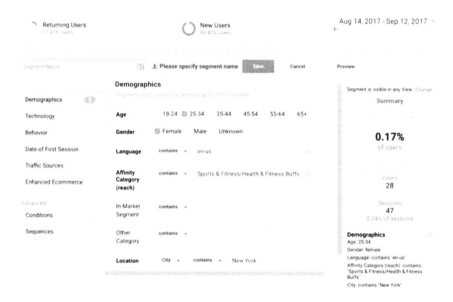

[Figure 32: Google Customer Segment Builder]

Behaviour-based or value-based customer segmentation are commonly used as these enable business to focus its marketing resources and efforts on profitable customer segments. Unfortunately, both segmentation methods are heavily based on information from current and past shopping activities, and information on needs and attitudes of customers tend to be ignored, making the segmentation results less reliable.

In the contemporary digital age, more information on customer needs and attitudes can be captured than ever before, through social websites and mobile devices. The captured information can feed into customer segmentation processes, making the segmentation results more reliable. Complaints made on a blog post may for example indicate a customer's negative attitude toward a brand, or a customer's needs that are yet to be met.

User-based Collaborative Filtering

Customer segments can also be used to facilitate a product recommendation by using User-based Collaborative Filtering in which products are recommended based on users' similarity.

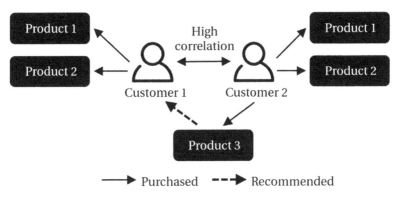

[Figure 33: User-based Collaborative Filtering]

If a customer belongs to the same customer segment as another customer, the two customers are considered similar and highly correlated. A product purchased by many customers of the customer segment can therefore be recommended to other customers of the same segment who have not yet bought the product.

Apache Mahout is a proven Machine Learning framework for implementation of User-based Collaborative Filtering.

MATURITY INDICATOR EXAMPLES

Level 0: Non-existent

- The organization may have performed shopping basket analysis, but the results have never been used for customer segmentation.

Level 1: Ad hoc

- Some customer demographics are analysed for customer segmentation on an ad hoc basis.
- Customer segmentation is a once-off activity for a marketing event or sales promotion.

Level 2: Basic

- Customers are grouped into a few customer segments based on demographics and purchasing history, annually or on a regular basis.
- Limited basket analysis is performed and only purchasing amount is considered for the segmentation.
- Customer segmentation is performed by each business unit, but is neither coordinated nor integrated at corporate level.

Level 3: Defined

- The organization has implemented corporate principles, policies, processes, standard methods and tools for customer segmentation in order to coordinate customer segmentations across multiple business units to ensure consistent customer segments.
- Comprehensive basket analysis is performed. Portfolio of purchased products, purchase amount, purchase frequency and purchase recency is for example taken into account.
- Further information on customer needs and attitudes is captured through big data analysis of social interactions, but

the data does not feed into customer segmentation processes readily.

Level 4: Optimized

- Customer segmentation is performed based on both customer value and need, and purchasing behaviour analysis is incorporated into value-based segmentation.
- Customers' preference of products and services are identified.
- Information from the front-office capabilities such as Social Listening and Social Servicing is readily available, and usable for the value-based and need-based segmentation to be more feasible and reliable.

Level 5: Progressive

- Customer segmentation is performed predominantly based on customer attitude towards a brand.
- The information required to identify brand loyalty, sensitivity to promotion and sensitivity to brand switch can be readily captured from other digital capabilities.
- 'Brand Loyalist' has been established as one of the customer segments.

CAPABILITY 8-4.
CONVERSION ANALYTICS

CAPABILITY DEFINITION

Conversion Analytics is a digital capability used to analyse a large amount of conversion data, capture trends and patterns, and help make decisions on future strategy to promote conversion in a conversion funnel.

The conversion data includes multi-year historical data of customer conversions during a digital customer journey from awareness towards purchase. The conversion data should be analysed for trends and patterns that have consistently occurred in the past and may therefore happen again in the future, so that decision makers can use the trends and patterns to develop insights into customer conversion.

This digital capability works closely with the Conversion Rate Optimization capability by providing conversion trends and patterns through deep-dive analysis of historical conversion data. The only difference between the two capabilities is that Conversion Rate Optimization is focused on the real-time status of a conversion funnel and recent progress in conversion to help determine ways to promote current conversion rate, whereas Conversion Analytics looks at historical trends of conversion to identify patterns and establish longer-term strategy to increase future conversion rate.

Conversion Data Population

Most data required for conversion tracking comes from weblog files, or webpage tagging. Weblog files are provided by a standard web server, while page tagging is an addition of a snippet of script code, such as JavaScript code, into a webpage to get more tracking data than what weblog data provides. The script codes tag a visitor with a cookie and sends interaction data back to a central server.

Once weblog data and webpage tagging data is created in the front-office and the middle-office operations, they are extracted, transformed and loaded into a data warehouse or data mart for analysis by the Conversion Analytics capability in the back-office on a regular basis, e.g. daily or weekly.

Conversion Pattern Analysis

After a large volume of historical data is populated in a data warehouse and/or data mart, historical trends of conversion can be identified through simple trending analysis and hidden patterns of conversion mined through complicated statistical analysis.

Although the primary purpose of the analysis of conversion patterns is to improve conversion 'rate', the metrics may be expanded to include 'cost per conversion' if relevant cost data is available, as conversion rates says nothing about cost effectiveness. Conversion can also be analysed against value metrics such as 'value per visitor' and 'customer lifetime value'.

What is chosen to be analysed through Conversion Analytics depends on the organization's strategy. If the strategy were to drive sales or market share strongly, then conversion cost analysis would not really be relevant.

MATURITY INDICATOR EXAMPLES

Level 0: Non-existent

- The organization may have a Conversion Rate Optimization tool that provides real time analysis functionalities, but it does not have a separate Conversion Analytics capability that enables a large amount of historical conversion log data to be extracted and stored in a data warehouse environment in the back-office.

Level 1: Ad hoc

- A large amount of weblog files is extracted, transformed and loaded onto a temporary data storage to analyse for web usage on an ad hoc basis.
- The analysis may produce a few historical reports, such as how many visitors were on each webpage and what they have clicked and selected, but they do not give a full picture of how conversion rate has changed and why.

Level 2: Basic

- Some business units have started analysing historical trends of conversion rates.
- Existing data warehousing and reporting capabilities are reused to store and analyse weblog files for trends in conversion rate through addition of a few more tables and reports.
- Webpage tagging is not available, and no data other than weblog is populated into the warehouse.
- Historical conversion rates are analysed based on multi-year weblog data on a regular basis.

Level 3: Defined

- Corporate-level Conversion Analytics principles, policies, analytics processes and data analysts have been established.
- Conversion Analytics tools are built on top of the enterprise-data warehouse capability and a data mart is enhanced for conversion analysis purposes.
- Webpage tagging and weblog files generate source data and both data sources are used to populate conversion data in the data warehouse.
- The reports can show historical conversion trends for 6 to 12 months, but sophisticated data mining functionality has not yet been introduced.

Level 4: Optimized

- The trend analysis of conversion has been optimized enough to identify invisible patterns in the trends by employing mathematical and statistical technique for sophisticated data mining.
- Metrics other than conversion rate has also been established to the optimized conversion funnel in terms of speed, cost and value, e.g. returning visitor conversion rate, bounce rate, cost per conversion, value per visitor, and customer lifetime value.

Level 5: Progressive

- The organization understands the reasons behind the conversion rate trends because the Conversion Analytics capability is integrated seamlessly with other front-office and middle-office capabilities, as well as other Digital Intelligence, e.g. conversion rate changes due to webpage layout changes, addition of new marketing offers and seasonal factors.

CAPABILITY 8-5.
DIGITAL MARKETING EFFECTIVENESS

CAPABILITY DEFINITION

Digital Marketing Effectiveness is a digital capability used to measure the effectiveness of digital marketing programs and other efforts in terms of whether they meet their objectives or not. The digital capability includes abilities to:

- Define effectiveness and establish corresponding KPIs and metrics.
- Identify and collect source data used for measurement.
- Measure performance against the KPIs and metrics.

Definition and Measurement of Effectiveness

Effectiveness of digital marketing can be defined in many ways, depending on the objectives of a digital marketing program or marketing strategy. Effectiveness may include: incremental profit, marginal contribution of incremental sales, net present value of profit, gross profit margin added, incremental revenue, incremental cost savings, number of new customers, incremental brand awareness, incremental customer satisfaction, and incremental sales, margin, profit, and customers per marketing cost, and many more.

When Marketing Effectiveness is defined as broadly as Return of Investment (ROI), the Return in the digital space is commonly measured via conversion rates in a conversion funnel. Here is an example of measuring digital marketing effectiveness by using conversion rate:

> "Digital Marketing Effectiveness = (Online Sales Amount from Lead-to-Purchase Conversion – Digital Marketing Cost) ÷ Digital Marketing Cost"

Different type of conversions can be used to calculate different Effectiveness, as there are many different conversions considering all different stages across the marketing funnel.

Integration of Measurements

Some of the Digital Marketing capabilities in the front-office may have their own performance evaluation functions within their capability. Digital Campaign Management capability for example often has a simple function to measure campaign results, and the function may provide real-time information on campaign performance. The simple function does however not necessarily reflect the whole spectrum of marketing activities and may not provide functionalities to perform deep-dive analysis.

To bridge the performance gap of the front-office, the Marketing Effectiveness capability should provide an enterprise-wide underlying capability, including marketing performance data population and multi-dimensional analytics capability, to define and measure the effectiveness of any type of marketing program and marketing effort.

Those performance measurement functions in the front-office should be integrated to the Marketing Effectiveness capability in the back-office to leverage the deep-dive, dedicated, and specialized analytics capability. This integration will also enable different marketing programs and efforts under the same marketing journey to be integrated readily for the measuring performance of the broader marketing journey.

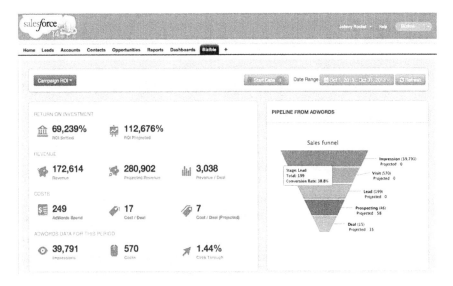

[Figure 34: SalesForce Marketing Effectiveness Measure]

MATURITY INDICATOR EXAMPLES

Level 0: Non-existent

- The organization has not defined marketing Effectiveness.
- Metrics to measure marketing effectiveness are not established.

Level 1: Ad hoc

- Although a few marketing performance metrics are available, marketing effectiveness is not clearly defined.
- Marketing performance in the back-office operations is measured against the metrics on an ad hoc basis, in addition to the front-office performance measure.

- Most of the data required for analysis for marketing effectiveness is collected manually.
- Metrics are focused on increasing sales, but the relationship between sales increase and the marketing program is unclear.
- Conversion is not considered when measuring marketing effectiveness.
- A productivity tool such as MS-Excel is used as an analysis tool.

Level 2: Basic

- There is a shared understanding of the definition of Marketing Effectiveness across the organization.
- Marketing effectiveness is measured by individual business units on a regular basis, without coordination at corporate level. Metrics and analysis methodology are not consistent across the organization.
- Many of the processes of gathering data required for marketing effectiveness analysis are performed manually.
- Conversion rate may be considered in addition to sales volume to measure marketing effectiveness.
- An analytics tool specialized in business intelligence is employed, but it is functionally limited.

Level 3: Defined

- Standard definitions and metrics of Marketing Effectiveness are established and enforced across the organization.
- Corporate principles, policies, processes, standard analytics models and methodologies, data analysts, and analytics tools are implemented.
- Conversion rates are a critical part of effectiveness measurement models.
- A substantial amount of performance source data is collected automatically, but there still are many manual steps involved to collect the rest of data and transform it into

a format suitable for analysis. Some of data required for analysis is unavailable.

- Measurement reports are readily accessible to management.

Level 4: Optimized

- When it comes to quantitative metrics, data collection processes have constantly been optimized to the point where manual intervention is only required intermittently.
- The measurement models and methods of Marketing effectiveness are consistently applied to the front office marketing performance measure, and they are therefore all readily incorporated into a single measurement of marketing effectiveness of a broader marketing strategy.
- The capability provides an integrated view of all marketing effectiveness metrics, including metrics from the front-office.
- A few qualitative metrics of marketing effectiveness are established and tied to financial metrics, but data collection for the qualitative metrics is limited and the metrics are not widely accepted by business units.

Level 5: Progressive

- Data capture for quantitative metrics is fully automated by integrating with other Digital Intelligence capabilities. Customer navigation data is for example delivered from Web Analytics capability seamlessly.
- Qualitative metrics have been accepted across the organization, as the reliability of the data gathered has improved and business communities agree to the importance of the metrics.
- Marketing Effectiveness reports are widely used by management for strategic marketing decisions.

CAPABILITY 8-6.
BIG DATA ANALYTICS

CAPABILITY DEFINITION

Big Data Analytics is a digital capability used to process and analyse a massive amount of data in un-structured or semi-structured format, in an effort to uncover hidden patterns, unknown correlations, or other business-meaningful information for social interaction, marketing, sales and customer service purposes.

Big Data Population & Storage

Big Data Analytics works together with other digital capabilities to collect source data such as weblogs, click streams, social media contents, emails, phone calls, messages, sensor data and many others.

Using traditional data integration technologies such as ETL (Extract, Transformation & Load) tools and data warehouse solution to collect, transform, populate and store these massive and ever-increasing data sources would be too slow and expensive. Distributed file stores and distributed data processing are therefore critical to successful Big Data implementation, as they provide high performance in analytical processing of massive 'big data' cost-effectively.

The Hadoop framework is a popular example of a suitable technology used for processing and storing big data in the contemporary digital environment.

New technologies such as In-Memory Database [26] (IMDB) and NoSQL Database provide underlying capabilities for Big Data.

---

[26] An In-Memory Database is a database management system that stores data in memory-based storage as main storage, as opposed to disk-

Some of these technologies are discussed in the following two sections: 'Mega Capability 9. Digital Data Services' and 'Mega Capability 10. Digital Infrastructure Services'.

Big Data Analysis

Once big data is populated in distributed file stores and ready for analysis, traditional Business Intelligence tools, as well as new tools specialized in big data analysis, can be used to retrieve, analyse and present the data.

Whereas traditional, structured data sources in relational databases are more suitable for calculating exact values, the massive, ever-increasing un-structured and semi-structured data sources in distributed file systems can be used best to identify patterns hidden behind the massive amount of the data. Big Data analytics is therefore commonly used for predictive analysis, and correlation analysis.

Big data sources gathered from the front-office are processed by Big Data Analytics and delivered to other digital capabilities that need the analysis results. The Social Listening capability of the front-office for example collects social media contents and passes the data onto Big Data Analytics for processing and analyses before being returned to the Social Listening capability for reporting. The results can also be distributed to the Customer Insights capability for customer profiling and Reporting & Dashboard capability for reporting.

Big Data Correlations

True value of big data analytics is derived from data correlation. Correlation is performed to capture hidden relationships between interactions, behaviours, events, content, products and many other actions and entities. It is not necessarily a causal

---

based storage to improve data access performance significantly. Traditional databases use disk-based storages as the main storage.

relationship where input results in output. Correlation does not tell us whether they have a causal relationship. It instead tells us how strong a relationship they have.

Correlation discovered in a case study that the more likely a female customer purchases unscented lotion and subsequently supplements like magnesium, calcium and zinc, the more likely she is 3 or more months pregnant. This was used by a retailer to proactively approach the customers because they may start going to new stores and developing new brand loyalties.

Correlation analysed in another case revealed that the more likely it is that a patient has a car, the more likely they take antibiotics as directed. This insight was used to establish 'Medication Adherence Score' by a credit scoring company. There is however nothing causal between car ownership and taking antibiotics as directed.

[Figure 35: Splunk Analytics for Hadoop]

Big data analytics should be able to provide decision makers with useful insights into customer behaviours through correlational analysis of big data. Artificial Intelligence and Machine Learning can be used to take big data analytics to the next level, because a machine learner can 'learn' how to produce useful insights and provide the insights with little involvement by human data analysts.

Business use cases, architecture and implementation of Machine Learning is discussed in the Epilogue of this book.

MATURITY INDICATOR EXAMPLES

Level 0: Non-existent

- Neither un-structured, nor semi-structured data is collected for analysis in the back-office.
- Neither distributed file storage, nor distributed data processing exists.

Level 1: Ad hoc

- Distributed file storage, distributed data processing applications, and a few other Big Data Analytics components have been tested, or a pilot system has been implemented.
- None of the Big Data Analytics components is being implemented under a Big Data strategy.

Level 2: Basic

- Some of Big Data Analytics components have been implemented for ongoing Big Data analysis purpose, but there is no strategic direction or road map for Big Data Analytics implementation.
- Big Data sources are constantly captured and stored in distributed file systems, but they are barely analysed for

meaningful business information such as correlations in products.

Level 3: Defined

- A corporate-level Big Data Analytics strategy and implementation roadmap has been established, and a comprehensive big data platform, analytics processes and data experts are implemented as per the maps.
- Not only are multiple big data sources collected, processed and stored in distributed file stores, but the data is also analysed to identify hidden patterns in customer navigation and behaviour across multiple digital channels and touchpoints. The effectiveness of the correlation analysis is however yet to improve.
- Click streams are analysed in real-time and simple statistics are produced as soon as they are captured in the front-office, without passing the data onto the back-office for later batch analysis.

Level 4: Optimized

- Big data analytics have been optimized to the extent that specific patterns of customer behaviour are identified and correlations of events in the digital channels are captured, e.g. correlation of the recent drop in conversion rate and the recent surge in negative feedback on social websites.
- Un-structured and semi-structured data sources are analysed, together with structured data sources to complement each other, and produce results that are unseen with each data source alone.

Level 5: Progressive

- This level of the capability allows the organization to discover, evaluate, optimize and deploy predictive models by analysing big data sources to improve marketing performance, such as conversion rate, or mitigate risks such as bad reputation spreading on social media.

- The Big Data Analytics capability is integrated seamlessly with front-office capabilities that feed big data sources and with back-office capabilities that consume the processed data, thereby supporting an enterprise data lake[27].

CAPABILITY 8-7. WEB ANALYTICS

CAPABILITY DEFINITION

Web Analytics is a digital capability to collect and analyse web data to understand effectiveness of a website and optimize web usage. It commonly analyses visitor's behaviour on a website and measures the effectiveness of each web page, and navigation and route to a destination page through hit, page view, visit, session, visitor, single page visit, visit duration, active time, exit rate, frequency, click path and many more metrics.

Source Data Collection

Data sources for Web Analytics can be collected in two ways: web server logging and web page tagging.

A web server generates web logs when a web page is requested by a web browser. Information about the request, including client IP

---

[27] The data lake is the largest data storage in an enterprise that holds unstructured, semi-structured and structured data sets in their native format, while the data warehouse and data mart store structured data only.

address, request date and time, the page requested, HTTP [28] response code, data bytes served, user agent and referrer are typically generated and combined into a weblog file. The weblog files are analysed to measure the effectiveness of webpages and the navigation structure of a website.

Web server logs do not collect user-specific information. This is where web page tagging comes in. Web page tagging inserts scripts such as JavaScript into web pages, and these return more specific information than web log data to a web server when the webpages are rendered on a web browser. This information can include a user's behaviour on the web pages, which is not captured into web logs, as well as cached pages that are not requested from the web server.

Complex web page tags can collect information that is more useful, but it would be costly to create and maintain those complex tags.

A common practice is to combine these two methods - web server logging and web page tagging - and collect data from both methods as they complement each other by balancing cost and benefit.

Data Store and Analysis

The amount of data collected from web server logging and web page tagging is enormous and the analysis of this data has been a challenge due to its massive volume. The data is often archived soon after it is captured to reduce the volume of data, rather than analyse it for marketing insights.

An organization can now take advantage of the Big Data Analytics capability to store, process and analyse the web data sources as if it is a Big Data source. The click-stream analysis function of the

---

[28] HTTP stands for Hypertext Transfer Protocol. The protocol defines how web content is 'transferred' between a webserver and a user when the user clicks on a 'hyperlink' in web content.

Big Data Analytics capability can also be used to analyse the data from web server logging or web page tagging to produce real time statistics of web transactions, so that businesses can respond to the real-time customer behaviours and the needs these behaviours may indicate.

Once the data is analysed through Big Data Analytics to identify online customer behaviours, it can feed the resulting information to the Customer Insight and Customer Segmentation capabilities for further analysis.

The resulting information can also feed to many other digital capabilities, e.g. Conversion Analytics for funnel analysis and Reporting & Dashboard for reporting.

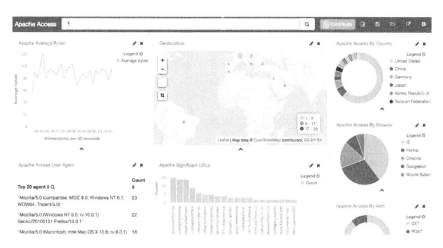

[Figure 36: Logz.io Apache Log Analysis]

MATURITY INDICATOR EXAMPLES

Level 0: Non-existent

- Web logs are captured and archived on a regular basis. The captured data may be analysed for security purpose, but are never analysed to identity patterns of customer behaviours.

Level 1: Ad hoc

- Web logs are analysed on an ad hoc basis to see a few simple metrics such as number of hits, page views, and sessions.
- Temporary data storage and productivity tools are employed for the ad hoc analysis.

Level 2: Basic

- Web logs are analysed on a regular basis to identify patterns in usage of the web site against quite a few metrics.
- The analysis is performed as part of on-going and consistent marketing activities, but the analysis is not coordinated at corporate level.
- Analysis on the patterns is limited due to the small amount of data mounted for the analysis and limited functionality of the analysis tools.

Level 3: Defined

- Corporate policies, processes, data analysts, models and methods for data capturing and analysis are implemented. A comprehensive web analytics tool is available to the data analysts.
- Web analytics are organized and coordinated by a central digital marketing function.
- The data source is not only web server logs, but web page tagging is also used. The large amount of weblog data enables comprehensive analysis of patterns of the weblogs, but identification of user-specific behaviour patterns is still limited.

Level 4: Optimized

- Web page tagging is widely used to identify patterns of user-specific behaviours on web pages, complementing web log analysis.

- Some of the behaviour patterns are identified through the correlation analysis of the massive amount of source data by Big Data Analytics.
- The results of Web Analytics are used to streamline page layout and user navigation on the websites by providing practical information for user experience design.

Level 5: Progressive

- Many different web usage patterns are identified and verified.
- Verified web usage patterns feed into other Digital Intelligence capabilities such as Customer Insight, Customer Segmentation, Conversion Analytics and Marketing Effectiveness to enrich the Digital Intelligence data by providing underlying insights into customer behaviours on the web pages.

CAPABILITY 8-8.
REPORTING & DASHBOARD

CAPABILITY DEFINITION

Reporting & Dashboard is a digital capability used to establish and maintain performance indicators and metrics, and measure and report performance of digital capabilities against the metrics to assist digital decision makers.

Collection of source data required to measure performance against indicators and metrics needs to be designed in such a way that it is captured automatically. The automated collection of source data is the most critical factor for the success to this capability. Online dashboards and reports should be comprehensive to provide a landscape of key metrics, but easy enough for management to understand.

While the other Digital Intelligence capabilities are more focused on data population, data storage, and data analysis, the Reporting & Dashboard capability is more focused on presenting analysis results to users.

The Reporting & Dashboard capability retrieves the analysis results from the other Digital Intelligence capabilities, combines the results, and presents them in such formats as tables, graphs, and charts to communicate the complicated results to decision makers in easier ways. The results can be presented as a dashboard on PC and mobile screens, and be printed as a paper-based report.

The layout of the online and offline reports may be pre-defined so that the reports can be created by a computer batch job before a user requests it. The batch jobs process a large amount of the analytical data using intensive computation, and are therefore performed outside business hours to avoid a negative impact on the performance of digital business transactions in the front-office and middle-office.

Requirements of a Reporting & Dashboard Tool

The primary role of the tool is to take data from the other Digital Intelligence capabilities, combine the data and create reports. The tool should include the functionalities to:

- Collate data from multiple data sources.
- Provide out-of-box standard report templates.
- Create ad-hoc report templates.
- Drill-down from a high-level view to detailed views.
- Provide web pivot-table analysis.
- Visualize data with a variety of graphs.
- Customize dashboard.
- Design workflows for collaboration on reports.

- Integrate to content management and communication tools.
- Import from, and export to spreadsheets.

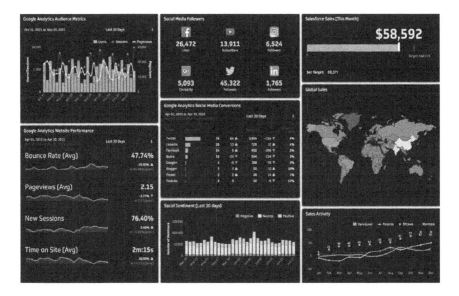

[Figure 37: Klipfolio Digital Business Dashboard]

MATURITY INDICATOR EXAMPLES

Level 0: Non-existent

- There is lightweight performance evaluation in the front-office digital capabilities, but no metrics, reports, or dashboard exists in the back-office for in-depth performance evaluation.

Level 1: Ad hoc

- A few simple metrics have been created for analysis of multi-year performance, e.g. online sales trending analysis, but the metrics are temporary and the performance is measured on an ad hoc basis.

- The data collection processes required to measure against the metrics are predominantly manual.

Level 2: Basic

- Several metrics have been created by business units for performance measure in the back-office, but those metrics are not well aligned with corporate-level KPI's.
- Performance is measured against the metrics on a regular basis and the standards reports are constantly reused.
- Report generation is partly automated, but heavy involvement of analysts is required to get the data, and an online dashboard is not available.

Level 3: Defined

- Corporate principles, policies, processes and tools are implemented. Corporate-level performance metrics and standard reports are established and aligned with those of business units.
- Reporting is semi-automated, but human involvement is still required for ad hoc, as well as standard report generation.
- The reporting tools have comprehensive functionalities, including an online dashboard and sophisticated data manipulation.
- The reports are predominantly pre-defined and batch-based, but data shows the past, not the present.

Level 4: Optimized

- Data quality of the report has significantly improved due to improvement in seamless and automated data capture.
- The capability shows current performance based on real-time reporting.

- Report generation and delivery is highly automated and little manual work is involved in data retrieval and report generation.
- Many customized reports are designed and created by end-users.
- Source data from the dashboard and reports can be tracked to a certain degree.

Level 5: Progressive

- Any report can be designed and created by end-users, with little involvement of IT staff.
- The Reporting & Dashboard capability is integrated seamlessly with the front-office capabilities as well as the Digital Intelligence capabilities, so that source data can be tracked easily, and the reasons for low performance may be identified.
- The Digital Planning capability is integrated to the Reporting & Dashboard capability seamlessly, resulting in many decisions on strategic digital planning being based on the dashboard and reports.

MEGA CAPABILITY 9.

DIGITAL DATA MANAGEMENT

Digital Data Management is a set of digital capabilities used to collect, store, distribute, control and search data that is used for all the Digital Capabilities. The data used in the Digital Capabilities includes master data, reference data, metadata, transactional data and analytical data.

The data used in digital transactions differs from the data used in traditional transactions in many ways. A significant amount of the data used in digital transactions is not in a structured format, and relational database and SQL (Structured Query Language), which have been around for more than three decades, is therefore no longer effective to manage the un-structured and semi-structured data generated from digital transactions. This is where a non-relational database, or NoSQL, technologies come in.

The amount of un-structured and semi-structured data generated from digital transactions poses a challenge for traditional data warehousing architecture in particular. It has such a massive volume that traditional data warehousing systems can't scale enough to keep up with the ever-increasing data volume. Digital

Data Management can address the challenge by introducing a new data store architecture.

Digital Data Management should also address the challenge of searching through the massive amount of un-structured or semi-structured data for information that users want.

We will look at the following digital capabilities sitting under Digital Data Management:

- Non-relational Data Management
- Distributed Data Store Management
- Enterprise Search
- Master Data Management
- Data Quality Management
- Data Policy Management

CAPABILITY 9-1.
NON-RELATIONAL DATA MANAGEMENT

CAPABILITY DEFINITION

Non-relational Data Management is a digital capability used to store and retrieve a massive amount of un-structured and semi-structured data coming from many sources, such as social listening, web logs, interactions on digital touchpoints and even digital sensor activities.

This digital capability gives database design simplicity, easy scaling, and high performance and availability compared to relational data management when dealing with a massive amount of un-structured and semi-structured data.

Disadvantage of SQL & Relational Data

Relational data models and SQL (Structured Query Language) have been the de facto standard for complex queries for transactional, structured and normalized data. It is however difficult and costly for relational databases and SQL to handle widely distributed and ever changing, un-structured and semi-structure data. This limitation causes negative impacts on availability and performance when manipulating both type of data sets.

NoSQL & Non-Relational Data

A NoSQL database provides a mechanism where data modelled in ways other than relational modelling, is stored and retrieved. It employs an approach that does not enforce a complex data schema, but brings the potential of high scalability.

Common approaches to a NoSQL database includes Key-Value stores, Columnar stores, Document databases and Graph databases.

Key-Value stores are the simplest non-relational model. A key is a unique identifier for an item of data, while a value is either the data that is identified, or a pointer to the location of that data, e.g. Key= Gender, Value = Male.

Columnar stores are more than Key-Value stores in that a key holds multiple properties, and each property can have a value e.g, Key = Name, Property = First Name, Value = Jace. Columnar stores give a certain level of structure to access data in the same columns. They don't however support the full feature set of a relational database. They use tables, rows and columns, but unlike a relational database, the names of column key and property, and format of the columns can vary from row to row in the same table. Google's BigTable, Amazon's Dynamo and Facebook's Cassandra are examples of Columnar stores.

Document databases are semi-structured rather than un-structured, providing some degree of structure. Using formats such as XML (eXtensible Markup Language) and JSON [29] (JavaScript Object Notation), each record of data may have different sets of data fields that can be determined by the application.

We can give the flexibility of a non-relational data model to a consistent, but rigid relational data model by combining NoSQL with SQL. Combining a JSON document with a CRM system can for example add non-relational but rich information from JSON into the CRM that the relational data model of the CRM application would not create or store otherwise.

---

[29] JSON is a human-readable text file format that uses JavaScript syntax to organize data attributes and values that can for example be used to contain the non-relational (key value) data. It is frequently used for easier data exchange between a server and a client program in the digital environment.

MATURITY INDICATOR EXAMPLES

Level 0: Non-existent

- NoSQL has never been tested.

Level 1: Ad hoc

- NoSQL has been tested to assess the feasibility of introducing it into the digital environment. A pilot system for a non-relational database management has been introduced, but there is no further plan to expand.

Level 2: Basic

- A simple form of NoSQL has been introduced as a quick fix. Un-structured or semi-structured data is constantly captured from such data sources as social websites, and stored in a NoSQL database. The data is however not retrieved for analysis on a regular basis.

Level 3: Defined

- The purpose and limitation of NoSQL database are fully understood, and NoSQL is officially introduced as a corporate-level strategic initiative.
- NoSQL design processes, tools and frameworks, and skilled developers are implemented.
- Stored non-relational data is retrieved and analysed on a regular basis, but business does not understand use cases of the analysis clearly.

Level 4: Optimized

- The capability has been optimized to the point where practical use cases are identified in the context of the organization, e.g. personalization analysis may require much demographic, contextual and behavioural data, and the relational database cannot cope with the volume of data.

- Different analysis models and architectures are developed for different business use cases.
- The semi-structured data has achieved higher consistency, while maintaining increased levels of availability and performance.

Level 5: Progressive

- The organization has successfully combined the advantages of both NoSQL databases and SQL databases, and both databases are well balanced to meet business needs of the combined data, adding rich NoSQL data on top of highly consistent SQL data.
- The capability is fully integrated with Digital capabilities such as Big Data analytics, Web Analytics, and customer & product analytics for them to take advantage of the massive amount of non-relational data.

CAPABILITY 9-2.
DISTRIBUTED DATA STORE MANAGEMENT

CAPABILITY DEFINITION

Distributed Data Store Management is a digital capability used to store non-relational data as well as relational data into memory-based or disk-based storage in such a way that the stored data is accessed and used by the front, middle, and back-office capabilities effectively and efficiently.

In other words, the capability should address the challenges arising from the fact that the data generated from digital transactions is massive in amount, unstructured or semi-structured in format, and highly distributed in the transaction environment.

The massive data should be stored in the memory layer or the persistent storage layer. As part of the efforts to address the challenge of massive data, an In-Memory Database architecture catering for high throughput and low latency has been evolving to store and process the massive data.

Distributed cache and file systems have been gaining momentum to address the challenges of storing and processing massive data.

Distributed Cache System

For the digital transactions in the front-office and middle-office, response times will be correlated directly to query latency. Access to data in memory is much faster than to that in disk storage, and there is therefore a strong incentive to store data in memory.

Specialized software is required to implement a pool of shared memory in a highly distributed environment such as the contemporary Digital environment. Memcached and Redis are examples of popular solutions to implement distributed caches. Memcached is for example used to cluster memory caches and implement a hash table distributed across multiple server machines. A hash table is a data structure that can map keys to values. A hash table is accessed with simple functions using a unique key to retrieve a corresponding value.

An In-Memory Data Grid (IMDG) is an advanced version of a distributed cache system for non-relational data, with some data processing functions embedded in the software.

Distributed File System

When a system fails, data in memory is lost. Critical data needs to be stored in data storage that supports persistence, such as file system. The file system needs to be scalable enough to accommodate the massive amount of unstructured or semi-structured data.

A distributed file system is used to store a large amount of data distributed across multiple server machines in a highly distributed environment, with each server having a set of inexpensive internal disk drives.

A distribute file system stores data reliably even when failures occur. Data availability is achieved by replicating the data across multiple nodes. Member nodes check the heartbeat of the other member nodes and communicate with one another to re-balance the data to ensure the data is as redundant as planned. There is therefore no need for additional hardware or software redundancy architecture such as expensive RAID[30] (Redundant Array of Independent Disks) systems, while a single point of failure can be minimized.

The Hadoop Distributed File System (HDFS) is one of the most popular distributed file systems. It stores large files across multiple machines that collectively represent a cluster of nodes, each of which feed data over the distributed network.

Data Lake

In the digital age, organizations commonly have both relational data and non-relational data in the back-office, and both are stored in a separate store architecture. A data lake is an architecture style used to accommodate both types of data in a single store.

A data lake is a logically centralized data repository and its tools used to populate processes and retrieve the data. The repository holds a vast amount of data populated from a wide variety of data sources, including unstructured or semi-structured data generated from digital channels. It also contains analytical data from data warehouses and operational data from ERP and CRM.

---

[30] RAID is an architecture that keeps data redundant across multiple storages, or establishes a data restoration mechanism in order to recover lost data, or increase data access performance.

A distributed file system can be used to implement storage for a data store architecture supporting data lake architecture.

MATURITY INDICATOR EXAMPLES

Level 0: Non-existent

- The storage architecture does not support distributed data processing environments.
- Neither distributed cache systems, nor distributed file systems have been tested.

Level 1: Ad hoc

- In-memory data access is available on a single machine and data in memory is not shared across multiple machines.
- A distributed cache system may have been tested, while a distributed file system has been tested and a pilot system implemented.

Level 2: Basic

- A distributed cache system is introduced, but not widely used across the organization. This is partly because the digital transaction environments are not highly distributed and there is a lack of understanding of use cases for the digital business.
- A distributed file system is implemented and a range of non-relational data has been populated and stored. The data storage is however becoming a data swamp where the massive amount of data keeps stacking up, as it is not used actively by business, nor properly cleansed.

Level 3: Defined

- A distributed cache and a distributed file system have been implemented as part of corporate-level strategic initiatives.

- The purpose, use cases, policies and standards of using the systems are clearly defined and agreed across the organization.
- The distributed file systems are used to gather all different data sources into a logically centralized repository. The data is organized as required by the business use cases, but data governance and meta-data management is not as mature as the existing data warehouse.

Level 4: Optimized

- The development policies and standards of the distributed cache system are well enforced, so that many digital applications take advantage of the distributed cache architecture, increasing performance of database transactions significantly in the highly distributed environment.
- Data governance is enforced and meta-data is well maintained so that the quality of un-structured and semi-structured data in the data lake has been optimized.

Level 5: Progressive

- Un-structured and semi-structured databases are integrated seamlessly with structured databases. This enables business to combine correlation analysis of unstructured and semi-structured data with dimensional analysis of structured data, thereby improving analytical insights significantly.
- The data lake lays the foundation for back-office analytical capabilities to produce meaningful business insights. It also integrates to the front and middle-office capabilities to find source data readily. This helps the business community to depend on the data lake more than on the traditional data warehouse for strategic business decisions.

CAPABILITY 9-3.
ENTERPRISE SEARCH

CAPABILITY DEFINITION

Enterprise Search is a digital capability to enable users to locate the content or information they want quickly and accurately, through keyword search into a variety of sources, such as file system, intranet, content repository, e-mail, database, data warehouse and/or data lake.

Before the contemporary digital area, the Enterprise Search capability was focused on searching through structured data stored in relational databases. Now the challenge is to search a massive amount of data with little-to-no structure; mostly textual information without any pre-defined format or layout.

[Figure 38: Microsoft SharePoint Enterprise Search]

Inverted Indexing

A contemporary Enterprise Search system can analyse documents in different formats and then create an inverted index data structure, storing mapping of content to its location in a database file. The purpose of an inverted index is to allow full text search as fast as possible.

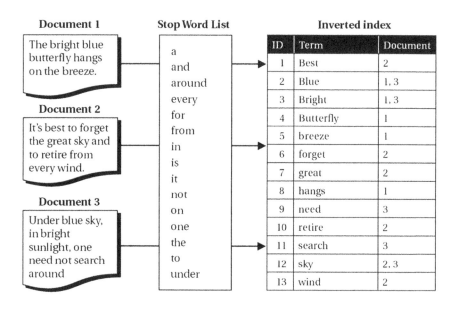

[Figure 39: Inverted Indexing]

Content Classification

Content Classification by topic allows users to navigate the content by topics, rather than only by metadata. Traditional enterprise search-engine software relies heavily on metadata when it groups search results. This approach caused many problems of inaccurate search results, resulting from incompatible and inconsistent metadata across multiple enterprise repositories.

Named-entity recognition functionality, also known as entity identification, of an Enterprise Search system can locate, identify, and classify named entities in text into pre-defined topics, such as the names of persons, organizations, locations, expressions of times, quantities, monetary values, percentages and many others.

Text clustering functionality of an Enterprise Search system can also group the search results into useful topics, by computing the search result descriptions on the fly. The topics may represent titles, excerpts, snippets and metadata.

Tagging & bookmarking functionality of an Enterprise Search system enable users to add social tags or bookmarks to capture knowledge across structured, semi-structured and un-structured enterprise data. The social tags or bookmarks can be utilized as topics when organizing search results.

MATURITY INDICATOR EXAMPLES

Level 0: Non-existent

- No search software specialized in keyword search exists.
- Keyword search by file name is supported. Other than that, there is no further enterprise search capability implemented.

Level 1: Ad hoc

- Simple keyword search software is implemented and used to perform search through relational databases, or metadata of content management systems.
- Software used to search un-structured and semi-structured data has been tested to assess the feasibility.

Level 2: Basic

- A basic commercial or open-source based Enterprise Search system has been deployed for some end users.
- Search results are not as accurate as the users expect, due to lack of data quality management and limited functionality of the system, such as limited connectivity and federated

search into multiple content sources, limited indexing functionality, and limited content classification functionality.

Level 3: Defined

- A data governance structure has been implemented to manage the quality of the search index data.
- The Enterprise Search system demonstrates rich functionalities in searching data with un-structured and semi-structured format.
- Search is limited to the content sources with un-structured and semi-structured data, and the system does not allow users to navigate the search results by customized topics familiar to an individual user.

Level 4: Optimized

- The topics used for content classification have been optimized by the robust data governance structure and data quality management.
- Even when a search query generates too many search results, the optimized search topics allow users to navigate through the search results easily for the data they are looking for.

Level 5: Progressive

- Search analytics is applied to Enterprise Search practice so that user search behaviours are analysed, and topics, taxonomy and indexes are updated accordingly.
- Almost all data sources and repositories within the organization are in the scope of search index, regardless of whether it is in structured, semi-structured, or un-structured format, so that users can search into almost all data within their environments.

CAPABILITY 9-4.
MASTER DATA MANAGEMENT

CAPABILITY DEFINITION

Master data represents critical business objects, such as customers, products, suppliers, sales, divisions, costs and many other business entities of the organization.

Master data is non-transactional, static data used to create transactional data. Customer data and product data, which are master data, are for example used to create a customer order, which is transactional data. Customer order data would have a product code and name, quantity of the product ordered, customer name, delivery address, etc. Most of the data fields on a customer order are captured from customer and product master data, while very few data fields are created by customer key-in.

Without rich master data, rich transactional data is not possible, which leads to poor analytical data. Master data is therefore at the core of all enterprise data.

Master Data Management (MDM) is a digital capability used to collect, aggregate, match, consolidate, quality-assure, persist and distribute master data, to ensure consistency in data use by different digital applications.

Master Data Management has been around as a critical component for data integration even before the contemporary digital age began. It has helped the organization identify and manage the same business entities of different systems in a consistent way. They could for example identify the same customer in different systems and serve the customer across the different systems seamlessly.

In the digital age, Master Data Management is becoming even more challenging because different master data of the same business entities is proliferating in new digital channels, new devices, social websites, and SaaS[31] applications, as well as traditional internal systems. Master data should therefore be integrated or consolidated more actively across the organization to function as master data properly.

Unfortunately, this is not the case in many organizations. Product data used on social media is for example not necessarily identified in the trusted product master data that is used by marketing, sales, customer services and finance departments. This can lead to inconsistent customer communication that can actually undermine sales or customer services.

Big Data, Customer Insight, and Customer Segmentation capabilities may be able to produce plenty of insights into a customer. Without knowing exactly who the customer is in the trusted customer master data, the insights can however not be used for social interaction, or digital marketing in the front-office.

Customer data and product data are the most important master data of all. Any organization can establish an effective Master Data Management capability by defining a standard customer and product data model, and consolidating all enterprise data similar to these into the centralized, standard customer and product data models. With proper access control to the master data and regular data cleansing activities, the robust foundation for Master Data Management required for digital business will be in place.

MATURITY INDICATOR EXAMPLES

Level 0: Non-existent

- Different applications have different definitions and scope of master data. Enterprise-wide master data is not defined.

---

[31] SaaS (Software as a Service) is a software delivery model where software, including business applications, is provided on the Cloud by a Cloud service provider. An enterprise or individual person uses the software without owning it.

- The importance of MDM to the digital business is not acknowledged by digital practitioners in the organization.

Level 1: Ad hoc

- Master data is managed, responding to operational issues and first awareness of issues resulting from lack of MDM has been raised on an operational level.
- A pilot system has been implemented to tackle the issues resulting from master data that is not integrated.
- No tool specialized in MDM is implemented.

Level 2: Basic

- Master data is defined and managed by each business unit that wants to solve its own problem and the definition and scope of master data is therefore not consistent across the organization.
- A MDM tool is introduced, but its functionalities are limited.
- An Enterprise-wide master-data governance structure is not established.

Level 3: Defined

- An Enterprise-wide standard definition and scope of master data has been established for master data, reference data and code data, as well as their usage and difference from transactional data.
- Corporate-level master-data governance processes, a dedicated MDM team and MDM tools are implemented.
- All core business objects are managed as enterprise master data, but there are still inconsistencies in master data quality.
- Non-relational data is not integrated with enterprise master data.

Level 4: Optimized

- The core business objects are managed as master data and are widely consistent across the organization.
- More business objects start to be included and managed as master data.
- Business objects from un-structured or semi-structured data started to be identified and integrated with the enterprise master data.
- MDM has enterprise-wide impact and business has ownership and stewardship of the master data. The owner and steward have KPIs to maintain high quality data.

Level 5: Progressive

- The MDM capability is integrated with Digital Intelligence capabilities so that master data is used as an analysis dimensions for data analytics.
- Master data is fully integrated with un-structured or semi-structure data, and is used to integrate structured data with un-structured and semi-structured data, creating synergy.

CAPABILITY 9-5.
DATA QUALITY MANAGEMENT

CAPABILITY DEFINITION

Data Quality Management is a digital capability used to ensure that data is complete, correct, accurate and relevant throughout its lifecycle. It involves profiling data, establishing quality metrics and targets, designing quality rules, implementing data quality processes and IT system, reviewing exceptions, monitoring quality and cleansing data.

Data Quality Management has been a discipline commonly applied to structured data within organizations, but quality-management initiatives for un-structured data are far less common. The effect of poor quality un-structured or semi-structured data can however also be profound. Poor data quality is one of the leading causes of failure or underperformance in Digital Intelligence capabilities.

Quality Measure Criteria

Data quality can be measured against completeness, accuracy, consistency, timeliness, uniqueness and interoperability.

- **Completeness** measures whether all the data required to perform a business process or generate a report is available.
- **Accuracy** measures whether the source data held is verified as correct and up-to-date, and how close the content of target data compared to source data is after the source data is captured and converted to the target data.
- **Consistency** measures whether the data held is the same in its definition, business rules, format and value, at any time or place, across channels and departments.
- **Timeliness** measures whether the data is made available in a reasonable period.
- **Uniqueness** measures whether the data (e.g. a customer) is recorded once, and once only.
- **Interoperability** measures whether the data coding complies as much as possible with agreed standards such as ISO, to facilitate data exchanges.

Quality Management Activities

As an initial step, data needs to be profiled to measure its quality. Data profiling is the systematic analysis of data to gather actionable and measurable information about its quality. Information gathered from data profiling activities is used to assess the overall health of the data and determine the direction of initiatives to improve data quality.

Data cleansing is the process of detecting and correcting erroneous data and data anomalies, both within and across systems. Data cleansing can take place in both real-time as data is entered, or afterwards as part of a data cleansing initiative.

Data monitoring is the automated and manual processes performed to evaluate the condition of an enterprise's data continuously. Information obtained from data monitoring activities is used to develop data-quality improvement initiatives.

Data compliance is the ongoing processes to ensure adherence of data to both internal enterprise business rules, and external legal and regulatory requirements.

MATURITY INDICATOR EXAMPLES

Level 0: Non-existent

- Data is corrected and fixes are applied only when significant problems are caused by poor data quality. There is however no operational capability to monitor and assess data quality, and establish and execute initiatives to improve data quality.

Level 1: Ad hoc

- Data is assessed against accuracy, and inaccurate data is cleansed on an ad hoc basis. Most of the effort is spent by reacting to urgent issues with quick fixes that will most likely not address any long-term improvement in data quality.
- Data Quality Management is mostly a manual process with little automation. It is challenging to trace flawed data back to the source.
- The ad hoc experience is not shared, and this limits the ability to repeat successes.

Level 2: Basic

- Data quality is assessed on a regular basis against pre-defined data quality metrics, with some practices shared to replicate good practices.
- Data profile analysis and data cleaning are performed as part of Data Quality Management.
- The rate of adoption of the Data Quality Management practices varies across different business units.
- Some data management tools specialized in data profiling, data quality monitoring, or data cleansing are implemented to automate the processes, but the functionalities of the tools are limited.

Level 3: Defined

- An Enterprise-wide Data Quality Management framework, principles, policies, quality metrics, management processes, roles and responsibilities, and specialized tools are established and enforced across the organization consistently.
- The practices include data profiling, data cleansing, data monitoring, data compliance, data quality assurance and data quality governance.
- A wide range of Data Quality Management tools is deployed and their functionalities are comprehensive enough to automate many processes of Data Quality Management.

Level 4: Optimized

- Measuring data quality against the metrics is highly automated with limited human intervention, and highly optimized to the extent that the business impact of the data quality can be assessed.
- It is much easier to trace flawed data back to sources, determine the root cause of the flawed data, and fix the problems, thereby preventing the reoccurrence of the same issues.

- Data quality is managed proactively with data issues identified early in the information workflow.
- Overall data quality against the metrics is consistent and predictable.

Level 5: Progressive

- Data quality is managed in a preventive manner. Data quality is for example checked and managed when data is created and updated. Controls for data validation are integrated into business processes.
- Data quality is highly consistent across structured, semi-structured and un-structured data, and across the front-office, middle-office and back-office capabilities.
- The opportunities for incremental quality improvements can be identified through the well-organized data-quality governance structure.

CAPABILITY 9-6.
DIGITAL DATA POLICY MANAGEMENT

CAPABILITY DEFINITION

Digital Data Policy Management is a digital capability used to create and update policies, standards, procedures and guidelines on creating, updating, retrieving, maintaining, archiving and deleting enterprise digital data, including master data, reference data, code data, transactional data and analytical data, to ensure the data is consistent, secure and compliant with internal control policies, and external laws and regulations.

Before the contemporary digital era, data was generated by, and mostly used within an organization, which is a controlled environment. The majority of users were employees and internal staff, and they mostly consumed the data.

In the digital age, a massive amount of semi-structured and un-structured data is generated and used outside an organization, due to social and mobile trends. The majority of users are customers and prospects, and they are both the providers and consumers of the data.

For this reason, the data needs to be generated, used, shared, stored and deleted in a way that not only creates new business value, but also protects existing business value, highlighting the importance of a data policy.

Data Policy documents commonly include policies, standards and procedures around the enterprise data scope, responsibilities for data management, and data life cycle management, from data creation to data deletion, data security, policy breaches, etc.

MATURITY INDICATOR EXAMPLES

Level 0: Non-existent

- Data policies may have been established, but the policies have nothing to do with data usage and management in the digital space.

Level 1: Ad hoc

- Some of the data policies can be applied to Digital Data Management, but the policies are not relevant because they are outdated.
- Users inside and outside the organization are unaware of the existence of the policies.

Level 2: Basic

- Some data policies on Digital Data Management have been developed and published to digital users to be compliant, not only to regulatory requirements, but also to internal control and security.
- The policies are neither comprehensive, nor in-depth.
- Users are aware of the existence of the policies, but the policies are not well communicated or enforced.

Level 3: Defined

- Corporate-level policies, standards, procedures and guidelines are implemented for the organization to comply with internal controls and external regulations fully.
- The policies are updated regularly and maintained by a team responsible for the policies.
- Compliance processes are established to ensure the policies are followed.

Level 4: Optimized

- Business risk of data creation and usage in the digital environments are well identified and included in the data policies, standards, guidelines and procedures to mitigate business risk, and thus preserve business value.
- The policies are well enforced due to matured compliance structure and continuous education and communication with internal and external users.

Level 5: Progressive

- The comprehensive data policies, standards, guidelines, procedures and compliances work as a tool for increasing business value, e.g. a few data policies are used as a marketing promotion message to increase sales.

MEGA CAPABILITY 10.

DIGITAL INFRASTRUCTURE MANAGEMENT

Digital Infrastructure Management is a set of digital capabilities used to provide reusable, standard and inexpensive infrastructure services that other Digital Capabilities consume.

The scope of digital infrastructure encompasses hardware infrastructure services such as server, storage and network, and technical software services such as application integration services, web presentation services and security services.

The purpose of Digital Infrastructure Management is to support unpredictable, massive transactional processing and big data analytical processing.

The proven practices for Cloud computing architecture patterns lay the foundation for Digital Infrastructure Services. This book does not cover all components of Cloud architecture, but focuses on essential infrastructure components used by the other digital capabilities.

Digital Infrastructure Management has the following capabilities:

- On-Demand Provisioning Services
- User Interaction Services
- Process Integration Services
- Parallel Processing Services
- Federated Access Management
- Digital Continuity Management

CAPABILITY 10-1.
ON-DEMAND PROVISIONING SERVICES

CAPABILITY DEFINITION

On-Demand Provisioning Services is a digital capability to scale up and down[32] or scale in and out[33] automatically when required, so that IT administrators, or the IT system itself can dynamically provision or de-provision application and infrastructure resources as requested.

In the digital environment, computational workload and computing resource usage are getting less predictable than ever before. Resource capacity and availability management should be prepared for an unpredictable surge in demand.

Dynamic Scaling

The dynamic scaling is to monitor current IT service levels and increase or decrease computing resources automatically to meet service levels for performance and availability at the lowest possible cost.

The dynamic scaling of resources commonly requires three technical services:

---

[32] When infrastructure scales up and down, it scales 'vertically' by adding or removing components within the single infrastructure unit, e.g. adding a CPU in a hardware machine. It requires high-end complex infrastructure to scale vertically. It was a common way of scaling infrastructure before the digital age.

[33] When infrastructure scales in and out, it scales 'horizontally' by adding or removing infrastructure units into the logical infrastructure pool, e.g. adding a physical machine into the logical server pool. It is considered the most effective way to implement Cloud architecture because it does not require expensive infrastructure to scale.

- **Monitoring Services**: to monitor service levels, meter resource usage and deliver monitoring results to the Optimization Services.

- **Optimization Services**: to analyse current service levels and resource usage against service policies in the policies database, come up with resource optimization plans and deliver the plans to the Provisioning Services.

- **Provisioning services**: to implement the optimization plans by provisioning or de-provisioning resources.

Below is how Monitoring Services, Optimization Services and Provisioning Services share responsibilities to perform dynamic scaling in an enterprise environment.

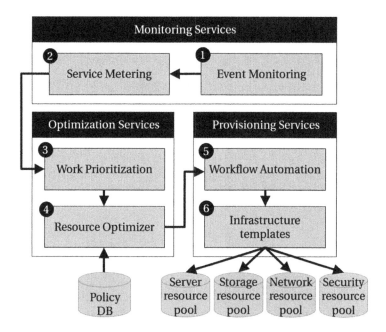

[Figure 40: Dynamic Scaling Architecture]

1. Event Monitoring monitors resources and reports monitoring results to Service Metering.

2. Service Metering analyses service levels achieved, and alerts Optimization Services of breaches in thresholds of service levels.

3. Work Prioritization prioritizes optimization works to improve service levels at minimum costs and informs Resource Optimizer.

4. Resource Optimizer develops resource optimization plans as prioritized based on business policies and rules.

5. Workflow Automation executes the optimization plans by provisioning, deprovisioning and repurposing resources.

6. Pre-defined templates are used by Workflow Automation to configure the multiple resource types dynamically.

Monitoring Services

The Monitoring Services are used to monitor and meter current service levels, and deliver monitoring and metering results to the Optimization Services.

The Monitoring Services monitor whether service level objectives are being met, service level thresholds are breached, and service incidents are occurring. The Monitoring Services also meter resource usage for delivering the current service levels and returns the information to the Optimization Services.

Optimization Services

The Optimization Services are used to decide whether the current capacity needs to be adjusted and, if so, to plan how much resource needs to be added or removed so that service level objectives are met at the lowest possible cost. When an optimization decision is made, the Optimization Services activate the Provisioning Services responsible for the implementation of resource provisioning and de-provisioning.

The Optimization Services consume the information provided by the Monitoring Services to identify the current state of service levels and resource usage. The Optimization Services then refer to the policy database that contains business rules, including service level objectives, thresholds and actions to be taken when the thresholds are breached.

The Optimization Services also calculate the cost of failure to prioritize service level objectives, depending on service impact and cost, and determine actions to optimize resources. Both the current state from the Monitoring Services and the decision-making rules from the policy databases are key inputs for the Optimization Services to make proper decisions.

After the Optimization Services make an optimization decision, the decision is delivered to the Provisioning Services to implement the decision by using automated workflows.

The Optimization Services may be configured to make a recommendation to a system administrator, instead of activating the Provisioning Services directly, so that human operators can intervene to make a final decision on resource optimization when necessary.

Provisioning Services

The Provisioning Services are used to provision or de-provision resources automatically according to the decisions made by the Optimization Services. The automation of scaling processes aims to replace routine, error prone, and time sensitive processes commonly performed by human operators.

The Provisioning Services have end-to-end provisioning or de-provisioning processes that consists of a series of independent workflows. A workflow contains many steps to provision services such as security, network, storage, server bare-metal and OS provisioning, and application deployment.

Each provisioning workflow can be implemented in several ways.

The Image-based provisioning approach is to create and use an image or snapshot of a known configuration or build as the basis for creating a new instance of the resources. The images can be stored on storage for rapid cloning. Image-based provisioning is the fastest option, especially in the unpredictable digital environment.

The Script-based provisioning approach is to use many existing functionalities of Command Line Interface (CLI)[34] programs. A built-in command line interface of infrastructure components, such as network and storage equipment, can be used for configuration. CLI enabled tools specific to an OS or infrastructure product can be used.

Script-based provisioning takes a more fine-grained approach so that each provisioning can be more customized than Image-based provisioning, which is more suitable for a standardized environment. An approach that combines Script-based provision and Image-based provisioning can be used for the Provisioning Services.

In order to enable heterogeneous infrastructure provisioning, a workflow-based provisioning tool is required. There are a number of GUI-based provisioning solutions available in the market. The aim is to create a number of workflows, one or more workflows for each technology deployed, which includes the set of dependent image or script-based provisioning tasks to create, modify and de-provision services.

Cloud Bursting

Cloud Bursting is another form of dynamic scaling. It is referred to as an automatic scaling of Cloud resources to redirect the traffic

---

[34] Common Line Interface (CLI) is a means of interacting with a computer program where a system user keys in commands to the program in the form of successive lines of text. Graphic User Interface (GUI) is a graphical representation in which a user can interact with a computer program through graphical icons and menus.

that overflows from an on-premises data centre to a public Cloud or Virtual Private Cloud, so that there is no interruption of services.

Cloud Bursting is suitable to ensure high performance of an application that handles non-critical transactions and non-sensitive information. A non-critical application can be deployed locally and then burst to the cloud to meet peak demands, or the non-critical application can be moved to the public cloud to free up local resources for mission-critical applications.

Cloud Bursting is the most challenging form of dynamic scaling due to its complex implementation. In order to redirect traffic successfully, a threshold for triggering re-direction of traffic should be defined, the same configuration and environments of the on-premises data centre should be replicated to the public Cloud, and on-premises data required for the transactions should be replicated to the public Cloud. The concept of dynamic porting of workloads between an on-premises data centre and a public Cloud has been around for quite a while, but the challenges have yet to be addressed for Cloud Bursting to be on the agenda of many enterprises.

MATURITY INDICATOR EXAMPLES

Level 0: Non-existent

- A small part of the infrastructure is virtualized and infrastructure resource utilization may be monitored.
- Provisioning of infrastructure is performed only by system administrators and on-demand, but automatic provisioning is not supported.

Level 1: Ad hoc

- A moderate portion of the infrastructure is virtualized and the utilization of the virtualized infrastructure are monitored on a regular basis.

- Automated provisioning has been tested for feasibility to help system administrators perform provisioning processes, but provisioning of infrastructure is performed manually by system administrators.
- Neither resource usage metering, nor resource optimization planning is implemented.

Level 2: Basic

- Infrastructure is highly virtualized into a logical resource pool.
- The usage of infrastructure is constantly monitored automatically, but actual service level achieved is not measured against service level objectives.
- When there is a request for infrastructure provisioning from users or developers, system administrators can use provisioning tools to automate some of provisioning processes to reduce the time to fulfil the requests significantly. The end-to-end provisioning processes are however not entirely automated.
- Resource optimization planning and decision-making are performed by system administrators without help from a resource optimization engine.

Level 3: Defined

- End-to-end resource provisioning processes are defined and many of the processes are automated by multiple tools.
- Infrastructure resources are virtualized into enterprise resource pools, and dynamic resource allocation from the resource pools is implemented.
- Current service levels and resource usage are monitored (near) real time. When a service level is about to be breached, the system administrator is informed of the event.
- The functioning of the Optimization engine is limited because the policies around dynamic scaling are not clearly defined, and thus system administrators are responsible for

coming up with optimization plans and making optimization decisions.

- Users and developers can request resource provisioning online and the requests are fulfilled by system administrators with help from provisioning automation tools.

Level 4: Optimized

- Horizontal scaling - scaling in and out - architecture is established as an enterprise standard, but vertical scaling - scaling up and own - architecture still has a large footprint.
- The majority of resource provisioning processes are automated by seamless integration of the Monitoring Services, the Optimization Services and the Provisioning Services.
- Service levels and resource usage are not only monitored, but also metered so that the metered usage and service level metrics are rated by the Optimization engine.
- The functionality of the Optimization engine is optimized enough to prioritize multiple service level objectives against the importance of the service and its corresponding cost.
- The policy database provides service level objectives (SLO) [35] , thresholds, actions to achieve the SLOs, and corresponding costs that are required for the Optimization engine to make an optimization decision.
- Cloud bursting has been tested and implemented for a pilot system to assess feasibility of technical implementation, but commercial terms of public Cloud pose challenges for introduction of Cloud bursting.

---

[35] A Service Level Objective (SLO) is an element of a service level agreement (SLA). A SLO is a means of measuring the performance of a service level delivered, e.g. "The availability SLO is 99.95%".

- Users or developers can automatically provision application and infrastructure resources in real-time on a self-service portal, without human intervention.

Level 5: Progressive

- Infrastructure is highly standardized and commoditized, and horizontal scaling is the predominant architecture.
- A utility-based metering, accounting and billing model is well established across the organization, and drives the entire on-demand provisioning of applications and infrastructure resources. The utility financial model combined with the Cloud computing model deliver optimized infrastructure services for the digital business.
- The Optimization engine has full control over the provisioning process workflows necessary to achieve service requirements automatically.
- Preventive operations that prevent IT services from being breached are integrated with the On-demand Provisioning capabilities, e.g. the capacity automatically increases before a service level is breached.

CAPABILITY 10-2.
USER INTERACTION SERVICES

CAPABILITY DEFINITION

User Interaction Services is a digital capability used to support interaction between users and digital applications, and communication and collaboration between users. User Interaction Services are responsible for delivering business functionalities of the digital capabilities in the front, middle and back-offices to users, and exposing the business functionalities as user interfaces on end-user devices.

User Interaction Services have frequently been referred to as presentation Logic by the layered or multi-tier architecture paradigm. The digital environment has posed a few new challenges for the traditional User Interaction services to transform to a digital capability.

Firstly, there are too many different digital device platforms. The ever-increasing and ever-evolving end-user digital devices have been creating different software platforms and hardware features that require different programming Logic for interfaces with users, and for communication with server-side digital applications, making digital practitioners' jobs even harder.

Secondly, digital transactions require real-time, dynamic changes of content on digital devices. Before the contemporary digital era, data was less frequently created or updated. Now, social websites are a prime example to see how frequently data is created or updated. Digital content needs to be delivered to digital devices as soon as it is created or changed.

A few architecture concepts of User Interaction Services will be examined to help address those challenges to better support interactions with digital users.

App Development Approach

Digital applications and infrastructure are built predominantly on standard technologies and commodity platforms, because the massive amount of digital transactions and data cannot be supported by the previous architecture and its cost structure. This is why all digital development should be based on Internet standards.

Most desktop applications are taking advantage of Internet standards to support digital transactions successfully, with a reasonable level of total cost of ownership. Mobile applications however, have not been moving fast enough toward using the standard technologies, because mobile apps need to tap into unique hardware features to provide improved customer experiences. This requires mobile app development to lean on the proprietary platforms and technologies, significantly compromising reusability of the presentation Logic.

There are three approaches to developing a mobile app: Web, Native and Hybrid.

- **Web approach**: to use standard Internet technologies only, such as HTML, CSS and JavaScript, along with server-side interpreting languages. HTML is used to manage the foundational structure of an HTML document and CSS determines how the HTML document is presented in terms of designs, layout, formatting, etc., while JavaScript manages dynamic actions and behaviours of an HTML document.

- **Native approach**: to develop mobile apps through different programming languages, runtimes and platforms, e.g. such OS-specific technologies as Objective-C with iOS, Java with Android, and C# with Windows.

- **Hybrid approach**: to combine both the Web and Native approaches.

App developers are commonly advised to choose a different approach depending on requirements, because each approach has its own advantages and disadvantages. The Web approach is for example cheap to develop and maintain, but cannot make full use of mobile hardware functionalities, whereas the Native approach can use all hardware features and thus provide improved customer experiences, but is the most expensive.

When the Native app development option is chosen, Controller components of the MVC (Model-View-Controller) model, as well as View components commonly reside on the device as part of a Native app, while Model components are also often incorporated into a Native app. This compromises the reusability of presentation Logic on the binary code level significantly.

As the Web approach works best when manipulating document type presentations that we are quite familiar with, while the Native approach works best when dealing with input from and output to mobile devices, the Hybrid approach may be the right one for many organizations, as it can combine advantages from both approaches effectively for synergy.

The concept of the Hybrid approach is to wrap a mobile-optimized Web app with a device-specific Native app. The Native app hosts a web browser controller that monitors URLs being requested by a user. When the user requests an URL that requires a native device functionality, the web browser controller invokes the native device functionality. When the native functionality completes, the Native app brings the web browser controller back into the appropriate location.

With the advent of HTML 5, the Hybrid approach has become even more popular, as HTML 5 helps meet digital transaction needs by filling much of the functional gap that exists. The current location of a mobile user can for example be obtained by using a simple function from HTML 5. HTML 5 also allows multimedia and graphical content to be readily integrated with static HTML documents, to meet the needs of digital media content. There are many reasons to recommend Hybrid app development as a standard approach to mobile app development for large organizations, as it will allow MVC architecture to be more easily implemented in presentation Logic layer.

The Native app approach will continue to be employed for use cases of non-document type mobile presentation, such as a mobile game app, but the Hybrid app, in which the Native approach is primarily responsible for device input and output, while the Web approach takes care of all the rest, is becoming a dominant app development option.

Real-time Web Architecture

Web applications using HTML are static, and therefore users don't get real-time update to the web page unless they make another request of the same web page. It would however be inefficient to request the entire web page when a user needs an update to only a single piece of data on the web page. This is where real-time web architecture comes in. Real-time web architecture allows users to get real-time updates without reloading the entire web page.

AJAX (Asynchronous JavaScript and XML) is a web-connection architecture pattern that allows a web browser to pull only updated data from a server. The idea is that once the entire web page is presented to the user, JavaScript on the web page asynchronously retrieves updated data as XML from the server and updates the corresponding portion of the web page. In AJAX, JavaScript can receive many types of documents such as HTML, XML, or even plain text as a response from a server, even though XML is implied in the name. JSON (JavaScript Object Notation) is also getting popular as a data format for updating information from a server, because JSON can easily be handled by JavaScript.

In some cases where AJAX is used, a web browser pulls data from a server for updates when there is no update in the server, or the web browser pulls data from a server when the update is not real-time information because the web browser does not know exactly when updates occur in the server. If this causes critical issues to a business, data push architecture patterns may be considered.

Comet is a web 'push' architecture pattern. A web browser establishes a Comet connection with a server once the entire webpage is loaded. In principle, the HTTP protocol disconnects a communication session between a web browser and a web server immediately after each response of the web server to the web browser. With a Comet connection, a long-held HTTP request allows a web server to push data to a web browser continuously, without the web browser explicitly requesting it.

WebSocket is used when both data pull and push are required to meet business requirements. It works better for business uses cases requiring a low latency, bi-directional and long-running connection between a web browser and a server. It provides similar functionality to TCP[36] socket connections, but it can pass through enterprise firewalls, whereas ordinary TCP socket connections cannot.

Content Aggregation & Syndication capability is heavily dependent on real-time web architectures to aggregate updates from data source web sites and syndicate updates to target web sites.

MATURITY INDICATOR EXAMPLES

Level 0: Non-existent

- Mobile apps have been developed without an agreed approach to presentation logic development. The development approach is solely decided by front-end developers.
- Some pulling or pushing technologies may have been employed to fulfil the business requirement of real time data retrieval, but there is no agreed approach to real-time web architecture. No one but the front-end developers knows what technologies are used for real-time web communication.

Level 1: Ad hoc

---

[36] TCP (Transmission Control Protocol) is a standard Internet network protocol that defines how data is transmitted from one computer to another on the Internet. A HTML webpage is for example transferred to users as a type of HTTP messages by a webserver, and HTTP messages are transmitted through TCP.

- A few concepts or architecture patterns have been tested and implemented by individual developers.
- Business owners, architects and developers discuss and make decision on the best approach to mobile app development. The architecture decisions are however not consistent across projects, and the best approach is therefore different from project to project.
- Real-time web architecture is discussed and decided on a project level. The architecture decisions are therefore not consistent across projects.

Level 2: Basic

- There are proven architecture patterns and repetitive processes shared across projects, architects, and developers, but these are not enforced as corporate standards by a central organization.
- A proven approach to mobile app development, and the pros and cons of each development approach are shared across architects and developers, but architecture decision the criteria and development approach are not enforced as enterprise standards.
- All types of real-time web architecture are being actively used, but what pattern is used for which business use cases are not entirely agreed across the organization.

Level 3: Defined

- There are architecture patterns, repetitive processes and tool sets established and enforced as enterprise standards through central architecture policies.
- Advantages and disadvantages of each approach to mobile app development are analysed, documented and agreed across the organization, with a set of development languages and tools enforced as enterprise standards.
- Standard use cases, architecture reference models and recommended implementation technologies of the real-

time web architecture patterns are defined to prevent individual developers from making inconsistent architecture decisions.

Level 4: Optimized

- The Hybrid approach to mobile app development is optimized to the level where architectural guidance is documented in detail, e.g. when to use Web technologies and which Native functions to use for what business use cases.
- Real-time web communication architectures are optimized to the extent that architectural decision guidance is documented in detail with some of the source and binary code reused, e.g. when to use which connection pattern, what are the criteria for decisions on patterns, and what are the standard implementation technologies.

Level 5: Progressive

- Presentation Logic of desktop and mobile apps are well aligned with MVC architecture and multi-channel architecture.
- Real-time web architecture supports Knowledge & Content Management capabilities so that it can provide an underlying capability for the content Aggregation & Syndication capability.

CAPABILITY 10-3.
PROCESS INTEGRATION SERVICES

CAPABILITY DEFINITION

Process Integration Services is a digital capability used to enable digital business processes to integrate seamlessly with one another by integrating applications with one another across on-premises and the Cloud.

The digital capability includes application connectivity, synchronous or asynchronous messaging, data transformation & formatting, workflow automation and process orchestration.

In the digital age, many applications should collaborate with one another in order to fully automate end-to-end business processes, regardless of whether they are deployed on-premises or in the Cloud, and whether inside or outside the organization. It is therefore necessary to create appropriate interfaces between the different deployment environments, and these should be different from the traditional integration architecture of the pre-digital era.

Loosely-Coupled Integration

If applications are coupled tightly with each other for integration, changes to the applications and integration are difficult and costly to implement. Applications and their integrations tend to change more often in the digital environments than in the past, due to the disruption and innovation in digital technologies. It is therefore recommended that integration of applications be loosely-coupled.

Having the integration 'Asynchronous' and 'Stateless' are two common ways to achieve a loosely-coupled integration:

- **Asynchronous**: The requesting application does not wait for the response from the responding application.

- **Stateless**: The responding application does not have any information on the state of the requesting application.

When two parties communicate at the same time, the communication is 'synchronous'. Communication over the phone is for example synchronous. One party 'waits' until the other is finished talking. When two parties communicate at different times, the communication is 'asynchronous'. Communication over email is for example asynchronous. When an email is sent, the sender 'does not wait' for the other party to send an email back right away. The receiver will respond to the email when it is convenient.

When an application residing within an organization communicates with another application outside the organization, it is recommended that the communication be as asynchronous as possible so that the internal application does not wait until the external application delivers the response. It is important to make sure that internal applications do not depend on the potentially unreliable and slow network outside and there is no delay resulting from waiting for external applications outside your immediate control to complete processes.

If an internal application makes a synchronous call to an external application when there is an incident or outage in the external network and the external systems, the internal application will wait much longer until a response is delivered, and will not release the system resources it is using during this time. This may cause problems in system performance and resource capacity.

To maintain high scalability of their Cloud, many Cloud service providers and social websites highly encourage asynchronous integration. Whichever protocol, e.g. SOAP[37] or REST[38], is chosen for application connectivity and messaging, these should be designed to integrate and communicate with external applications asynchronously.

A stateless application does not have any information on the state of the application it is communicating with. Digital applications should be as stateless as possible so that they can be independent from other applications they are communicated with. 'Stateless' application is an important concept for digital infrastructure to scale 'out', which is to scale 'horizontally' with cheap commodity hardware platforms. To support the ever increasing data and transactions in the digital space, the luxury of scaling 'up', which is to scale 'vertically' with expensive high-end hardware platforms is not affordable.

Analogous to business, call centre agents are stateless so that a user can call any agent and they can pick up the user's state from a database. If there is a call centre agent who remembers a user's state from his memory and not from a database, then that agent is the only one who can serve that user. The agent is dedicated to the user, and no other agent can be assigned to that user. If every agent is dedicated to a small group of specific users, the call centre cannot scale efficiently.

This also happens when it comes to applications serving other applications. If application A for example makes a request and asks for approval from 'Stateful' application B, and application B

---

[37] SOAP stands for Simple Object Access Protocol. It is a technology specification used to exchange messages between applications. The specification is maintained by the World Wide Web Consortium (W3C) as an Internet standard. It is robust and secure in architecture, and thus popular for critical applications.

[38] REST stands for REpresentational State Transfer. It is an architectural pattern, not a technology specification, used to exchange messages between applications. It is much easier and simpler to use than SOAP, and thus popular for lightweight web applications.

keeps the state of the progress with application A within itself, it would be impossible for a new instance of application B to serve application A. The newly installed instance of 'Stateful' application B on scaled-out Cloud infrastructure will not know the state of application A.

The state of the application making a request should be kept somewhere else so that any application responding to the application will have access to the state. It could be a memory location or permanent storage on the client side, such as a cookie or AJAX, or a server-side database if the state is critical.

Web Feeds

A web feed is a set of data or a content item that includes web links to the source of the data or the content item. Blogs and podcasts are common sources for web feeds, but web feeds are also used to deliver structured information, e.g. weather forecasts, or top ten search results.

RSS (Really Simple Syndication) and Atom are two common web feed formats. RSS is used widely, while Atom is more recent. Both technologies are pull-based and rely on the requesting application, the subscriber, to pull data from the providing application, the publisher. The pull-based approach has similar disadvantages that AJAX of the User Interaction Services has. The subscriber may pull data from the publisher for feed updates when there is no update in the publisher, or the subscriber may pull data from the publisher when the feeds are outdated because the subscriber does not know exactly when updates occur in the publisher.

The push-based approach may address the issues by having the publisher push web feed updates to the subscriber. This approach does however have another disadvantage, as the publisher website should maintain a constant connection to provide data feeds. With a large number of subscribers and connections, this can cause an unacceptable load on the publisher side.

The distributed Publish-Subscribe messaging pattern has been established to solve all these issues at once. The distributed Publish-Subscribe is called PubSubHubbub or WebSub. The idea is to put a middle layer, called a Hub, between publishers and subscribers.

Any publisher can run a hub for the distributed Publish-Subscribe, but WebSub commonly operates in an ecosystem of publishers, hubs and subscribers in digital business environments.

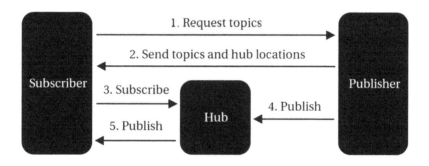

[Figure 41: PubSubHubbub Architecture]

Digital Process Orchestration

Applications and data are integrated with other applications and data for many purposes. A piece of data may for example need to be moved from one place to another, multiple systems need to be synchronized, or a functionality of an application needs to be reused by another application. As the digital infrastructure of an organization matures, the integration architecture moves toward the goal of business process automation and orchestration. This enables business to adapt to business process changes resulting from digital innovation readily.

Digital Process Orchestration is used to design and change digital business processes, and automate the digital business processes with little programming by IT staff. When an internal application for example receives digital content from an external content partner on a weekly basis to assemble a web page, the whole processes to get digital content, generate a web page and publish the web page can be designed, changed and deployed by business users for automating the processes. In a business scenario such as a field service application that is used to ask and get approval of a worker dispatch from an HR application, the whole processes to ask, give, receive and display the approval of the worker dispatch can be designed, changed and deployed by business users for automation of the processes.

There are three components required to implement process orchestration: a process design tool, a process execution engine, and a process administration tool.

- **A Process Design Tool** provides the facilities needed to analyse and model digital business processes. The tool automatically maps the processes to the technical components supporting them. An important function of the tool is the ability to perform simulation on the designed processes. Designed processes are deployed to the Process Execution Engine for process execution.

- **A Process Execution Engine** is the actual platform responsible for the execution of the business processes. The process flow control is central to the process execution engine and it may contain support for a business rules engine and scheduler.

- **A Process Administration Tool** provides the operational support for the process execution with the capability of general process tracking, administration and event management. Business process monitoring is an essential part of this tool.

MATURITY INDICATOR EXAMPLES

Level 0: Non-existent

- Data is copied and replicated for use by other applications, and functionalities of an application are called by other applications. These are however the traditional ways of integrating data or applications, rather than meeting the integration needs of digital applications such as web feeds and digital process orchestration.
- There is no loosely-coupled integration between on-premises and the Cloud.

Level 1: Ad hoc

- The integrations between on-premises and the Cloud are mostly synchronized communications.
- The stateless design concept has been tested, but has not been designed or implemented.
- RSS or Atom is implemented for data syndication. This is fully pull-based data distribution.
- Workflow is partly automated by each digital application where workflow automation is supported, but not all workflow functions imbedded in the applications are activated and used.

Level 2: Basic

- Use cases and designs of asynchronous calls are shared by a few developers or architects across a few projects where an on-premises application connects to a Cloud application.
- A few stateless applications have been implemented as a pilot system.
- RSS or Atom is implemented and a push notification is added to complement the pull-based approach.
- Many workflows embedded in the digital applications are activated and used, but enterprise-wide business process modelling and execution engines that enable the organization to integrate the workflows across the digital applications is not implemented. There is no central tool

implemented to model, deploy, execute and monitor end-to-end enterprise digital processes.

Level 3: Defined

- Use cases, design principles and guidance, and reference architecture for asynchronous message design have been established and enforced as enterprise standards, e.g. asynchronous SOAP message design.
- Stateless design is recommended for communications between applications, but is not enforced as an enterprise standard due to its complexity of design and implementation.
- A PubSubHubbub (or WebSub) architecture is implemented. RSS or Atom is implemented and connected to the hub responsible for data feed distribution.
- A process design tool is implemented to model and deploy business processes onto the process execution engine. The process orchestration system is integrated with the participating applications and their workflow components, but only small portion of business processes are managed by the process orchestration system due to the complexity of integration with the applications.

Level 4: Optimized

- Interfaces of applications are asynchronous wherever an asynchronous call is possible and recommended, and application programming is moving toward asynchronous patterns to take advantage of high scalability of private or public Cloud architecture.
- Use cases, design principles and guidance, and reference architecture for stateless design have been established and are enforced as enterprise standards. States of applications are mostly delivered through messages that are exchanged between the integrating applications, and the applications

therefore get 'stateful' by reading the messages, and become stateless again after completing the tasks.

- The PubSubHubbub architecture has been optimized and fine-tuned for improved performance and availability of data feed delivery, e.g. such architecture principles as 'Publish or subscribe to more than one hub for better availability', 'Publisher should retry pings to their hubs in case of failure of notifications', 'Subscriber should process a notification asynchronously for improved performance', etc.

- All three components of the process orchestration system are implemented, i.e. process design tool, process execution engine, and process administration tool. Most processes that can be automated by the process orchestration system are in the scope of the system. The integration of the process orchestration system with the participating applications is mostly loosely-coupled, e.g. wrapping application functionalities into reusable services.

Level 5: Progressive

- The enterprise architecture practice for digital business is predominantly based on a loosely-coupled architecture pattern from object design, all the way up to process orchestration, e.g. application integration through asynchronous calls, stateless application and communication programming, asynchronous database access and data feed, applications wrapped into interfaces for services, etc.

- The scope of process orchestration is extended to include the processes of collaboration with partners, suppliers and customers to automate the collaboration processes further.

CAPABILITY 10-4.
PARALLEL PROCESSING SERVICES

CAPABILITY DEFINITION

Parallel Processing Services is a digital capability used to process massive sets of semi-structured and un-structured data, as well as structured data, in parallel on distributed computing nodes.

This capability lends itself well to digital transactions and many Cloud service providers have created Cloud service offerings built on the parallel processing paradigm to efficiently process and analyse the massive amount of data coming from digital transactions, e.g. AWS EMR (Elastic MapReduce).

Parallel Processing Services are primarily used by Digital Intelligence capabilities to sort, calculate and summarize the massive amount of data during their analytical processes. The capability can also lay the groundwork for some of the front-office digital capabilities. The Social Listening capability can for example take advantage of this processing power to filter and sort raw data from social websites, and find patterns in customer voice.

The idea behind the Parallel Processing concept is to break down a large set of un-structured or semi-structure data into many smaller segments of data, process the data segments on distributed nodes in parallel, and assemble the outputs from all participating nodes.

A common architecture for parallel processing has two types of components: Master and Slaves. The Master component plans the entire job consisting of many tasks and allocates the tasks and data to multiple Slave components. Slave components execute the tasks and analyse the data, and return their outputs to the Master component for final assembly of the output.

Parallel Processing Framework

There are two popular implementations of the parallel processing concept: MapReduce and Spark.

MapReduce was the first into the market and is in widespread use across all industries that deal with a massive amount of data from their digital transactions. The MapReduce framework consists of two major functions:

- Map, and
- Reduce.

The Map function is to map and transform the input data structure to an output data structure, and the Reduce function is to reduce the number of output data sets.

When an input data structure is for example "Apple, Apple, Apple, Peach, Peach, Banana":

- during the Map process, the input data structure is transformed into the following output data structure of (name, count) pair: "(Apple, 1), (Apple, 1), (Apple, 1), (Peach, 1), (Peach, 1), (Banana, 1)"

- during the Reduce process, the number of the output data pairs is reduced to "(Apple, 3), (Peach, 2), (Banana, 1)"

MapReduce is one of two components of the Hadoop framework designed for distributed processing and storage of a large data set. The other component of Hadoop is the Hadoop Distributed File System (HDFS) explained in 'Capability 9-2. Distributed Data Store Management'.

MapReduce works well when a very large amount of data is processed, as it uses the Hadoop Distributed File System (HDFS) to store working data. Its Slave nodes scale up to approximately 15,000. It works better for batch processing than for real-time processing.

Spark is relatively new and has been growing, thanks to its more advanced architecture using in-memory processing of data for better performance in real time analysis of data flows. For faster processing of sizable data on a real-time basis, Spark is more suitable than MapReduce, e.g. real-time fraud detection of banking transactions.

MATURITY INDICATOR EXAMPLES

Level 0: Non-existent

- A batch-processing system is implemented for traditional batch jobs, such as bulk data copy and pre-defined report generation. This is however not built on a distributed parallel processing framework for handling un-structured or semi-structured data coming out of digital transactions.

Level 1: Ad hoc

- One of the distributed parallel processing frameworks available in the market has been tested for feasibility.
- IT agrees that a parallel processing framework should be introduced as part of digital innovation, but there is little awareness or consensus from business on business use cases, and a strong business case has therefore not yet been developed.

Level 2: Basic

- IT has implemented one of the popular parallel processing frameworks to gather and store a large amount of data from social websites and digital devices.
- The parallel processing framework is used to capture, filter, and store the data for later analysis, but the stored data is barely used by business due to the lack of understanding of where and how to use the data.

- IT staff actively use the parallel processing framework for IT internal purposes such as full-text indexing, web log processing, etc.

Level 3: Defined

- A few use cases of the parallel processing framework have been agreed by business and a business case has been created based on the use cases and business requirements, e.g. real-time dashboard displaying statistics of major business events from website click streams, order and payment transactions, social website posting and feeds, field worker real-time location and movement, etc.
- All baseline components required for parallel processing are implemented, e.g. Hadoop MapReduce, Hadoop distributed file system, Hadoop Yarn, and Hadoop Framework Common.
- A few other optional components to complement Hadoop are also introduced to help access data sources and data mining.
- The Parallel Processing Services function as a standalone application, but the integration with other Digital capabilities is not seamless.

Level 4: Optimized

- Two or more parallel processing frameworks are deployed and integrated to fulfil both real-time data processing and batch processing needs. They are loosely coupled with each other, while sharing storages for data integrity.
- The integration with other Digital capabilities are improving and becoming seamless.
- Data integration processes are optimized. The data integration processes include different data layers, such as data staging and a database, as well as naming standards and locations.

- The parallel processing frameworks are configured with a fully distributed mode to make the most of the distributed, scale-out architecture of the digital infrastructure.

Level 5: Progressive

- The parallel processing frameworks are not a standalone capability, but an integral part of all digital capabilities that actively generate, collect, use, and analyse a massive amount of un-structured and semi-structured data. Parallel Processing Services are used directly by the digital capabilities' run-time as underlying services, or parallel processing processes are integrated seamlessly with the digital capabilities processes.
- Any new business opportunities involving heavy data transactions, such as Internet of Things (IoT) and machine learning is successfully enabled by the Parallel Processing Services.

CAPABILITY 10-5.
FEDERATED ACCESS MANAGEMENT

CAPABILITY DEFINITION

When a user tries to access an application, the application performs access management processes before granting the access. Access management consists of authentication and authorization. Authentication is a process to verify who the user is, and authorization is to verify what access rights or privileges to what resources the user has.

Federated Access Management is a digital capability used to authenticate the identity of a user and to authorize the user for access to all digital resources inside and outside the organization, based on trust in a federated access service provider.

A user's credentials are always stored with a federated access service provider. When the user logs into an application, the application trusts the federated access service provider to validate the credentials, instead of taking the credentials from the user.

As users have immense opportunities to access a wide variety of digital applications in the digital space, the need to share and reuse the data required to authenticate and authorize users inside and outside the organization is ever increasing, in order to provide improved the digital experience when accessing the various digital touchpoints.

Federated Access Management can meet this need by allowing a digital application and a website to perform authentication and authorization of a user through another party that has identity and access rights information, without actually having or seeing the sensitive, private data.

The fundamental premise of the use cases is that the requested website or system resides in a different security domain than the federated access service provider holding identity and access rights information.

The basic idea of the concept of Federated Access Management is that a federated access service provider authenticates and authorizes a user on behalf of the website or application the user is trying to access, and the website or application grants access to the user based on the response from the federated access service provider.

A common scenario of how authentication and authorization are performed using Federated Access Management is shown below.

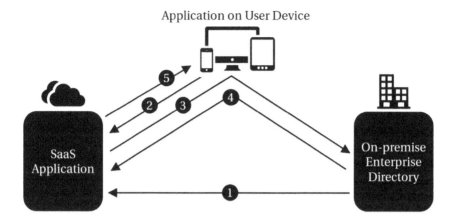

[Figure 42: Federated Access Processes]

1. The on-premises enterprise directory system[39] delivers a key used to verify the digital signature of the on-premises system to the SaaS application.

2. The user visits the SaaS application and tries to log on with their own credentials residing on the on-premises enterprise directory system.

3. The SaaS application redirect the access request to the enterprise directory system through the client program of the user device. The enterprise directory system asks the user for their credential, and the user provides the credentials.

4. The enterprise directory system completes authentication and authorization based on the credential, and returns the result along with its digital signature to the SaaS application through the client program of the user device.

---

[39] A directory system provides directory service by which users can locate resources distributed throughout the enterprise network, e.g. employees, printers, servers, and services. It is also used to grant access to those resources.

5. The SaaS application verifies whether the result is signed by the enterprise directory system by using the key used to verify the digital signature, and grants or rejects access based on the result.

Federated Access Management should not be confused with Single Sign-On (SSO), in which users are not required to enter their log-on credentials each time they access a different website or application.

Federated Access Management Practices

OpenID Connect is an open standard that offers a framework for authentication functionality. OpenID Connect is deployed onto OAuth, which is also an open standard that offers a framework for authorization functionality. OAuth, combined with OpenID Connect, provides complete capability of federated authentication and authorization.

For federated authentication, OpenID allows the server responsible for authentication to send a user's web browser an ID token that is to be sent through to a website server the user is trying to access. After performing authentication, OAuth allows the website to ask the server responsible for authorization to send an access token directly back to the website for federated authorization of the user.

OAuth can be used without OpenID for a website to grant an access to a user whose identity is not known. This is similar to be given a key to a friend's house. This will allow access to the house, without having to be the friend.

Another open standard, SAML (Security Assertion Markup Language), offers a complete framework for both federated authentication and authorization. A SAML-compliant server providing central authentication and authorization services returns a user's ID and requested URL to the web browser in an encrypted message. The web browser in turn forwards the message to the website.

Whatever standards or technologies are employed to implement Federated Access Management, the overall approach remains the same. Each of the standards and technologies do however provide different functionalities to be able to meet different business requirements and needs.

In a SAML environment, a strong encryption-based digital signature is used to verify the integrity of federated authentication and authorization, instead of the identity and access tokens used in OpenID Connect and OAuth. The websites registered by a central authentication and authorization server can only participate in SAML-based federated access management, whereas any websites compliant to OpenID Connect and OAuth specifications can participate in OpenID and OAuth-based federation.

This is why SAML is more widely used in enterprise digital environments, while OpenID and OAuth are commonly used in digital environments that are more open.

MATURITY INDICATOR EXAMPLES

Level 0: Non-existent

- There is no federated access management in place that allows users to have access with single credentials to multiple digital touchpoints sitting in different security domains.

Level 1: Ad hoc

- Two or more enterprise directories are synchronized to identify users and allow them to have access to different systems from different security domains, regardless of whether on-premises or on the Cloud.
- Federated access management has been tested to assess the feasibility of replacing the directory synchronization, but

federated authentication and authorization has not yet been implemented.

Level 2: Basic

- A trust relationship has been established between two or more security domains through proprietary protocols, as they have the same identity management solutions, e.g. Microsoft Active Directory forest trust.
- Federation servers of the directory services such as ADFS (Active Directory Federation Server) may be deployed, but are not actively used across the environment and is used for limited purposes only, such as access to Office 365 Online.

Level 3: Defined

- Federated Access Management has been established as a standard approach for distributed authentication and authorization in the distributed environments.
- Standard internet protocols such as SAML, OpenID Connect and OAuth are used for non-intrusive authentication and authorization of users.
- The federation services support all different directory servers.

Level 4: Optimized

- Additional functionalities have been built on top of the Federated Access Management to provide better sign-on experience or improved security, e.g. Single-Sign On (SSO) and multi-factor authentication (MFA)[40] built on federated access services.
- The federation services have been optimized to take advantage of the openness of OpenID and OAuth to have

---

[40] MFA is an authentication practice in which extra authentication methods are used on top of ID and password.

access to a wider customer base. OAuth in particular is actively used to expose the services of the organization and enrich customer experiences, by tapping into a variety of applications from other organizations.

Level 5: Progressive

- The level of the digital capability has been a strong IT enabler for the multi-channel and omni-channel business strategy to work.
- The Federated Access Management provides opportunities to use other organizations' multiple channels to access different customer bases to devise a different product mix which innovates not only digital sales and delivery, but also the whole digital business model.

CAPABILITY 10-6.
DIGITAL CONTINUITY MANAGEMENT

CAPABILITY DEFINITION

Digital Continuity Management is a digital capability used to ensure that digital business continues if availability solutions fail and cannot restore digital capabilities because of such natural disasters and disastrous external incidents as fire, floods, earthquakes, strikes and war. The capability encompasses the assessment of the impact of such events on digital business, continuity planning, solution implementation and communication with users.

Availability management solutions such as system clustering and local backup cannot ensure the availability of the digital systems with such an extreme incident. On-Demand Provisioning Services include an ability to provision new or more resources when there is an availability issue. When such an extreme incident occurs and the production data centre cannot provide services for digital business any more, Digital Continuity Management should enable critical digital capabilities to recover so that critical digital business processes can continue.

There are 77 digital capabilities described in this book. Some of them may be critical to your digital business, and some may not. Whether a digital capability is critical to a digital business is commonly assessed against the probability of the incident happening and the impact of the incident on digital business.

Disaster recovery solutions should be focused on the critical digital capabilities rather than all the digital capabilities.

You can simply back up applications and data supporting the critical digital capabilities into removable storage media and keep them offsite. The most common way is however to set up a separate, remote data centre for disaster recovery purpose on-premises or on the Cloud, and electronically replicate applications and data to the data centre on a regular basis.

The frequency of replication depends on the Recovery Point Objective (RPO) metric that describes the maximum-targeted period in which data might be lost from a disaster. If the RPO is for example one day, the replication must be made at intervals of 24 hours or less.

The Recovery Time Objective (RTO) is another metric frequently used for disaster recovery. It represents the targeted period within which a system supporting a digital capability must be recovered after a disaster, in order to avoid unacceptable consequences associated with a disruption in digital business. If the RTO is for example one day, the system must be recovered within 24 hours or less.

MATURITY INDICATOR EXAMPLES

Level 0: Non-existent

- The organization does not know which digital capabilities are critical to its digital business.
- A disaster recovery solution is not implemented to enable digital business to continue operating.

Level 1: Ad hoc

- Disaster recovery planning has been performed, but the plan is neither official, nor comprehensive.
- Business is not involved in the disaster recovery planning.
- Some of the data considered critical is copied to removable storage media that is stored outside the production environment on an ad hoc basis.

Level 2: Basic

- Business has come up with a rough idea on which business functions or processes are crucial to digital business.
- The disaster recovery plan is updated on a regular basis, but the plan is managed in such a way that they are not readily available for use by business during an emergency.
- The majority of critical data is electronically replicated to a remote site outside the production environment on a regular basis.

Level 3: Defined

- Digital continuity policies, processes and IT systems are implemented as part of the enterprise business-continuity management.
- All plans required for digital business continuity are developed, e.g. Emergency Response Plan, Escalation Plan, Declaration Plan and Crisis Management Plan.

- The impact of disasters on all digital business functions or processes are assessed and documented with business involved.
- All critical digital capabilities have redundancy in the disaster recovery centre.
- All employees that would be impacted by disasters are trained.

Level 4: Optimized

- The business impact analysis is updated quarterly by both Business and IT.
- All required continuity plans are readily available to employees during an emergency. Employees are trained and updated as required. The plans are revised on a regular basis.
- Rigorous audit and testing of disaster recovery is performed on a regular basis, and the result is used to improve the digital capability.
- The majority of digital services can recover within a day after a disaster occurs and critical services takes a few hours to recover.
- The critical digital capabilities can recover and operate within a few hours.

Level 5: Progressive

- Through rigorous business case analysis, costs for maintaining disaster recovery systems are balanced against the benefit digital continuity management can generate.
- Full redundancy of digital capabilities is maintained. Disaster recovery plans and implementations are a critical part of digital business continuity.
- Critical digital capabilities can recover and operate within a few minutes.

MEGA CAPABILITY 11.

DIGITAL ALIGNMENT

Digital Alignment is a set of digital capabilities used to establish overarching directions of digital capabilities to align with corporate business strategy, plan digital initiatives to improve digital capabilities and facilitate effective decision making on digital investment and value realization. It also includes the capability to collaborate across different business units and departments to plan and implement digital initiatives, and organizational readiness to change.

Digital Alignment has the following digital capabilities:

- Digital Innovation
- Digital Planning
- Digital Governance
- Cross-Boundary Collaboration
- Digital Journey Readiness

CAPABILITY 11-1.
DIGITAL INNOVATION

CAPABILITY DEFINITION

The speed and scale of digital business change requires creating a flow of new, innovative ideas to remain competitive.

Digital Innovation is a digital capability used to monitor and analyse digital trends, capture their implications for industry dynamics, customer, competition, products, services, and supply chain, and apply them to digital capabilities to innovate the digital business.

Any organization can start building a Digital Innovation capability by setting up a small, virtual and multi-disciplinary team responsible for conducting digital trend research, and compiling research result reports.

When you consider the fact that many promising ideas won't make it through the various and rigorous processes of scrutiny, a well-defined methodology with supporting tools and a proper time frame will equip the team with the means to stay focused and efficient, and not to waste their valuable time.

The processes of Digital Innovation may include the following:

- Gather management expectation on Digital Innovation.

- Set goals and objectives according to the expectation.

- Capture information on industry dynamics into a reality map.

- Assemble a list of candidate digital business or technology solution ideas.

- Conduct proof of concept and develop usage scenario.

- Assess applicability, feasibility, time horizon, cost and other factors.

- Classify into quick-wins, short-list and long-list portfolios.

- Obtain approval from management.

- Develop implementation plans.

Organizations are well advised to create an Innovation Funnel to manage the progress of taking innovative ideas from concept to reality as you go through the Digital Innovation processes repeatedly and create more ideas.

A mandate for budget allocation to Digital Innovation will accelerate improvement of the innovation capability. Consistent, mandatory budget allocation to Digital Innovation can have a positive impact on digital business performance.

MATURITY INDICATOR EXAMPLES

Level 0: Non-existent

- Research into trends of digital technology or digital business is not performed.

Level 1: Ad hoc

- Ad hoc research into trends of digital technology or digital business is performed.
- The ad hoc research may lead to a new idea of adopting emerging digital technology or digital operations, but it is neither significant nor consistent.

Level 2: Basic

- Research into trends of digital technology or digital business is performed by individual business units or departments on a regular basis, but multi-disciplinary research is not in place.

- The regular research may have an operational impact on digital capabilities, but it does not have a significant impact on shaping top-down digital strategy.

Level 3: Defined

- Corporate principles, policies, processes, tools and roles required to perform research and analysis are defined and implemented.
- A multi-disciplinary team across business and IT may be established for the innovative research.
- Digital Innovation is an integral part of digital strategy planning processes.
- Technology scanning capability is limited mainly due to lack of internal expertise in digital research and collaboration with an external research network, such as academia and vendors specialized in Digital Innovation.

Level 4: Optimized

- The organization understands where Digital Innovation can have substantial business impacts, has developed a reality map and focuses research efforts as per the reality map.
- Innovation ideas are actively assembled from vendors, start-ups, academia and multiple other sources. Prototypes, mock-ups and other types of proof of concept (PoC) may be leveraged to come up with brand new ideas. Multiple innovation portfolios of quick-wins, short-list and long-list are maintained.
- A fast follower is still preferred to a digital innovator to avoid potentially high risks that implementation of the innovation portfolios could bring.
- The Digital Innovation budget is consistently planned and is proportionate to the total discretionary budget on an annual basis.

Level 5: Progressive

- A Strategic alliance with capable partners specializing in Digital Innovation is strongly pursued as a critical factor, as they are the most reliable sources for digital trend analysis.
- Digital Innovation portfolios and action plans are highly implementable, because of the ability to identify risks from implementing the portfolio and enforcing controls to mitigate the risks.
- Pilot environments and a fast fail culture prevails.
- Digital Innovation processes are fully integrated with the processes of other digital capabilities, so that innovative ideas can infiltrate into many digital operations and value chains that can benefit from Digital Innovation.
- Digital Innovation is the primary source of competitive advantage of the organization.

CAPABILITY 11-2.
DIGITAL PLANNING

CAPABILITY DEFINITION

Generally, if a strategy is in place, the following three aspects should be understood:

- where you are,
- where you want to go, and
- how to get there.

This is also the case when it comes to Digital strategy. The current state of all digital capabilities available, the desirable future state of the digital capabilities, and a road map that guides the organization from the current to the future state of digital capabilities should be understood.

Digital Planning is a digital capability used to establish digital strategies by:

- Identifying the current state of digital capabilities,
- Designing a future state of digital capabilities, and
- Creating a road map.

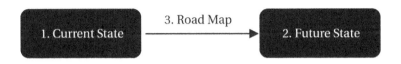

[Figure 43: The Sequence of Digital Planning]

The Digital Planning processes are described in detail in the final section, 'Digital Transformation Planning Methodology'.

In this section, the concept of the three stages for Digital Planning will be discussed.

Identification of the Current State

The current state of a digital capability is assessed in terms of how People, Process and Technology are combined to work together to create business outcomes:

- **People**: How people are organized into an organizational structure, what are their roles and responsibilities, and what proficiency levels are required to perform the responsibilities.

- **Process**: What activities the people perform, what activities are missing or redundant, and whether the flow of the activities are streamlined or not.

- **Technology**: What technologies and tools are utilized to help the people to perform their roles and the business processes, whether the functionalities of technologies are rich enough, and whether the processes are automated enough or not.

If the maturity model of The Digital Capability Model is employed, it will help identify where the organization is on the maturity scale of each digital capability.

The current state assessment provides a snapshot of how an organization operates in its current digital environment, and identify potential areas of improvements, including quick-fix opportunities, even before moving to designing a future state.

Development of a Future State Blueprint

If a specific and measurable goal of the digital business is available, the job of setting up a desirable future state is easier. In most organizations, this is however not the case. A digital capability maturity model can come to the rescue again. The aim could be to lift the digital capability by 1 to 2 levels, depending on the availability of resources and the urgency of the capability lift. It now becomes easy to pinpoint exactly where the organization wants to go on the maturity scale.

Another important deliverable of this stage is a blueprint of digital capabilities. The blueprint shows how people, processes and technology of a digital capability will be combined to work together to produce better outcomes than the current state. The target level of maturity provides directions on how the blueprint is designed to achieve the future state. Some of the current combinations of people, process and technology may be sustainable, depending on what the target is.

Development of a Road Map

A road map is all about "What to do" and "When to do it" to achieve the future state blueprints. "What to do" is commonly referred to as initiatives, programs and projects. Whatever they are called, each one of them should have information on how to perform the works and may include objectives, scope, a high-level solution, a set of tasks, time frame, required human resources, cost and benefit. "When to do it" stands for a sequence of the programs or projects with their dependency identified.

Milestones and waves along the digital journey can also be identified as part of the roadmap.

A business case for a program or project should also be developed as part of identifying projects or programs. A business case is a justification for a proposed program or project that includes benefit and a cost analysis. Business case reports are provided to a governance committee that makes a decision on an investment that a digital project or program needs. The business case will be discussed in the next section, 'Capability 11-3. Digital Governance'.

MATURITY INDICATOR EXAMPLES

Level 0: Non-existent

- A few projects have been identified and implemented in relation to the digital business. The projects have however been initiated to quick fix burning platforms, and there were neither a structured assessment of the current state, nor agreement on the target maturity of the future state.

Level 1: Ad hoc

- The current state of the digital business and operations are assessed on an ad hoc basis, but the current state is not assessed against a structured framework.
- Projects are identified from the assessment of the current state, but those projects predominantly represent bottom-up needs for quick fixes.
- A specific future state is not envisaged, and the state of a digital capability and the level of maturity digital projects would achieve is unclear.

Level 2: Basic

- Quick-hit plans are developed by a single person or a small group of people annually to address internal & external burning issues on digital business.
- A structured digital framework or approach to assessing the current state, setup of future state, and creation of a roadmap is not yet employed.
- A desirable future state is discussed as part of each project plan, rather than across all projects.
- Business cases are developed in most cases, but the level of analysis is too shallow to make an investment decision.
- The digital plans are aligned with neither business strategy, nor IT strategy.
- Digital planning is not coordinated by a central body, and the plans are therefore not consistent across business units.

Level 3: Defined

- A standard digital capability model, planning processes, digital strategists and planning tools are implemented.
- Digital plans are developed annually and revised quarterly or bi-annually.
- Digital plans are well aligned with business and IT strategy.
- Digital planning is strongly coordinated by a central digital organization and the digital plans are therefore consistent across business units, with the dependency of all digital projects well identified and coordinated.

Level 4: Optimized

- Performance targets of the future operating model are clearly defined and documented to measure the progress of the digital journey, and the success of projects that are to achieve the future state, making the business cases much stronger.
- Digital plans are revised and optimized based on the performance measurement along the digital journey, so that

the projects can have a substantial impact on digital business performance.

- Costs are traceable to the specific benefits it creates. The Digital organization understands what they get for their digital spending.
- Through effective performance planning, the organization can develop a longer-term digital strategy that is effective and sustainable in the long-term.

Level 5: Progressive

- Digital plans are an integral part of the corporate business strategy, business unit strategy and IT strategy.
- The Digital capability model and principles are used on executive level to make digital decisions.
- Digital Innovation drives the Digital Planning process to come up with disruptive idea and projects. The digital practices of the organization lead the digital trends in the industry.

CAPABILITY 11-3.
DIGITAL GOVERNANCE

CAPABILITY DEFINITION

Digital Governance is a digital capability used to make, sponsor and enforce the right decisions on digital business across the board. The capability encompasses leadership, accountabilities, responsibilities and processes to make, sponsor and enforce the right decisions around digital demand capture, digital planning, digital investment, digital programs and digital operations.

Digital Decisions

Digital decisions should be made on digital investment, digital program oversight and digital operations.

Digital initiatives are planned through the Digital Planning processes and the digital initiatives are then reviewed and approved through investment decision-making processes, which are part of the Digital Governance processes. A set of business cases is the key documents for a decision-making body to review, prioritize and approve digital initiatives.

Once a digital initiative is approved, a digital program is organized to execute the initiative. A program may consist of multiple projects. A governance body should be accountable for oversight of the program to see if the business value promised in the business case is being realized as planned in the business case. The oversight involves making decisions on any issues or agenda to facilitate the realization of business value.

When a digital program is complete, the output of the program is maintained through daily operational processes. When a Marketing Automation capability is for example implemented by a digital program, the capability should be maintained to be sustainable in the longer term. The digital operations also involve making a decision on any issues or agenda to make the capability sustainable and operable.

Governance Archetype

Decisions on digital business and digital capabilities can be made in a centralized or decentralized manner, or it can be in between the two, namely in a federal way. If most digital decisions are made by a central digital organization, the digital governance structure is centralized. If the digital decisions are made by business units, the structure is decentralized. If the central digital organization and business units share the accountabilities of making digital decisions, the digital governance structure is a federal model.

How centralized a digital governance structure should be typically depends on two factors:

- how autonomous the business unit is in making a decision in the entire organization, and

- how different the nature of the business is from the corporate business portfolio.

If the business unit is autonomous and the nature of the digital business does not share much in common with the other business units in the entire organization, the digital governance structure should not be centralized. If the business unit does not have much freedom in business decision making and the digital business of the business unit share many features in common with those of the other business units, the digital governance structure tends to be centralized.

A federal governance structure is preferred by many organizations in practice, because it seeks to utilize the advantages of both centralized and decentralized models, achieving such benefits as enterprise wide perspective, scale economies, critical mass of skills, control of digital standards and responsiveness to diverse needs of business units.

Decision-Making Accountability

Defining 'which governance body is accountable for what decision' is critical to successful Digital Governance.

When an organization has a federal structure of Digital Governance, a digital executive board that is the highest in the decision-making hierarchy for digital business is created. The members of the board are from all parties involved in the digital business. They may include business units, IT department, marketing department and the central digital organization. The primary accountability of the board is to make decisions on digital investment and oversight of digital programs.

The highest executive board may empower multiple sub-committees to discuss the digital agenda and even make decisions in relation to oversight of small digital initiatives and digital programs.

The central digital organization assists the board and committees around digital investment and digital program oversight, while having accountability for making decisions on daily digital operations.

MATURITY INDICATOR EXAMPLES

Level 0: Non-existent

- Decisions on digital investment are made by the gut feeling of an individual executive, without business case analysis and initiative prioritization.

Level 1: Ad hoc

- Digital initiatives are governed to reduce and minimize their cost, even if the investments can be justified by business cases.
- The alignment of digital initiatives with business strategy and the oversight of digital programs are conducted on an ad hoc basis.

Level 2: Basic

- Digital initiatives are governed to control their cost.
- Decisions on digital investment are made by ad hoc meetings.
- The alignment of digital initiatives with business strategy is discussed during the ad hoc meetings, but strategic alignment is not always made.
- Program oversight is performed, but whether the benefits promised in the business case is realized, is not assessed.

Level 3: Defined

- All governance bodies and governance processes are defined, and the roles, accountabilities and responsibilities of all governance bodies are documented. The processes and roles are however not well enforced.
- Many investment decisions on digital initiatives are made based on business cases, considering both benefit and cost with more focus on cost, as Digital investment is not seen as a means for business innovation.
- Key executives are involved in the governance bodies to support and make decisions on digital investment and programs.
- A governance body oversees the program to assess whether the programs and projects are realizing the business benefits promised in the business case document.

Level 4: Optimized

- Digital governance roles and processes have been optimized and fine-tuned.
- Investment decision on digital initiatives are made based predominantly on business cases, considering both benefit and cost.
- Whether digital initiatives realize the business value promised in the business case is tracked, even after the program is finished.

Level 5: Progressive

- All digital decisions across the board are driven, measured and rewarded based on business value realized.
- Digital initiatives are considered one of the key sources of business innovation and the digital initiatives identified as 'innovative' are therefore encouraged to be implemented, even if they do not promise any immediate business value in the business cases.

- Critical digital decisions are included in the business agenda and discussed by top management.

CAPABILITY 11-4.
CROSS-BOUNDARY COLLABORATION

CAPABILITY DEFINITION

Cross-Boundary Collaboration is a digital capability used to foster collaboration across all business units, functional departments, suppliers and partners, and consolidate or harmonize their digital strategies and efforts to maximize the synergy of digital investments, and prevent redundant efforts of establishing digital capabilities within each silo of department and organization.

The collaboration is important because an individual business unit or a functional department tends to build their digital capabilities in a silo that is not shared or leveraged across the organization, costing the organization a lot more and benefiting a lot less.

Collaboration in Digital Planning is the most critical part of the Cross-Boundary Collaboration capability. If a central digital organization is implemented, it may take the lead on Digital Planning and coordinate the processes. Collaborative planning processes should otherwise be defined clearly and enforced to make sure the collaboration is performed effectively.

Effective Digital Governance structure can lay the foundation for effective Cross-Boundary Collaboration. A committee consisting of representatives from business units and functional departments can be organized to discuss and capture common digital requirements across the organization.

Collaboration in daily digital operations is far more challenging, as it requires seamless integration of digital processes of business units or departments. It is a good idea to implement collaborative business processes into technical tools, because it would be much easier to rely on technology than human behaviour to implement collaborations across different business units and departments.

MATURITY INDICATOR EXAMPLES

Level 0: Non-existent

- No governance structure, process, or tool is defined or implemented for collaboration across different business units and functional departments.

Level 1: Ad hoc

- Some business units and functional departments discuss digital plans on an ad hoc basis, for a seasonal event or once-off promotion, but there is no structured, consistent operating model for Cross-Boundary Collaboration.

Level 2: Basic

- Many business units and functional department collaborate with one another and the collaboration involves suppliers or partners in some occasions. The effort made by the individual business units and functional departments are however far from the practices that are centrally organized, coordinated, aligned and are not consistent across the organization.

Level 3: Defined

- Corporate-level digital collaboration principles and policies, collaborative processes, collaboration channel and automation tools are implemented to drive and enable

Cross-Boundary Collaboration on digital planning and digital program implementation.

- Coordination by a central digital organization may be available to help collaborate on digital planning and implementation.

Level 4: Optimized

- Digital collaboration extends to external parties, including service providers, suppliers and partners on a regular basis.
- A Digital business eco-system exists where the participating parties inside and outside the organization share digital plans, and implement some of initiatives together to mitigate the implementation risks and maximize benefits from collaboration.

Level 5: Progressive

- The collaborative eco-system gives sustainable competitive advantage and cannot be copied easily by competitors, because the eco-system participants hold strategic alliance and the competitive advantage is generated from their collective efforts.

CAPABILITY 11-5.
DIGITAL JOURNEY READINESS

CAPABILITY DEFINITION

Digital Journey Readiness is a digital capability used to manage organizational readiness to change themselves, to implement digital initiatives according to the roadmap to achieve target levels of digital capabilities described in future digital blueprints. The organizational readiness can be measured against two criteria:

- Organizational willingness to change
- Organizational competency to change

Willingness to Change

It is typical human nature to resist change rather than willingly accept it. The extent and type of resistance or acceptance varies depending on the digital change. Several criteria can be used to assess the extent to which each of the following conditions exist now, or will exist because of the digital change:

- Perceived threat to current job security
- Loss of current expertise
- Need to learn new skills
- Shifts in influence, authority and control
- Shifts in communication patterns
- Change to organizational structure
- Change to organizational culture
- Loss of social status
- Change in habits or customs
- Ignorance of the digital change
- Limited understanding of the digital change and its implications
- Low tolerance for the digital change

It is recommended that surveys and workshop techniques be used to gather employees' feeling and opinions on the checklist above to assess the level of willingness to change.

Competency to Change

Even if the level of organizational willingness to change were high, the organizational readiness would not be high if the level of organizational competency to change is not as high. Below are common criteria to assess the level of organizational competency to change.

- **Leading ability**: Organizational ability to get support, buy-in, or commitment from key leaders within the organization undergoing the digital change.

- **Visioning & articulating ability**: A clear and concise picture of how the organization will work, and how it will be organized after the digital change is implemented.

- **Proactive planning ability**: Organizational ability to assess the impact the change will have on the organization, in order to be proactive in defining and preparing for impacts, rather than reactive to impacts after they occur.

- **Selling & marketing ability**: Common sales or marketing techniques and skills to promote the digital change, and emphasize the benefits.

- **Participating ability**: People's ability to be actively involved in creating and managing the digital change as a means of building ownership.

- **Communication ability**: Organizational ability to create and get across regular and accurate information about the digital change in a proactive and open manner.

- **Training ability**: Organizational ability to train the concepts and skills required to implement the digital change, and to perform operational work after the change.

- **Integrating ability**: Organizational ability to coordinate the multiple activities and initiatives likely to be implemented as part of a major digital change.

- **Supporting ability**: The infrastructure required to support the changes that will need to occur.

- **Transitioning ability**: Organizational ability to move smoothly from the current environment to the target environment.

Previous experience in executing any types of change in the past can be a good source of information to assess the current ability of the organization to change.

MATURITY INDICATOR EXAMPLES

Level 0: Non-existent

- The organization has never have gone through this type of the change in the past.
- The organization is never ready for this extent of the change and may have to learn how to change by going through a set of pilot changes before launching a transformative change.

Level 1: Ad hoc

- The level of organizational readiness to change is low with low willingness and low competency.
- The organization has gone through a few small organizational changes in the past.

Level 2: Basic

- The level of organizational readiness to change is medium-low, with either a combination of medium-low willingness and medium-low competency, a combination of medium willingness and low competency, or a combination of low willingness and medium competency.
- The organization has gone through a few medium-sized organizational changes.

Level 3: Defined

- The level of organizational readiness to change is medium, with either a combination of medium willingness and medium competency, a combination of medium-low willingness and medium-high competency, or medium-high willingness and medium-low competency.

- The organization has gone through quite a few medium-sized organizational changes and one or two major changes.

Level 4: Optimized

- The level of organizational readiness to change is medium-high, with either a combination of medium-high willingness and medium-high competency, a combination of medium willingness and high competency, or high willingness and medium competency.
- The organization has gone through quite a few large organizational changes.

Level 5: Progressive

- The level of organizational readiness to change is high, with high willingness and high competency.
- Changes are deeply integrated with the daily digital operations and there is no clear boundary between large changes and daily operations, due to frequent large change programs implemented.

MEGA CAPABILITY 12.

DIGITAL DEVELOPMENT & OPERATIONS

Digital Development & Operations is a set of digital capabilities used to develop digital capabilities in development environments, deploy them into production environments, and maintain and support the digital capabilities to be sustainable for a longer term.

Digital Development includes designing digital processes, roles, responsibilities and organizational structure, and implementing tools and technologies to automate and support the digital processes and responsibilities of employees. When a digital development is complete, the outputs are deployed into a production environment for use by employees, and maintenance and operations by digital administrators.

Digital Development & Operations has the following digital capabilities:

- Digital Program & Project Management
- Digital Design Authority
- Digital Capability Development

- Digital Capability Introduction
- Digital Service Operations
- Digital Quality Management

CAPABILITY 12-1.
DIGITAL PROGRAM & PROJECT MANAGEMENT

CAPABILITY DEFINITION

Digital Program & Project Management is a digital capability used to manage digital programs and digital projects. The digital capability includes performance metrics, management methodologies, management tools and skilled staff.

The 'program' management part of the digital capability is to lead and guide multiple digital projects that collectively fulfil the scope of a digital program.

The 'project' management part is to produce specific deliverables such as digital organization designs, digital process flows, digital role and responsibility designs, digital applications, and digital infrastructure under the guidance of program management.

Digital Program Management

Digital program management focuses on giving consistent direction and guidance to the delivery of a digital capability, through multiple digital projects and digital capability releases. In order to achieve the objective and scope of a digital program, and lead, guide and support constituent digital projects, digital program management commonly includes the following as its management scope:

- **Resource management** to define an approach to sourcing, and managing human and physical resources of a program.

- **Vendor management** to define an approach to selecting resources from outside the organization and managing relationship with vendors.

- **Quality management** to define quality requirements, quality processes and quality metrics used by projects.

- **Scope change management** to set a framework for managing the scope of a program and its constituent projects, and controlling changes to the scope once the baseline scope has been set.

- **Capability release management** to establish a framework for allowing a digital program to deliver a release of a digital capability for use by digital users.

- **Issue management** to define program-level processes and project-level processes for issue identification, analysis, escalation, resolution and reporting.

- **Problem management** to establish a structure to identify, prioritize, track and resolve all problems logged by quality validation and testing.

- **Program risk management** to set an approach to identifying, assessing and mitigating program-level risks.

- **Financial management** to define financial controls and processes for budgeting, tracking, costing and reporting.

- **Contingency management** to specify the processes for reserving and allocating budget contingency, and schedule contingencies within a digital program over time.

- **Performance management** to set performance metrics and performance measure processes for use by projects, and measure and report the performance of a program.

Digital Project Management

Digital project management focuses on creating and providing specific deliverables that are deployed into digital business environments for use by digital users. The project deliverables may include designed processes flow, documented job responsibilities, developed business applications, or configured hardware. In order to deliver those deliverables successfully, Digital project management commonly includes the following as its management scope:

- **Scope management** to identify and manage the project-level scope, aligning with the digital program-level scope.

- **Resource management** to estimate resources needed for a project by organizational breakdown structure, resource skill and type, and weekly or monthly periods.

- **Schedule management** to develop a schedule of key project events such as milestones as well as start and finish dates, and identify the critical path between start and finish dates.

- **Task management** to develop task-level work plans containing scope, effort (workdays), time (schedule) and resources.

- **Communication & collaboration management** to specify meetings, processes and tools used to facilitate communication and collaboration among project team members.

- **Quality management** to set specific methodologies, procedures and measurement techniques so that all deliverables and work performed meet or exceed the predefined functional, technical and contractual requirements, as well as the expectations documented for program-level quality management.

- **Project issue management** to identify and resolve issues according to the procedures defined by program management.

- **Project risk management** to set an approach to identify, assess and mitigate project-level risks.

- **Functional Change management** to set a framework for controlling changes to the outputs, such as business requirements, process designs and software configuration once the baseline outputs have been set.

MATURITY INDICATOR EXAMPLES

Level 0: Non-existent

- There is no clear definition of program and project, and their difference.
- Standard methodologies or tools for digital program management or digital project management do not exist. Programs or projects do not share management practices.
- A program plan or project plan may be created, but the program or project does not stick to the plan.

Level 1: Ad hoc

- In some instances, a program has multiple projects, although there is no standard definition of program or project within the organization.
- There is no standard methodology or tool for digital program management or digital project management, but a few management practices are shared across some of digital programs and projects.
- A digital program plan or digital project plan is created, but the plan is often abandoned during a crisis.
- The success of a project still relies heavily on a few skilled people, rather than industrialized processes.

Level 2: Basic

- People understand the difference between programs and projects, but there is no structured approach to sharing the scope and responsibility between programs and projects to develop digital capabilities.
- Many programs or projects have shared good practices, methodologies and tools within the organization, and they became the de-facto standards for digital development.
- Basic disciplines for program and project management are institutionalized, but program and project plans may differ

considerably from program to program, and from project to project.

- The methodologies and tools still have limited functionalities.

Level 3: Defined

- The difference between a digital program and a digital project is centrally defined, and there is a standard approach to shaping a program and its constituent projects.
- Standard management methodologies, program-management office structure and management tools for managing programs and projects are defined and enforced.
- The management methodologies offer detailed processes, job aids and deliverable templates, and the management tools have comprehensive functionalities to enable the methodologies.
- Program and project plans are widely consistent from program to program, and from project to project.
- The standard program and project management processes enable consistent quality across the organization.

Level 4: Optimized

- The digital program and project management practices have been optimized and industrialized enough for the program and project managers to monitor and measure the progress and quality automatically.
- The significant increase in the ability to measure and optimize the performance of a program and project enables the program and project to be more successful in terms of on time and on budget, and meeting critical expectations of key stakeholders.

Level 5: Progressive

- Program management focuses more on realizing business value promised in a business case, rather than monitoring project tasks, thanks to the highly industrialized and automated management processes.
- Constituent projects of a program are re-aligned and re-structured in a way that helps the program realize the business value.

CAPABILITY 12-2.
DIGITAL DESIGN AUTHORITY

CAPABILITY DEFINITION

Digital Design Authority is a digital capability used to review digital designs and enforce decisions on the designs to ensure the integrity of programs and projects are maintained.

Digital Design Authority maintains a consistent, coherent and complete perspective of the landscape of a range of digital designs, such as digital process design, role & responsibility design, data model design and infrastructure design. It also manages critical dependencies and interfaces between programs and projects, so that digital operations are changed and benefits secured in a coordinated manner across the organization.

Digital Design Authority has the following characteristics:

- **Program-level view**: The Digital Design Authority reviews digital designs developed by different projects under the same program from an integration perspective to verify if the designs can collectively achieve the program's scope and objective.

- **Independence**: the role of the Digital Design Authority sits outside program governance so that the review and design decisions can be made without any influences from the program.

- **Authority**: The Digital Design Authority role is given the power to accept or reject a design.

More often than not, the role of the Digital Design Authority is ignored due to limited budget and time of a digital program. Even if a program officially establishes a Design Authority role as part of the program's structure, the decisions by the Digital Design Authority to correct and change the designs would often be ignored for fear of being behind schedule, or short on the budget.

The lack of enforcement of the Digital Design Authority often causes unacceptable quality problems and the program therefore has to spend more time and money on fixing these. On the other hand, a full-fledged Digital Authority would add a significant overhead to the time and budget of a program.

How could a well-balanced trade-off be found? It is important to understand that the objective of the Digital Design Authority is not to improve the overall quality of digital designs, but to ensure the consequences of low quality designs are understood by the program manager and stakeholders, so they can make a final decision on whether the program can accept the consequences.

A program cannot fix all design problems and should choose what to change and what not. One of the responsibilities of the Digital Design Authority role is therefore to prioritize the design changes against two criteria:

- the importance of the change, and
- the cost and time of the change.

The prioritization can help the program manager and program governance board to make a final decision on how many changes the program can accept.

It is also recommended that an organization develop corporate standards of digital design principles, policies and guideline to help Design Authority practices be consistent across all programs

MATURITY INDICATOR EXAMPLES

Level 0: Non-existent

- No role or function to ensure design integrity for a digital program has been implemented.

Level 1: Ad hoc

- A solution architect role may be established within a program on an ad hoc basis, to see the landscape and integration of all designs. The role is however neither independent from program management, nor authorized to make decisions on designs from the projects.
- No design principles, policies, or guidelines are available for the solution architect to refer to.

Level 2: Basic

- A senior chief architect role is established within every large program to maintain the architectural integrity across the projects. The role is however neither independent from program management, nor authorized to make decisions on digital designs developed by the projects.
- A number of digital design principles, policies and guidelines are established as de-facto standards, and referred to by the senior chief architect when reviewing digital designs.

Level 3: Defined

- An independent Digital Design Authority role is considered vital, and therefore created as a trusted advisor for every program, residing outside the program.
- The trusted advisor refers to digital design principles, policies and guidelines that are established as standards and enforced across the organization.
- The trusted advisor makes designs recommendations, but the role does not have authority to reject designs.

Level 4: Optimized

- An independent Digital Design Authority role is considered vital to achieving a higher level of maturity of a digital capability.
- The design decisions made by the Digital Design Authority provides multiple options for the decision maker or decision board to choose from when implementing the design changes.
- The role is given the power to accept or reject designs of digital capabilities considered mission-critical to digital business.
- The Digital Design Authority practice has constantly been optimized to the point where the organization maintains its own knowledge of reference architectures and proven designs.

Level 5: Progressive

- Design decisions by the Digital Design Authority role includes a cost and benefit analysis of each change. This helps the decision maker or decision body to prioritize design changes and determine what to change, from business value and implementation effort perspectives.
- The Digital Design Authority is part of the core competency of Digital Development and Operations that provide a competitive advantage.

CAPABILITY 12-3.
DIGITAL CAPABILITY DEVELOPMENT

CAPABILITY DEFINITION

Digital Capability Development is a digital capability used to analyse, design, implement and test the three elements of process, people and technology, which are required to achieve the future blueprint of a digital capability. Digital Capability Development is managed by Digital Program & Project Management.

Development of People, Process & Technology

A business process model supporting the blueprint of a digital capability is commonly defined at the beginning of the development of a digital capability. The business process model may include a business process hierarchical structure, business process flows, business rules, inputs and outputs of each process.

When the business process hierarchy is developed, a big business function is broken down into smaller processes in the functional silo. There would also be multiple levels of business processes with different granularity in the business process hierarchy. Business process flows are also designed in parallel with the business process hierarchy to establish a seamless flow of processes, not only from a functional silo perspective, but also from a cross-functional integration perspective.

The fine-grained processes at the bottom of the business process hierarchy are commonly called tasks or activities. The tasks or activities that are inherently cohesive and require a similar type of human skill are typically classified into a smaller number of groups called responsibilities. The responsibilities that are inherently cohesive and require a similar type of skill are then grouped into a single role. Similar roles can also be grouped into a team or a department. This is how the organizational structure, roles and responsibilities are built from the bottom up. A top-down perspective can be added to the top of the bottom-up organizational designs if a strategic direction has been established for the digital organization.

An organization may have to design the skills and proficiency levels required of staff to perform the role and responsibilities. Organizational structure, role, responsibility, skill, and proficiency level are major parts of the people element. In some instances, an organizational culture is designed as part of the people element when there is urgent need to transform into a new organization, culturally different from the current organization.

Digital applications and digital infrastructure are designed and implemented as the technology element. The designs for the process and people elements provide the technology element with a baseline of business requirements.

When digital applications and infrastructure are ready for testing, the three elements of process, people and technology can be put to the test to see if they collectively fulfil the vision of the target blueprint of a digital capability.

Agile Development Approach

Agile Development is a new paradigm of capability development that is iterative, incremental and continuous in its approach. It has been shaped to address the challenge of meeting frequent changes in requirements, designs and implementations.

This approach makes more sense when digital development is done, because digital technology and business is much more dynamic than average industry, and the digital operations of an organization need to embrace the changes in digital technologies and behaviours of digital users to survive.

Waterfall Development is non-iterative, sequential approach to capability development. There is no going back to the previous phase to change once a phase is complete. This approach is proven and reliable when applied to a larger, long-term development. When the approach is however applied to a development that frequently changes, the development may risk irrelevance.

Agile Development offers the ability to change and adapt rapidly. It helps divide a scope initially identified into independent units of work. An iteration is made to implement some of the units of work, and an iteration may represent a release of a small part of the digital capability, thereby making the development incremental and the deployment continuous. Changes are made through either changing an independent unit of work, adding of a new unit of work, or prioritization of the units of work.

Scrum and Kanban are among the most popular methodologies that implement the Agile Development approach.

The Scrum methodology provides a set of principles, processes and roles to make iterative, incremental and continuous development. In Scrum, an iteration is called a Sprint where a piece of capability is developed and released in approximately 2 to 4 weeks. Analysis, design, implementation, test, communication, collaboration, review and all the rest of it are focused on committed delivery of the outcome in 2 to 4 weeks, with a rolling plan for the next few Sprints.

Kanban is a Just-In-Time (JIT), lean manufacturing method developed by Toyota. The basic idea is that a previous process delivers the exact amount demanded by the next processes. This will eliminate, or at least reduce, Work-In-Progress (WIP) and stocks unused by the next process. It is often referred to as 'demand-pull' supply chain management, which is the opposite of 'supply-push' supply chain management where finished goods and stocks are manufactured or procured before demands are generated. A Kanban, which literally means a signboard in Japanese, is used to communicate the demand of the next process to the previous process. Entire work progress and bottlenecks in digital development can be collected and monitored through the signboards, and changes can be made readily, based on the work progress and bottlenecks.

MATURITY INDICATOR EXAMPLES

Level 0: Non-existent

- A Standard methodology or tool used for digital development does not exist.
- The organization does not have official processes to share proven development practices.
- A development plan and schedule may be created, but the development project does not stick to the plan or schedule.

Level 1: Ad hoc

- No standard methodology or tool for digital capability development exists, but some of the practices for digital development are shared by a few architects, designers and developers.
- One of the Agile development approaches has been tested for feasibility.
- A digital development plan is created, but during a crisis, the plan is often abandoned.
- The success of the development still relies heavily on a few skilled architects, designers and developers, rather than on industrialized development processes and tools.

Level 2: Basic

- Some methodologies and tools are shared by many digital architects, designers and developers, and they therefore became the de-facto standards for digital development.
- The basic disciplines for digital development are institutionalized, but development practices may differ considerably from development to development.

- One of the Agile development approaches is applied to digital capability development, but the benefits of Agile development are not realized as expected, due to the lack of enterprise-wide support and cultural shift.
- The development methodologies and tools still have limited functionalities.

Level 3: Defined

- Corporate standard methodologies and tools are implemented for digital development.
- The development methodologies and tools offer detailed processes, job aids and deliverable templates, and the development tools have comprehensive functionalities to enable the processes.
- The standards are predominantly based on the waterfall approach. One of the Agile development methodologies is also recommended as a standard, but cultural transformation required for successful Agile development has not yet been made.
- The development methodologies and tools are in place, predominantly for the Technology element of a digital capability, and the development of the People and Process elements of a digital capability need to be enabled further.

Level 4: Optimized

- The digital development practices have been optimized to the extent that the development of the People and Process elements of a digital capability are well supported by the development methodologies and tools.
- Significant improvement in measuring the quantitative quality of digital development has been made, helping optimize the performance of the digital development.
- Cultural transformation toward Agile development has been made around collaboration, automation, incremental release, speed and quality.

Level 5: Progressive

- The quality of digital development is measured through qualitative information, enabling continuous innovation of digital development practices.
- Digital capability development is primarily focused on realizing business value and requirements, and releases are therefore prioritized against the business value to be realized.

CAPABILITY 12-4.
DIGITAL CAPABILITY INTRODUCTION

CAPABILITY DEFINITION

Digital Capability Introduction is a digital capability used to introduce part or all of newly developed digital capabilities into the organization, without disrupting existing digital business operations. It includes the ability to transition People, Process and Technology elements that are required to build the maturity level of a digital capability, in accordance with the future state blueprint established through Digital Planning. The Digital Capability Introduction may be repeated for each release of a new capability to the organizational or geographic unit (e.g. location or role) that will receive the new digital capability.

Before the new digital capability is activated, it should be verified that the organization is prepared for using the new digital capability, both for the first day and from there on forward.

Workforce Transition

The existing workforce is evaluated in terms of roles and skills, and a gap analysis against the future roles and skill levels is performed.

The gap analysis identifies which roles can be filled by the existing workforce, which workforce resources need to be re-deployed, and which gaps can be addressed with training, recruiting and selection. This process helps to establish plans for workforce recruiting, training and deployment.

Business Policy & Procedure Deployment

The transition to the new business policies and procedures of a new digital capability needs to be planned, managed and controlled, to enable the organization to follow and execute all the new digital business policies and procedures related to the digital capability.

Digital Application Deployment

The new application and its operating environment needs to be transitioned. Data required by the new digital application needs to be populated. The operating environment needs to be configured to the needs of the organization, after which the application is installed and its parameters configured. Whether the application is correct and consistent for the deployment is then verified.

Digital Infrastructure Deployment

Different business units or departments may have different infrastructure environments, and the potential differences in digital infrastructure environments need to be addressed before deployment of new releases. The goal is to bring the business units or departments up to the digital infrastructure baseline required for the digital capability to function properly. Deployment of the digital infrastructure may include the commissioning and decommissioning of digital infrastructure components.

Hand-over to Digital Service Operations

The IT operation team should verify whether a released digital capability meets operational requirements or not when the new digital capability is introduced into a production environment. Operability and supportability requirements and service acceptance criteria can be used to conduct a maintenance and support impact assessment. Operability testing, go/no-go decision, warranty timeline, service catalogue and service level agreements need to be incorporated into hand-over planning.

MATURITY INDICATOR EXAMPLES

Level 0: Non-existent

- No planning or activities are performed to ensure that the organization is prepared and ready for the introduction of a new digital capability.

Level 1: Ad hoc

- Planning and activities ensuring readiness for the introduction of a digital capability into the organization are performed, and the scope of the plans and activities defined on an ad hoc basis.
- When planning and activities are performed, only the Technology element, including digital application and infrastructure, is in the scope of the plans and activities.

Level 2: Basic

- Planning and activities to ensure the organization is prepared and ready for the introduction of a new digital capability are performed on a regular basis.
- The plans and activities are however focused on the Technology element, resulting in people not always being well prepared for the transition in roles and responsibilities, and the changes in business policies and procedures.

Level 3: Defined

- Standard methodologies and tools are implemented to ensure all People, Process and Technology are considered when preparing the organization for the digital capability introduction.
- IT operational requirements are part of the digital development so that they are planned, designed, implemented, tested and deployed according to standard methodologies, making sure digital operations are ready for the capability introduction.

Level 4: Optimized

- Significant improvement has been made in measuring quantitative readiness for the introduction of a new digital capability.
- The Digital Capability Introduction practices have been optimized to the extent that new workforces are well prepared to meet the skill proficiency levels required for the changed responsibilities and tasks.

Level 5: Progressive

- The quality of Digital Capability Introduction is measured through qualitative information, enabling continuous innovation in ensuring organizational readiness for a new capability introduction.
- Digital Capability Introduction is primarily focused on realizing business value. Any risks involved in the introduction of a new digital capability are identified, the probability of risks and their impact on business values are measured, and mitigation actions are implemented.

CAPABILITY 12-5.
DIGITAL SERVICE OPERATIONS

CAPABILITY DEFINITION

Digital Service Operations is a digital capability used to plan, deliver and measure day-to-day operational services that maintain digital capabilities and support users with the digital capabilities.

After a new digital capability is developed through Digital Capability Development and introduced through Digital Capability Introduction, the new digital capability is maintained and users are supported with incidents and requests associated with the new digital capability through Digital Service Operations.

The technology element of a digital capability needs to be maintained for digital applications and digital infrastructure to be sustainable in the longer term. Users need to be supported when there is an incident with and users make a request regarding the digital applications and infrastructure.

The people element of a digital capability needs to be maintained for roles, skillsets and proficiency levels to be current and optimal in the longer term. The process element of a digital capability needs to be maintained for business policies to be relevant, and for business processes and procedures to be efficient in the longer term.

While all three elements need to be maintained, the technology element is the primary focus of Digital Service Operations, because the technologies behind digital applications and infrastructure tend to change faster and more frequent than the other elements.

ITIL (Information Technology Infrastructure Library)

The Technology element of a digital capability is commonly provided as a service by internal IT within an organization, or external IT service providers in accordance with service level agreements. ITIL is a set of best practices for managing and providing technology as a service. The best practices are utilized by many organizations for IT service management, in which the technology element of digital capabilities is provided to business as a service.

The ITIL lifecycle has five stages: Service Strategy, Service Design, Service Transition, Service Operation and Continual Service Improvement. Although IT organizations and IT service providers may employ all five stages to manage their end-to-end IT operations, Service Operation is the most relevant to Digital Service Operations capability. A quick summary of the five stages is given below.

During the Service Strategy stage, customer needs are captured, the service portfolio is assessed against the needs, and service improvement plans are established. The stage has the following management processes.

- **Business Relationship Management** is to identify customer needs and ensure that appropriate services are delivered to meet those needs.

- **Demand Management** is to forecast future demand and capacity for services, and influence the demand.

- **Service Portfolio Management** is to maintain a healthy service portfolio to meet business needs.

- **Strategy Management** is to establish initiatives, blueprints and a roadmap to change and develop services.

- **Financial Management** is to plan the budget and track costs.

Service levels and requirements are designed in terms of capacity, availability, security and service continuity during the Service Design stage.

- **Service Level Management** is to design service levels and get agreement from service users.

- **Capacity Management** is to design system capacity to achieve the service levels.

- **Availability Management** is to design system availability to achieve the service levels.

- **Security Management** is to design system security to achieve the service levels.

- **Service Continuity Management** is to design disaster recovery to achieve the service levels.

- **Service Design Coordination** is to coordinate all design activities to achieve the service levels collectively.

- **Service Catalogue Management** is to create a catalogue describing services and service levels.

- **Supplier Management** is to procure components required for services and service levels.

Throughout the Service Transition stage, changes to services are initiated, conducted, tested and deployed. The Service Transition stage includes the following management processes.

- **Change Management** is to request, prioritize, approve and monitor changes to the services.

- **Transition Planning &. Support** is to plan and manage the implementation of changes

- **Service Validation & Testing** is to validate and test services changed or created.

- **Release & Deployment Management** is to deploy new or changed services without disruption to current services.

This management process is integrated with Digital Capability Introduction.

- **Asset & Configuration Management** is to manage, log and track the configuration information of released services and assets.

The Service Operation stage of ITIL is to run the deployed services, address incidents and fulfil user requests to keep business running as usual.

- **Event Management** is to monitor and identify events that may affect services proactively.

- **Incident Management** is to address breaches in service level agreements.

- **Problem Management** is to solve root causes of incidents previously unknown.

- **Request Fulfilment** is to fulfil requests made by users.

- **Access Management** is to grant access to authorized users, while preventing authorized access.

- **Service Desk** is a function to perform the Incident Management process.

- **Application Management** is a function to maintain applications and support users.

- **Technical Management** is a function to maintain the IT infrastructure and support users.

Continual Service Improvement is to assess the current state of services and processes, and to implement plans to improve the services and processes.

DevOps

DevOps stands for Development & Operations. It has been initiated to apply the idea and concept of Agile Development to IT operations, so that IT operations can also be 'Agile'. When Agile Development is introduced into an organization and incremental and iterative releases are developed, Operations can often not cope with the frequent releases, compromising the advantage of Agile Development. DevOps intends to solve the issue by introducing the culture and methods behind Agile Development into IT operations, so that IT operations can be aligned with the incremental, iterative and continuous approach of Agile Development.

DevOps can help IT operations to handle the frequent releases through fully automated deployment and monitoring, and seamless collaboration between operations teams and development teams. The close collaboration can also lead to improvement in Incident Management and Problem Management.

MATURITY INDICATOR EXAMPLES

Level 0: Non-existent

- There is no service level agreement through which digital services are provided and maintained.
- No structured approach or formalized process is implemented for Digital Service Operations. Changes to a Digital Capability are for example not conducted in a consistent way, and outages in services are managed in many different ways.

Level 1: Ad hoc

- Few services are managed by a service level agreement, but it lacks comprehensiveness and depth in describing services.
- High-level Change Management processes and Incident Management processes are documented, but the

documents lack details of policies and procedures to enforce the processes.
- The operations tools are focused on recording the list of changes, incidents or requests, and their functionalities are therefore too limited to automate the end-to-end service operation processes.

Level 2: Basic

- Basic service operation management processes are established.
- A very basic service catalogue is available, but the catalogue does not have details on available service options.
- A few critical services are managed by a service level agreement that describes expected levels of services. Some of the relationships between services are identified through service mapping, e.g. X service is required for Y service to be delivered.
- Availability levels of critical services are assessed, but the scope of the assessment is focused on infrastructure. Some of the critical services are protected by a disaster recovery solution.
- Configuration management practice is in an early stage.
- Continuous deployment has been tested to integrate deployment management to Agile Development.
- Change management, Incident management and Request fulfilment policies and processes are well established and enforced.
- Comprehensive tools for service operations are implemented, and their functionalities are rich enough to automate the workflows of management processes such as Change management and Incident Management.

Level 3: Defined

- Almost all management processes and corresponding automation tools required for service operations are defined, documented and enforced as standards.
- The service portfolio is assessed in terms of functional and technical health against customer needs at least annually, and service portfolio improvement plans are created. Service costs are tracked and measured.
- A comprehensive service catalogue is implemented. The catalogue contains details of standard services, service levels and service options, along with a price table.
- Service levels of all critical services are planned and monitored in terms of availability, capacity, security and service continuity across applications and infrastructure.
- A Configuration Management Database is implemented to store configuration item information, but the definition and scope of the configuration items are unclear. Management of configuration items is therefore not mature.
- Release & Deployment Management processes are automatically integrated with Agile Development for iterative and continuous deployment.
- Events are captured, stored and analysed for proactive detection of incidents.
- Service on-boarding and off-boarding processes are automated.
- The service operation tools implemented are comprehensive enough to automate and support the end-to-end processes.

Level 4: Optimized

- The management processes are streamlined due to seamless integration of corresponding tools, and optimized business rules and policies built into the tools.
- User's demand for future capacity is estimated through well-calibrated models and parameters embedded in the demand forecasting tool.

- Service costs are tracked automatically and related back to actual usage of services consumed by an individual or group.
- SLA (Service Level Agreement) developed from a business service perspective is managed independently from OLA (Operation Level Agreement)[41] developed from a technical component service perspective. Almost all Operation Levels are measured consistently, whereas not all Service Levels can be monitored. A breach in OLA can be traced back to a breach in SLA.
- Configuration items are well defined, tracked, audited and accounted for.
- Release & Deployment Management and event monitoring are highly automated and seamlessly integrated with Agile Development.
- Correlation analysis of events are performed to predict possible incidents.

Level 5: Progressive

- More effort is spent on Continual Service Improvement than on other management processes, as the routine management processes are highly automated, increasing business benefits and decreasing costs of Digital Service Operations.
- The Financial health of the service portfolio is assessed to increase the business value of digital service operations.

---

[41] An operational-level agreement (OLA) is the agreement with other support groups, whereas a SLA is the agreement with business or customers. An OLA defines the interdependent relationships of IT support groups responsible for IT operations to achieve service level objectives of service-level agreement (SLA) collectively. The OLA describes the responsibilities of each group toward other support groups, including their IT processes and timeframe for delivery of their services.

- End-to-end monitoring enables accurate measure of business service levels. Any incidents can be linked back to business services.
- Configuration item control is highly integrated with release and change management. Incidents are seldom traced back to incorrect or missing configuration items.
- Event correlation analysis has improved to the extent that Digital Service Operations can take preventive measures to avoid incidents that would breach the SLA.

CAPABILITY 12-6.
DIGITAL QUALITY MANAGEMENT

CAPABILITY DEFINITION

Digital Quality Management is a digital capability used to ensure that digital capabilities are developed in a way that the quality of digital capabilities is predictable and consistent during digital development, and that the quality is maintained throughout the lifecycle of the digital capabilities.

The focus of Digital Quality Management is not only on the final output of a digital capability, but also on the means and processes to produce it. Digital Quality Management therefore includes 'quality assurance' activities to prevent defects, as well as 'quality control' activities to correct defects.

Quality plans commonly include the following:

- Expectations from stakeholders on quality.
- Overarching principles to govern quality management.
- How quality work is to be performed in terms of how to prevent defects from a quality assurance perspective, and how to correct defects from a quality control perspective.

- How to improve quality management ability.

Quality Improvement is a set of activities to identify opportunities to improve quality assurance and quality control abilities, and build and implement quality improvement initiatives.

Preventive & Corrective Quality Management

The purpose of quality assurance is to prevent defects in the final outputs of Digital Development & Operations by managing how a digital capability is developed and maintained. The focus of quality assurance is not on the final outputs, but on interim steps to produce the final outputs. Regular reviews of the quality of processes, people and tools employed for the Digital Development & Operations capabilities against pre-defined quality metrics is essential to predicting and preventing defects.

The purpose of quality control is to correct defects in the final outputs of Digital Development & Operations by validating, verifying and testing the outputs. Quality control focuses on the final outputs, not on the interim steps to produce the outputs. Quality control is commonly performed at every gate to the next stage of a digital development.

Many organizations have implemented a quality management framework that is aligned to an international standard to perform quality assurance and quality control. When it comes to the Digital Development & Operations capabilities, the traditional quality management frameworks do however not always work due to the iterative, incremental and continuous nature of development and delivery of Digital Development & Operations.

The validation, verification and testing of deliverables from the Digital Development & Operations capabilities should be as automated as Agile Development or DevOps is, in order to cope with the repetitive nature of deliverables and deployments. Test automation in particular is the most critical to the contemporary quality management, as it allows testing to be as continuous as Agile Development and DevOps.

Quality Criteria for Digital Capability

In addition to traditional quality criteria, Digital Quality Management should include the metrics to measure the quality around digital customer experiences across multiple digital touchpoints along the digital journey. It may cover the following areas to validate whether a digital capability meets expectations on improved customer experiences.

- Whether user interfaces, including menu structure and user navigation, are easy to use.

- Whether customer navigation processes across multiple digital channels are seamless and does not need swivel chair integration.

- Whether application functionalities are comprehensive enough to accommodate different customer needs for services.

- Whether content and information is rich enough to facilitate the transition and progress on a marketing & sales funnel.

It is also important to include the criteria that validate whether the digital applications, data and infrastructure built into a digital capability is truly Cloud computing-based in its architecture. The following may help to establish the criteria:

- Whether IT resources can be populated by a user without help from IT staff, using the service catalogue on the self-service portal.

- Whether the capacity of IT resources can automatically increase or decrease as directed by service level objects.

- Whether the usage of IT resources can be tracked and costed to the consumers automatically.

- Whether the infrastructure is built on cheap, commodity hardware to support horizontal scaling, rather than on high-end machines for vertical scaling.

- Whether the application is stateless enough to take advantage of the horizontal scalability.

- Whether the applications are designed for failure and are coupled loosely enough to integrate between the Cloud and on-premises.

MATURITY INDICATOR EXAMPLES

Level 0: Non-existent

- Testing is performed during digital development, but there is no quality management principles or framework to govern the testing processes, testing tools or test cases.

Level 1: Ad hoc

- Quality is managed for large projects and programs only. A Quality principle or framework is applied, requirements are validated, deliverables are verified, and final output are tested according to the quality principles or framework.
- Because the quality management is performed on an ad hoc basis, most projects do not have proper quality management in place.
- A brief quality review may be performed by many projects, but the review practices are not consistent across the projects.
- No quality management practice is implemented for Digital Service Operations.

Level 2: Basic

- A de-facto standard quality framework, methodology and practices through which requirements are validated, interim deliverables are verified and final outputs are tested is shared across many projects.

- Quality criteria, are however not consistent across the projects, resulting in inconsistent quality deliverables across the projects.
- Quality management is focused more on quality control than on quality assurance, resulting in digital development spending more time fixing problems than planned.
- Digital operation teams have established quality plans, but the plans are not always enforced.

Level 3: Defined

- A central quality management team is responsible for assuring quality throughout Digital Capability Development and Digital Service Operations. Roles and responsibilities of the other players in quality management are also defined.
- A standard quality-management framework, principles, policies, quality criteria, processes, tools, templates and job aids are all established to facilitate quality management.
- Digital quality is an integral part of the corporate quality management framework.
- The enterprise-wide support and enforcement in quality management have increased consistency in deliverables across many projects.

Level 4: Optimized

- Quality improvement initiatives have been created and implemented to optimize the quality management practices.
- Quality management process are highly automated by quality management tools. Not only are the workflows automated, but quality is also measured automatically.
- Quality metrics for Digital Service Operations have been established and incorporated into the quality management framework and tools.
- The quality criteria are predominantly quantitative metric-based. The quantitative measurements are summarized and

presented on a dashboard view. The dashboard does however not necessarily provide information explaining the reasons behind the quality levels achieved.

Level 5: Progressive

- This level of the Digital Quality Management capability provides qualitative explanations for the quantitative measurement of the quality.
- Quality management is an integral part of continual improvement in Digital Capability Development and Digital Service Operations, e.g. Continual Service Improvement (CSI[42]) of the ITIL is focused on quality management processes and quality metrics to improve service levels.

---

[42] The Continual Service Improvement (CSI) continually improves the effectiveness and efficiency of service delivery and support processes, and services delivered. The CSI processes may use methods from quality management in order to learn from past successes and failures. CSI initiatives to improve the effectiveness and efficiency are commonly established and implemented.

DIGITAL TRANSFORMATION PLANNING METHODOLOGY

This section is a guide on performing strategy planning on digital capabilities, offering a digital transformation planning methodology and deliverable samples. The digital capabilities and maturity models explained throughout this book are aligned with the planning methodology. The Digital Capability Model is used as a framework for the assessment of current digital capabilities and the design of future digital capabilities. The assessment and design tasks are all critical parts of the planning methodology.

This planning methodology aims at supporting a full-scale digital capability improvement journey that diagnoses current digital capabilities, identifies needs for future digital capabilities, develops future digital capability blueprints and digital strategies, delivers one or more digital capabilities to meet those needs, and ensure that the value of those digital capabilities can be sustained over time.

The planning methodology consists of the following 3 stages:

- Stage 1. Identify current state.
- Stage 2. Design future state.

- Stage 3. Develop roadmap.

The purpose of Stage 1 is to assess the current operating model for digital business and translate it to maturity levels of digital capabilities to measure the current state of the digital capabilities quantitatively to run the digital business. Stage 1 has the following 2 tasks:

- Task 1-1. Assess the current state operating model.
- Task 1-2. Define the maturity level of the current digital capability.

The purpose of Stage 2 is to define future maturity levels of digital capabilities to run a successful digital business, and to translate it to a future operating model for the digital business. Stage 2 has the following 2 tasks:

- Task 2-1. Set the maturity level of the future digital capability.
- Task 2-2. Design the future operating model.

The purpose of Stage 3 is to identify gaps between the state of current digital capabilities and the state of future digital capabilities, and define initiatives and a roadmap to bridge the gaps. Stage 3 has the following 3 tasks:

- Task 3-1. Identify gaps and improvement opportunities.
- Task 3-2. Develop initiatives and business cases.
- Task 3-3. Develop a roadmap.

TASK 1-1.
ASSESS CURRENT STATE OPERATING MODEL

This task is to understand how the organization operates to run its digital business. The Digital Capability Model is used as a framework to analyse the current operating model.

It is important to consider the three elements of People, Process and Technology of a digital capability when assessing the operating model. The result of the assessment of the current operating model state is to be used to evaluate the maturity levels of the digital capability.

The steps to perform the task are described in detail below.

1. Review the documents describing the digital processes, organizational structure, digital roles & responsibilities and digital systems including application, data and infrastructure if available. Not many organizations have these documented, and it is therefore often difficult to obtain relevant documents. If a response to document requests is delayed, it is often a signal that the documents don't exist. In this case, it is wise to move on to other sources of the information quickly.

2. Review the digital systems by assessing the menu structure of the websites and business functionalities of the digital applications. The digital system review is often more helpful to obtain accurate information on the current state of digital processes, information and roles & responsibilities than other information sources, especially when there is little to no documentation of the operating model in place.

3. Conduct interviews with stakeholders, digital practitioners, internal users, external users and customers. Questionnaires need to be prepared for the interview in order to gather information that could not be determined from the document and system review. The capability

definitions and maturity indicators of the Digital Capability Model may provide a baseline for questions relevant to the context of the organization. For example, "Do we have a digital customer journey map?" or "Do we perform correlation analysis of products that are viewed and purchased by customers?"

4. Summarize the findings from the document review, system review and the interviews into the digital capabilities if possible. Issues and needs, as well as a snapshot of the current state digital capabilities may be identified in this way. The issues and needs will be incorporated into the requirements used to define the future state of digital capabilities.

Key Inputs

Any information on the current state of digital processes, digital organizations and roles and responsibilities, digital application, and digital infrastructure can be used as inputs. A digital capability diagnostic tool may be created and utilized to collect and organize the information gathered from the document review, system review and interviews.

Key inputs include:

- The Digital Capability Model customized for the organization.
- Digital capability diagnostic tool, e.g. MS Excel-based template to organize all key information received.
- Documents on the digital operating model, e.g. digital process models, organizational structure diagram, digital role description or job manual, digital application portfolio and infrastructure inventory.
- Interview questionnaire.

Key Outputs

Findings from the document review, system review and interviews should be summarized and organized into relevant digital capabilities.

- Interview questionnaire answered.
- Digital capability diagnostic tool with current state information.
- Current state assessment summary.

Digital Capability Diagnostic Tool

Digital Capability		Capability urgency (A)	Capability importance (B)	Capability priority (A,B)	Weight	Current Maturity level	Future Maturity level (~2yrs)	Future Maturity level (~4yrs)	Current issues and requirements for future state of the digital capability which are gathered from the client
	User experience testing	3	4	Medium	70	2	3	4	
Digital marketing		4	5.0	Medium high	82	0.6	3.2	4.2	
	Digital brand marketing	5	5	High	100	1.5	4	5	
	Paid search	2	4	Medium low	55	1	3	4	

[Figure 44: Digital Capability Diagnostic Tool Example]

TASK 1-2.
DEFINE MATURITY LEVEL OF CURRENT DIGITAL CAPABILITY

The purpose of this task is to translate the findings from the assessment of the current state operating model into maturity levels of the digital capabilities.

The detailed steps to perform the task are described below.

1. Review whether the Process, People and Technology elements of each digital capability are implemented and combined properly to create the required business outcome. Evaluate each element against the indicators shown as illustrative examples of the maturity levels of a digital capability.

2. Assign a maturity level to each digital capability based on the evaluation of the three elements. If a digital capability is considered to have both aspects of maturity level 2 and maturity level 3 for example, then give a median value such as level 2.5. The digital capability diagnostic tool can be used to log maturity levels. Internal workshops may be required to discuss and agree on the maturity levels given to digital capabilities.

3. Add rationale behind the maturity level of a current digital capability. The rationale is to be used to set up future state maturity levels, design future operating models and develop business cases.

Key Inputs

- Interview questionnaire answered.
- Digital capability diagnostic tool with current state information.
- Current state assessment summary.

Key Outputs

- Digital capability diagnostic tool with current state maturity levels.
- Current state assessment report.

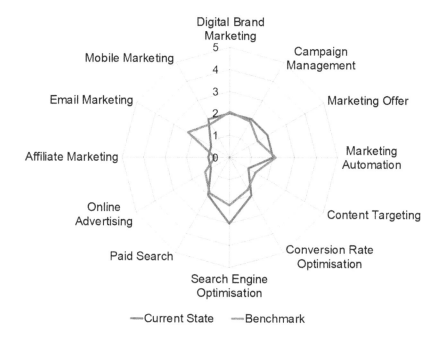

[Figure 45: Current State Maturity Level Example]

TASK 2-1.
SET MATURITY LEVEL OF FUTURE DIGITAL CAPABILITY

The objective of this task is to set target state maturity levels of digital capabilities in order to provide specific directions for the future operating model of the digital business.

The target state maturity-level of a digital capability sets a goal that the digital capability is to achieve in the future through its operating model where the People, Process and Technology elements are combined in a unique way to produce the expected business outcome.

The steps required to perform the task are:

1. Understand the corporate business strategy, business unit strategy and the goal of digital business. The strategy and goal provide critical inputs into setting specific target state maturity levels and operating model. Unfortunately, many companies do not have these documented. If this is the case, interview a few executives who can explain the intentions and expectations of the leadership on digital business. This provides top-down requirements for future state digital capabilities.

2. Benchmark the digital capabilities against those of major competitors and the top tier players in your industry, or even other industries based on information available. The information on their digital capabilities of the front-office and middle-office may be obtained by researching online, while information on the other capabilities may be difficult to obtain because it is not visible to anyone outside their organization.

3. Set future state maturity-levels of digital capabilities based on the business strategy and digital business goal, and the benchmark. The maturity level indicators and examples of the Digital Capability Model should be read carefully and each maturity level of a digital capability understood in terms of what it means for the People, Process and Technology elements, before setting the desirable target states. It would be unrealistic to set a target maturity level too aggressively. If the current state maturity level of a digital capability is level 2, then aim to achieve maturity level 3 or 3.5 in 1 to 2 years' time. It would also be unwise to set target maturity levels for other digital capabilities too differently. If the target maturity level of one digital capability is 2 and that of another digital capability is 4 when the two digital capabilities have significant dependencies on each other, the two capabilities will not work together properly. It is strongly recommended that all maturity levels of digital capabilities be balanced against one another.

Key Inputs

- Corporate and business unit strategy, and goal of digital business.
- Digital capability diagnostic tool.

Key Outputs

- Implication of business strategy and digital business goal on digital capability.
- Digital capability benchmark result.
- Digital capability diagnostic tool with future state maturity levels assigned.

[Figure 46: Digital Marketing Maturity Level Example]

TASK 2-2.
DESIGN FUTURE STATE OPERATING MODEL

The purpose of this task is to translate the future maturity levels of digital capabilities into a future state operating model. If the implication of a maturity level for the People, Process and Technology elements are understood, this translation task won't be challenging.

It is important to remember that all digital capabilities have a certain level of dependency on one another, and they should therefore be designed in such a way that they can be integrated as seamlessly as possible.

The operating model designs should be high-level enough to see a big picture, but detailed enough to calculate benefit and costs of implementation of the digital capabilities. This design is not to be used for the implementation of the digital capabilities, but for the development of the business case for them.

The steps to build a digital operating model translated from the maturity levels of digital capabilities are described below.

1. Determine the operating principles that are aligned to 'Operational Excellence' or 'Customer Intimacy'. A good example of the principles is "Streamline digital business processes by extensive digital tool automation", because the principle can drive the design of digital processes that 'Technology' automates, rather than processes that are dependent on the proficiency of 'People'.

2. Establish operating performance targets that set the objectives the future operating model should achieve. The performance targets are set across digital capabilities and for a specific digital capability. The performance targets can give criteria against which a design option of the future operating model can be assessed, to see whether the option can live up to the maturity level of a digital capability.

3. Create options for the operating model of a digital capability. First, establish business processes with the assumption that those processes can be automated by digital tools, or the digital tools can at least help and support users to perform the processes. Where digital tools cannot automate or support, design People element to perform the processes. Current business processes may be reused to build future business processes where the processes have the potential for competitive advantage. The issues and needs identified during 'Task 1-1' may be considered. Assess the Current State Operating Model as part of the requirements for the future state operating model. Do not dive deeply into detailed designs such as detailed activities of a process, detailed responsibilities of a role, or detailed functionalities of a tool which are required for implementation projects. This is not an implementation project but strategic planning. Stop at the level of design where benefits and costs to be analysed in 'Task 3-2' can be estimated reasonably.

4. Integrate the operating models across all digital capabilities. Some designs around the boundaries of the digital capabilities would probably be redundant, missed, or misaligned. A process of a digital capability may for example not be integrated to another process of another digital capability. Re-align and re-structure the processes, people and technology elements of the digital capabilities in the scope.

If there is a shortage of time or skills to design future operating models, this task may be skipped and the next task executed. Define digital initiatives with future state maturity-levels of the digital capabilities without the future state operating models. The development of business cases of the digital initiatives would however be less accurate as future operating models on which the business cases are based will not be available.

Key Inputs

- Digital capability diagnostic tool with future state maturity-levels assigned.

Key Outputs

- Future operating model per digital capability.
- Integrated future operating model across all digital capabilities.

TASK 3-1.
IDENTIFY GAP AND IMPROVEMENT OPPORTUNITY

Both the current and future state models of the digital capabilities in scope are now available. During this task, critical gaps between the current state and the future state of the digital capabilities are assessed, and solutions to bridge the gaps are identified and organized into opportunities to improve the digital capabilities.

The future state operating model is 'what' needs to be achieved, while the opportunities are 'how' the future state operating model is achieved. It is important to separate 'how to achieve it' from 'what to achieve' in order to establish a road map and implementation plans. Stage 3 is all about 'how to achieve' the future state maturity level and the operating model defined in Stage 2.

The steps to take to establish 'how to achieve' the future state are described below.

1. Compare the current maturity levels of the digital capabilities with the target maturity levels to see what the critical gaps between them are. This high-level gap analysis

can help highlight the big picture of the differences between the current state and the future state.

2. Compare the current operating model of the digital capabilities to the target operating model to find gaps between them. This gap analysis will identify the differences in the people, process and technology elements. If a gap between both operating models is not strongly aligned with the high-level gaps identified during step 1, it may be considered as not being important.

3. List the gaps identified from both comparisons. Although there may be a certain level of redundancy and misalignment in the gaps, not all of them need to be fixed at this stage. Identify actions to bridge the gaps. For example:

   - Gap: "The functionality of the social listening tool is limited."
   - Action: "Improve the functionalities of the social listening tool."

4. Consolidate similar or related actions into a smaller number of actions, removing redundancy and misalignment in actions. The restructured actions represent opportunities to improve the digital capabilities.

Key Inputs

- Current state maturity levels of digital capabilities.
- Current state operating models of digital capabilities.
- Future state maturity levels of digital capabilities.
- Future state operating models of digital capabilities.

Key Outputs

- Gap list.
- Improvement opportunity list.

Capability	Priority	Improvement opportunities
Social listening	●	· Develop a social listening plan including a list of social media to listen to, what contents to gather, how to gather, frequency of gathering, how to translate the contents and decide trends and user's intents, how to summarize the analysis, how to apply them for business, etc. · Design end-to-end processes from listening to business change, implement a social listening system, and designate a market analyst with clear role & responsibilities defined.
Social marketing	◑	· Develop a social marketing plan, which is tightly aligned with the customer journey maps, the digital brand marketing plan, and the campaign programs. It should include the role of the social website channel as a viral marketing tool, and marketing objectives including increasing brand awareness for what products, and services to market to whom with what messages & contents. · Design end-to-end processes of integrating social marketing activities with other marketing channels/efforts, and designate a social marketer with clear role & responsibilities defined.
Online community management	◑	· Develop a strategy how to create a strong 'fan' base enthusiastically supporting the X client brand and apply it to the guideline for building and maintaining online communities. · Designate a social manager with clear role & responsibilities defined.
Ratings and reviews management	◐	· Implement a system for taking ratings & reviews from clients within the X client channels, and develop system for gathering and analyzing ratings & reviews data from all relevant websites. · Develop guidelines to responding to those ratings and reviews based on possible scenarios.
Content moderation	◐	· Develop internal guidelines for monitoring, identifying, and responding to the contents that need to be moderated. · Develop clear rules to be applied for community operations and notify to the communities.

[Figure 47: Improvement Opportunity Example]

TASK 3-2.
CREATE DIGITAL INITIATIVE & BUSINESS CASE

The purpose of this task is to aggregate the improvement opportunities identified in the previous step logically into digital initiatives. Generally, improvement opportunities within the same digital initiative will share many functions, processes, responsibilities and technology in common.

In many cases, the principles of aggregating opportunities into initiatives is driven by the way the digital organization is structured and decision-making accountabilities for digital business are shared. Relying on the organizational structure or the governance structure as a means for organizing digital initiatives has the advantage of making leadership and accountability assignments clear within the organization.

Follow the steps below to shape implementable digital initiatives.

1. Document overarching objectives that can provide direction and guidance to identification of digital initiatives. The objectives can give top-down focus, stakeholders' intentions and expectations, and the scope of the digital initiatives. The organization may for example indicate a desire to expand their customer base into a younger generation through digital channels with a specific target of a 10% increase in the number of customers in the younger customer segment. If this is not given from top-down, a desirable but achievable target can be established from the bottom up. Establishing objectives focuses the digital initiatives on a more specific business goal so that the investment is not wasted. The objectives may:

   - Capture the organization's major concerns.
   - Identify the specific business results that the organization hopes to achieve, e.g. improved market share in digital channels.
   - Single out the mechanism by which the organization expects to achieve its business results, e.g. improved social support services.
   - Lend itself to the creation of measures of success, e.g. stock availability and online order fulfilment accuracy.

2. Group the improvement opportunities into a smaller number of digital initiatives. When an opportunity is dependent on another, both opportunities should be grouped into the same initiative. Opportunities are dependent on each other if:

- An opportunity is in the same digital capability as another.
- An opportunity is managed by the same function, team, or organization as another.
- An opportunity is in the same process flow as another.

Initiatives should be created and organized in a way that the initiatives can be implemented as independently from one another as possible. When initiative X is for example dependent on initiative Y and the investment in initiative Y is not approved by the decision-making body, then initiative X can't be implemented as initially planned.

3. Develop a business case per digital initiative. A business case includes a benefit and cost analysis. Refer to the future operating model and the corresponding improvement opportunities to quantify the benefits the digital initiative can generate, and the costs the initiative requires. A variety of standard-value analysis techniques may be used to determine the relative value that each digital initiative will create for the organization, including Discounted Cash Flow (DCF) and Return on Invested Capital (ROIC).

4. Escalate the business cases to the decision-maker or decision-making committee for approval. Anyone or any committee that has accountability for making decision on investment in digital initiatives should review the business cases, prioritize the digital initiatives based on the business case review and decide whether to approve, reject, or hold off on each one of the digital initiatives. The approval process may occur after a road map is developed.

Key Inputs

- Opportunity list.

Key Outputs

- Overarching digital objectives.

- Digital initiative list.
- Business cases.

TASK 3-3.
DEVELOP ROADMAP

This task defines a road map that will be used to reach the future state operating model and maturity levels of the digital capabilities. A road map includes a high-level sequence of the digital initiatives approved by decision-makers.

The sequence of the initiatives should consider dependencies among the initiatives. The completion of a Big Data architecture may for example be a prerequisite for proceeding with other initiatives, such as a Social Listening architecture.

A road map may also include quick-wins. A quick-win is a solution that can be implemented easily with little effort. Quick wins may be found easily during 'Task 1-1 Assess Current State Operating Model'. They require relatively little capital investment and have low risk. Success cases from quick-wins may be used to build momentum to get buy-in and sponsorship of a longer-term digital transformation across the organization.

1. Develop a profile per digital initiative. An initiative profile commonly contains the initiative's name, sponsor, owner, objective, scope, high-level solution, high-level tasks, budget estimation, human resource requirements, period, dependency, constraint, assumption, etc.

2. Develop a road map, considering all the dependencies between the initiatives. All the initiative profile data may have to be reviewed to determine the optimized sequence of the initiatives.

Key Inputs

- Digital initiative list.
- Business cases.

Key Outputs

- Digital initiative profile.
- Road map.

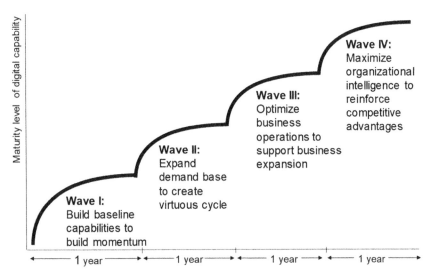

[Figure 48: High-level Roadmap Example]

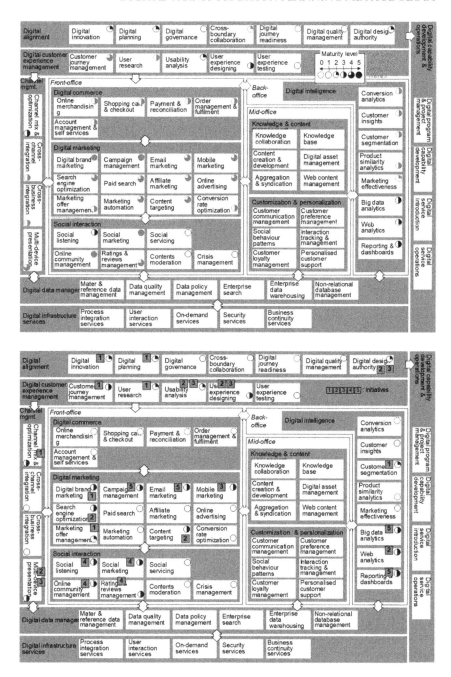

[Figure 49: Roadmap Example - Wave 1 and 2]

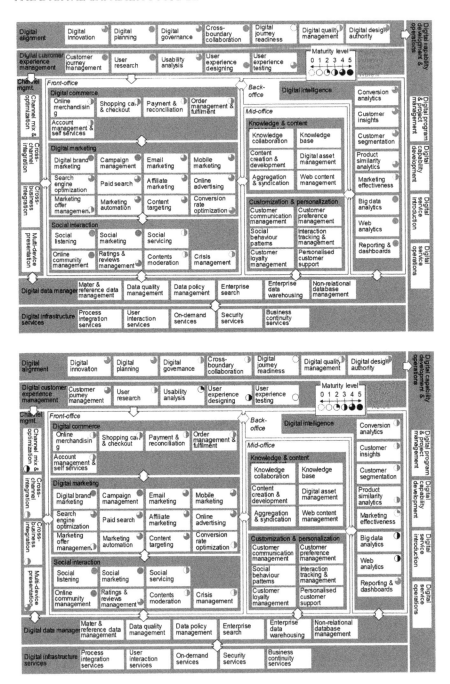

[Figure 50: Roadmap Example - Wave 3 and 4]

Epilogue:

APPLYING ARTIFICIAL INTELLIGENCE

Machine Learning-based Artificial Intelligence

Artificial Intelligence (AI) and Machine Learning are gaining traction in the digital space. Machine Learning is a subset of AI, as AI has a larger scope that may include unconscious perception and decision-making based on for example gut feeling. Machine Learning is however believed to be the most feasible way of implementing AI for now.

Machine Learning was mentioned earlier in this book, but not established as a standalone capability of The Digital Capability Model. This is because, in my opinion, it is in the early stage of operational maturity in the digital space and has therefore a lot more potential to mature than the other capabilities, despite the fact that Machine Learning has been around for decades.

One simple example of the immaturity of Machine Learning-based AI in the digital space, is that many of the business use case of adopting Machine Learning technologies is not based on Big Data architecture and scale-out (horizontally-scaled) architecture. This AI architecture is not truly optimized for digital business and operations to take advantage of massive amounts of unstructured and structured data, with significantly cheap and elastic infrastructure. As those digital characteristics are not met, it is essentially the same Machine Learning as decades ago when IBM's expensive host, Deep Blue, beat the world champion at chess.

As the level of adoption of Machine Learning technologies into digital business operations matures, it will be established as a standalone digital capability in the Digital Capability Model.

Business use cases, conceptual architecture and practical development of Machine Learning are briefly described in this epilogue from a business user perspective. When Machine Learning is included as a standalone digital capability in the next edition of this book, its maturity levels and indicators will also be discussed.

Business Use Cases

Machine Learning based AI is gaining momentum, particularly in the security and risk management areas in businesses. Threat detection, vulnerability assessment, fraud detection and credit risk assessment are good examples. Machine Learning has however a potential to have broader and more widespread impact on digital business operations, due to the abundance of digital data to be used for learning by the machine.

Machine Learning can support digital business operations in two ways:

- **Strategic support**: to help strategic decision makers make informed decisions by providing practical insights into unseen patterns behind the scene and offering predictions about the future.

- **Operational support**: to automate business processes by capturing business events real-time, making operational decisions and responding to the events based on the decisions.

The strategic and operational support offered by Machine Learning can be implemented with the following uses cases within The Digital Capability Model context. Not all the use cases have great potential, but they are worth investigating to see the big picture of the profound impacts that Machine Learning may have on digital businesses behind the individual use cases.

Use-cases in the Front-office

- **Digital Customer Journey Management**: Machine Learning can recommend an optimal customer journey and route to purchasing stage for each customer segment.

- **Social Listening**: Machine Learning can understand what customers are talking about much better and possibly why, by detecting unseen patterns behind the words and pictures. Social Listening is one of the digital capabilities where Machine Learning has great potential.

- **Social Media Marketing**: Machine Learning can send optimal messages and content to the right customers at the right time on social media.

- **Rating & Review Management**: Machine Learning can sense negative tones in review comments, and alert Social Managers or respond to the negative comments in an intelligent way.

- **Social Crisis Management**: Machine Learning can detect the possibility of a business crisis, prioritize them and alert Social Managers.

- **Paid Search**: Machine Learning can calculate the optimal price for Google AdWords bidding to optimize Return On Investment.

- **Marketing Offer Management**: Machine Learning can create effective marketing offers, including dynamic prices based on the customer's responses in the past.

- **Marketing Automation**: Machine Learning can create optimal, dynamic workflows to automate marketing processes and perform the marketing activities as defined by the workflows.

- **Conversion Rate Optimization**: Machine Learning can create a new conversion model in which marketers can see how conversion rate will change when they make a change to the marketing mix, such as price and marketing offer.

- **Lead Management**: Machine Learning can nurture many different leads effectively through optimal channel, message, marketing offer and timing for effective engagement, considering the contexts and interests of individual customers. It can perceive the level of buying intent behind the words qualified prospects use. Lead Management is another digital capability where Machine Learning has a great potential.

- **Online Merchandising**: Machine Learning can make personalized product recommendations. This is a proven practice.

- **Channel Mix & Optimization**: Machine Learning can recommend the optimal channel mix for each customer segment.

Use-cases in the Middle-office

- **Social Behaviour Management**: Machine Learning can identify patterns of user behaviours on social websites and recommend optimal grouping of users based on the behaviours.

- **Interaction Tracking & Management**: Machine Learning can track customers' interactions with the organization and learn how to respond better next time, and respond accordingly or recommend optimal responses.

- **Digital Customer Services**: Machine Learning can communicate with customers over chatting apps, email, phone, and other messaging tools for customer services, take customer service requests, create service tickets, prioritize the tickets, and respond to the requests or escalate to the appropriate staff by capturing words like refund requests, technical issues and delivery issues.

Use-cases for Digital Intelligence

- **Product Similarity Analytics**: Machine Learning can analyse and update similarity of products, services and content without involvement from human analysts.

- **Customer Segmentation**: Machine Learning can detect profitable commonalities in customers and recommend optimal customer segments. It can create a number of micro-segments resulting from analysing individual variables required for this level of granular segmentation. This includes predicting customer lifetime value and performing user-based collaborative filtering without human involvement.

- **Conversion Analytics**: Machine Learning can find hidden patterns of conversions from the customer interactions and purchasing history in the sales funnel.

Use-cases for Digital Data Management

- **Enterprise Search**: Machine Learning can understand the context of the search requests, take in a long sentence as search keywords, and find more relevant search results than traditional indexing methods can. It can learn based on how a user responds to the search results.

- **Master Data Management**: Machine Learning can find duplicate customer records and inconsistent customer data.

Architecture & Development

Machine Learning-based AI can be taught by humans or learn by itself. The former is referred to as Supervised Learning, and the latter as Unsupervised Learning.

The AI is given 'inputs' and 'outputs' by humans for Supervised Learning, so that it can learn what is expected for outputs in relation to inputs. An AI can learn whether a blog post contains a critical incident or not, whether a customer request has high priority or not, or which marketing offer can produce the best response from a customer through Supervised Learning. Algorithms such as Classification[43] and Regression[44] are examples of those employed for Supervised Learning.

On the other hand, the AI is only given 'inputs' for Unsupervised Learning, so that the AI can discover unexplored patterns behind the inputs based on its algorithms, and produce new insights into the data. Algorithms such as Clustering[45] is an example of those employed for Unsupervised Learning.

Supervised Learning is discussed here to explain Machine Learning architecture and development, as it is much more frequently used in business.

Let's take an example where human intelligence can be replaced with Machine Learning-based AI to explain how a Machine Learning system is developed and used for business in an easy way.

---

[43] A Classification algorithm is used to classify input into different categories, which is output.

[44] A Regression algorithm is used to discover the relationships among variables in order to create a functional equation out of inputs and outputs.

[45] A Clustering algorithm is used to group a set of inputs in such a way that inputs in the same group are more similar to each other than to those in other groups.

"A real estate company wanted to estimate a proper sales price of its customer's property. An external financial <u>consultant</u> was invited by the company to create an optimal financial <u>formula</u> through which the sales price of a property is predicted. The consultant extracted <u>factors</u> which affect sales price of a property from historical sales data, such as number of rooms and land size, and combined the factors to come up with the financial formula. The consultant used some of historical property sales data to create the formula, and used some other historical property sales data to verify if the formula calculates the sales price of the properties sold correctly. Now, the property sales rep can use the formula to predict the sales price of a property on the market."

The consultant in the example can be replaced with a <u>Machine Learning framework</u>[46] that contains mathematical algorithms. The financial formula created by the consultant represents a <u>Model</u> created by a Machine Learning framework. The processes through which a Machine Learning system is implemented to replace the financial consultant are shown below.

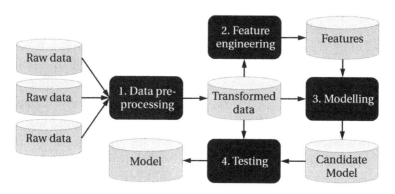

[Figure 51: Machine Learning Development Processes]

---

[46] A Machine Learning framework is a set of software programs that contains one or more mathematical and statistical algorithms such as Classification, Regression, Decision Trees and Clustering.

1. **Data Pre-processing**: Raw data - historical property sales data - is collected, cleansed, normalized, combined and transformed for the Machine Learning framework and algorithm to understand and consume. These processes are mostly done by data engineers skilled in database management and data manipulation.

2. **Feature Engineering**: Features are extracted from transformed data. Features are structured data that have an impact on the output of a Machine Learning model. In the example, the factors, such as size of land, that have an impact on property sales price are features. Human data analysts and Machine Learning algorithms are commonly used to identify the right features.

3. **Modelling**: A Machine Learning framework uses the features and some transformed data to develop the right model through which output - property sales price - is calculated. Multiple Machine Learning frameworks and algorithms may be tested to see which framework or algorithm develops the model that produces the best results. While the model is optimized, the features are also optimized for the model to produce the best output.

4. **Testing**: Some 'other' transformed data, which has not been used to develop the model, is used to verify that the candidate model produces reasonable results. The transformed data used for modelling should not be used for testing. In the example above, some other historical property sales data is used to see whether the model produces sales prices that are close to the prices at which the properties sold.

When the testing is successful, the model is deployed into a production environment. As soon as the sales rep in the example above records a property on the real-estate website, the web site will give him a reasonable sales price.

A Machine Learning model can act as a human worker in the digital space. When a customer request for after-service is for example recorded on a tool used for Digital Customer Services, the tool forwards the request to the Machine Learning model and not to customer service staff. After receiving the request, the model decides which customer service category it belongs to, which priority level it has, and to whom it should be allocated for resolution, and acts accordingly.

Many Digital Intelligence capabilities can also make use of Machine Learning. Machine Learning can for example be applied to identify relationships among products, services and content for 'Capability 8-1. Product Similarity Analytics'. Apache Mahout is a famous Machine Learning framework for collaborative filtering ready for immediate use. Apache Mahout is deployed on top of Hadoop using MapReduce.

The beauty of applying a Machine Learning framework is that in-depth and specialized knowledge of the complex statistical algorithms is not required to implement AI for the digital capabilities.

GLOSSARY

Term	Description
BPM	Business Process Management. A discipline that uses methods to design, automate and monitor processes. See See the footnote 22 of 'Capability 7-2. Customer Communication Management'.
CTR	Click-Through Rate. ratio of users that click on a web link to the total users who view the webpage or email containing the web link. See the footnote 9 of 'Capability 3-4. Content Targeting'.
Data Mart	A subset of the data warehouse. The data in the data warehouse is re-organized into the data mart. See the footnote 26 of 'Capability 8-2. Customer Insights'.
Data Lake	The largest data storage that holds unstructured, semi-structured and structured data sets. See the footnote 28 of 'Capability 8-6. Big Data Analytics'.
ETL	Extraction, Transformation and Loading. ETL is performed when data is moved from OLTP to OLAP. See the footnote 25 of 'Capability 8-2. Customer Insights'.
HTML	Hyper Text Markup Language. The standard markup language for creating web pages. See the footnote 6 of 'Capability 3-2. Search Engine Optimization'.

Term	Description
HTTP	Hyper-Text Transfer Protocol. A protocol that defines how web data is transferred between two systems. See the footnote 29 of 'Capability 8-7. Web Analytics'.
IMDB	In-Memory Database. A database management system that stores data in memory as main storage. See the footnote 27 of 'Capability 8-6. Big Data Analytics'.
JSON	JavaScript Object Notation. A text file format that uses JavaScript syntax to organize data . See the footnote 30 of 'Capability 9-1. Non-relational Data Management'.
Metadata	Metadata is a set of data that describes information about other data. See the footnote 21 of 'Capability 6-3. Content Lifecycle Management'.
OLAP	On-Line Analytics Processing. A processing style of compurer programs that perform comlex data analytics. See the footnote 24 and 25 of 'Capability 8-2. Customer Insights'.
OLTP	On-Line Transaction Processing. A processing style of computer programs that perform simple, but frequent business transactions. See the footnote 22 of 'Capability 8-2. Customer Insights'.
Relational Database	A database in which data entities are structured in a way to identify relations between the data entities. See the footnote 5 and 6 of 'Capability 2-3. Social Media Servicing'.
SaaS	Software as a Service. A software delivery model where software is provided on the Cloud. See the footnote 32 of 'Capability 9-4. Master Data Management'.
SQL	Structured Query Language. A computer language used to create and access structured data held in a relational database management system (RDBMS). See the footnote 5 of 'Capability 2-1. Social Listening'.
XML	eXtensible Markup Language. A markup language that defines markup tags to encode documents in a format that is both human-readable and machine-readable. See the footnote 8 of 'Capability 3-2. Search Engine Optimization'.

REFERENCES

Multiples sources have been consulted to crosscheck and verify the facts and trends of the digital technologies and business operations. Although a biased selection of sources has not been made, not all sources are listed below.

* * *

Caylar, P., Dmitriev, M., Fletcher, B., & Grieder, P. (2014). Change the Channel: A New Multitouch Point Portfolio. McKinsey&Company.

Capgemini Research Report (2012). Digital Shopper Relevancy: Profiting from your customers' Desired All Channel Experience. Capgemini.

Mayer-Schönberger, V & Cukier, K (2013). Big Data: A Revolution That Will Transform How We Live, Work and Think. John Murrav.

Hensle, B. (2014). Customer Experience Reference Architecture - Today's Winners Are Defined by Customer Experience. Oracle Corporation.

Nielsen, J. (1995). 10 Usability Heuristics for User Interface Design. Available at https://www.nngroup.com/articles/ten-usability-heuristics.

Chrzanowska, N. (2017). 12 Powerful Ways Social Listening Can Help Your Business. Available at https://brand24.com/blog/12-powerful-ways-social-listening-help-business/.

Haines, B. (2015). 14 Amazing Social Media Customer Service Examples. Available at https://blog.bufferapp.com/social-media-customer-service.

SalesForce.com (2016). Campaign Management Implementation Guide. Available at https://resources.docs.salesforce.com/210/latest/en-us/sfdc/pdf/salesforce_campaign_implementation_guide.pdf.

Gilliland, N. (2017). Six Successful Examples of Online Brand Communities. Available at https://econsultancy.com/blog/68720-six-successful-examples-of-online-brand-communities.

Bassig, M. (2017). 8 Amazing Examples of Business Owners Responding to Reviews. Available at https://www.reviewtrackers.com/examples-responding-reviews/.

Symes, B. (2013). 13 Best Practices for Improving Organic Search Rankings on Google. Available at https://www.dialogtech.com/blog/call-tracking/13-best-practices-for-improving-organic-search-rankings-on-google.

Google. AdWords Help - Google Best Practices. Available at https://support.google.com/adwords/answer/6154846?hl=en-AU.

Google. AdWords Help - Contextual Targeting. Available at https://support.google.com/adwords/answer/1726458?hl=en.

Google. AdWords Help - Topic Targeting. Available at https://support.google.com/adwords/answer/2497832?hl=en-AU.

Haddon, M (2017). Display Advertising Best Practices 2018. Available at https://blog.bannerflow.com/display-advertising-best-practices-2018/.

Thornton, K. (2013). 7 Best Practices for Lead Management. Available at https://www.salesforce.com/blog/2013/08/lead-management.html.

SAP. SAP Real-Time Offer Management. Available at https://help.sap.com/saphelp_crm700_ehp01/helpdata/en/61/7cb0a79d8f4ca0ac8de36dcfb2e20f/frameset.htm.

Cohen, H. (2010). 11 Point Marketing Offer Check List. Available at https://heidicohen.com/11-point-marketing-offer-check-list/.

Google. AdWords Help – About Conversion Tracking. Available at https://support.google.com/adwords/answer/1722022.

Korbut, D. (2017). Recommendation System Algorithms: Main Existing Recommendation Engines and How They Work. Available at https://blog.statsbot.co/recommendation-system-algorithms-ba67f39ac9a3.

Johnson, R. et al. (2014). Part V. The Web - 17. Web MVC framework. Available at https://docs.spring.io/spring-framework/docs/3.2.x/spring-framework-reference/html/mvc.html.

Moore, A. et al. (2010). Best Practices in Knowledge Management. Available at http://www.kmworld.com/WhitePapers/BestPractices/Knowledge-Management-November-December-2010_2339.pdf. KMWorld Magazine.

EMC Whitepaper (2008). Understanding Content Management and Digital Asset Management Functionality. Available at https://uk.emc.com/collateral/emc-perspective/h5654-understanding-content-management-ep.pdf.

Kandler, J. (2015). 23 Creative Content Syndication Ideas. Available at http://mysiteauditor.com/blog/23-creative-content-syndication-ideas/.

Sengupta, S. (2015). Best practices on Workflow for Content Aggregation, Authoring and Publishing. Available at https://www.linkedin.com/pulse/best-practices-workflow-content-aggregation-authoring-sengupta/.

Ewald, B. (2012). 5 Tips for Painless Customer Preference Management. Available at https://www.targetmarketingmag.com/article/5-tips-painless-customer-preference-management/all/.

Capgemini Research Report (2016). Customer Communications Management for Banking and Financial Services. Capgemini.

Premier Technologies (2016). The pros and cons of customer interaction tracking. Available at https://www.cio.com.au/mediareleases/26992/the-pros-and-cons-of-customer-interaction-tracking/

Robinson, D. (2011). Customer Loyalty Programs: Best Practices. Haas School of Business, University of California, Berkeley.

Mangalindan, J. (2012). Amazon's Recommendation Secret. Available at http://fortune.com/2012/07/30/amazons-recommendation-secret/.

Apache Software Foundation (2018). The Hadoop Distributed File System (HDFS) Architecture. Available at http://hadoop.apache.org/docs/current/hadoop-project-dist/hadoop-hdfs/HdfsDesign.html.

Simon, P. (2016). The next wave of MDM: Integrating structured and unstructured data. Available at https://blogs.sas.com/content/datamanagement/2016/06/13/the-next-wave-of-mdm/.

Chatzakis, A. (2016). AWS Best Practices - Architecting for The Cloud: Best Practices. Available at https://aws.amazon.com/whitepapers/architecting-for-the-aws-cloud-best-practices/. Amazon Web Services, Inc.

Apache Software Foundation (2018). MapReduce Tutorial. Available at http://hadoop.apache.org/docs/current/hadoop-mapreduce-client/hadoop-mapreduce-client-core/MapReduceTutorial.html.

Lightfoot, J. (2016). Authentication and Authorization: OpenID vs OAuth2 vs SAML. Available at https://spin.atomicobject.com/2016/05/30/openid-oauth-saml/.

DataRobot (2012). Machine Learning Applications | Use Cases By Industry. Available at https://www.datarobot.com/use-cases/.

Hakim, N. & Keys, A (2014). Architecting a Machine Learning System for Risk. Available at https://medium.com/airbnb-engineering/architecting-a-machine-learning-system-for-risk-941abbba5a60.

* * *

The multiple software review websites listed below have also been consulted to investigate software solutions available on the market.

- Capterra at https://www.capterra.com
- FinancesOnline at https://financesonline.com
- G2 Crowd at https://www.g2crowd.com
- GetApp at https://www.getapp.com
- Software Advice at https://www.softwareadvice.com
- Software Suggest at https://www.softwaresuggest.com/us
- TechnologyAdvice at https://technologyadvice.com

Wikipedia at http://en.wikipedia.org/wiki has also been referred to in order to crosscheck current trends and facts of the digital technologies with other sources.

INDEX

D

R

S

T

U

W

X

ABOUT THE AUTHOR

Jace is a Sydneysider, living with his family on the Hills Shire in the northern part of Sydney. As a seasoned management consultant with more than 23 years' experience in business operations and technology strategy, he has worked with Deloitte as a partner and a few other multinational management-consulting firms.

He is passionate about exploring cross-boundary, multi-disciplinary areas of business operations as he strongly believes those are where competitive advantages for an organization can be created. He has always dreamt about developing a business capability model in which business and IT work together as a truly single team to generate unique values. This book is the first fruit borne from these never-ending thoughts.

When away from work, he spends time on learning cosmology, genetics, classical German philosophy and the Bible, and their relationship in a quest for the fundamental truth of life. During the weekend, he loves to play golf with his family and friends in a beautiful golf course around Sydney.

You can reach him at jace.an@yahoo.com for any questions or comments.

SPECIAL OFFER

"Provide a Quick Review, and

Get the Digital Planning Toolkit for Free"

Thank you so much for purchasing and reading this book. We would love to hear your feedback, and we would be incredibly grateful if you could take a couple of minutes to write a quick review for other readers. To appreciate your review, we would like to offer the Digital Planning toolkit for free. The comprehensive toolkit has two files: one is a MS-Excel-based digital capability analysis tool and the other is a MS-PPT-based digital transformation strategy report template. Please refer to the next pages for a few screenshots of the toolkit.

Here is how you can get the toolkit:

1. Provide a review where you bought the book, or leave a review post on any social website.

2. Email the link to your review to info@digitabilitymodel.org.

3. You will receive the toolkit via email.

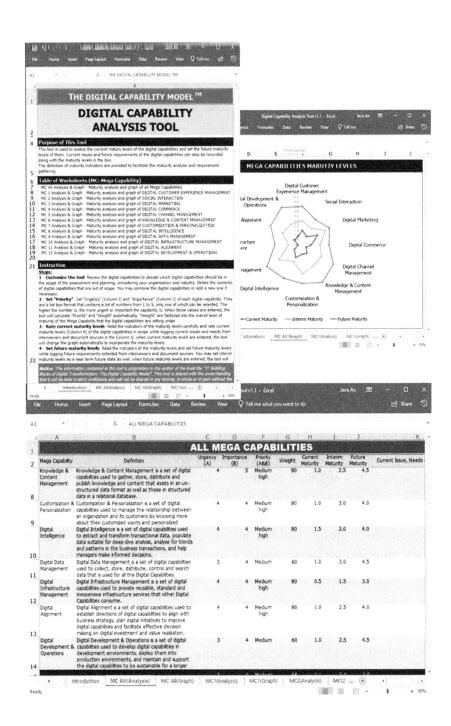

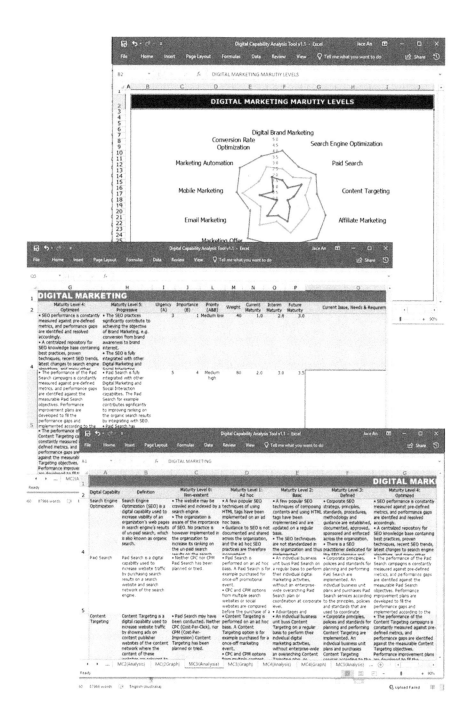

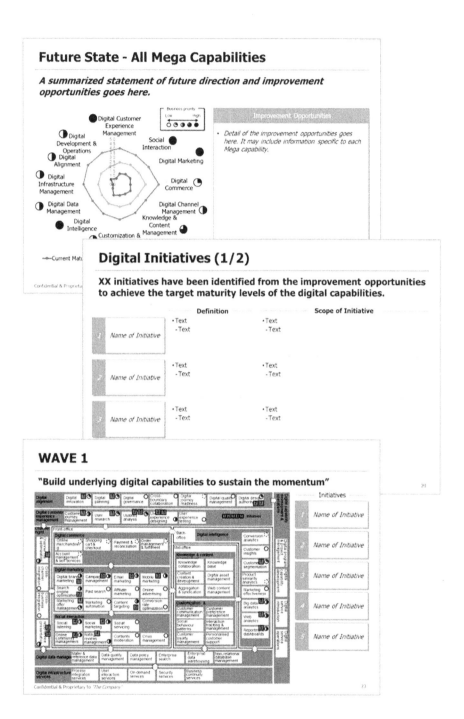

34087519R00258

Made in the USA
Middletown, DE
22 January 2019